Green Books

One Magic Square

Lolo Houbein's great-great-grandfather was a market gardener in North-West Frisia who passed on a food gardening gene down every generation. In Lolo's youth she saw her hometown in western Holland implode under the impact of war, until all animals, birds and rodents were eaten, all fish angled, all trees used for firewood and a long winter of famine ensued during which 24,000 people died of starvation in an area approximately a sixteenth the size of Tasmania. Food security has been Lolo's life-long preoccupation and this book is an offering for survival to those who have never even grown a radish.

Lolo Houbein was educated at the universities of Adelaide and Papua New Guinea in the literatures of Australia, Britain, Papua New Guinea, the Pacific and Africa, classical studies, world religions and anthropology. She is well known as an author of fiction and non-fiction. Her novel *Walk a Barefoot Road* won the Bicentennial/ABC Fiction Award.

By the same author

Fiction
Everything Is Real, 1984
Walk A Barefoot Road, 1988, 1990
The Sixth Sense, 1992
Lily Makes a Living, 1996
Island Girl, 2009

Non-Fiction
Wrong Face in the Mirror, 1990
Tibetan Transit, 1999

Revised for the UK climate

ONE MAGIC SQUARE

Grow your own food on one square metre

LOLO HOUBEIN

This edition has been revised for UK and Northern European climates and published in the UK in 2015 by
Green Books
An imprint of UIT Cambridge Ltd
www.greenbooks.co.uk

PO Box 145, Cambridge CB4 1GQ, England
+44 (0) 1223 302 041

Original edition published in 2008 by
Wakefield Press, Australia
www.wakefieldpress.com.au

Photograph of author on opposite page and on page 92 by Jo Schild.
Photographs on pages 319, 321 and 329 kindly donated by an enthusiastic gardener on the staff of Green Books.
Page 291: iStockphoto
All other photographs and illustrations by Lolo Houbein.

Edited by Bethany Clark, Wakefield Press
Typeset by Clinton Ellicott, Wakefield Press
Designed by Liz Nicholson, designBITE

ISBN: 978 0 85784 280 0 (hardback)
ISBN: 978 0 85784 281 7 (ePub)
ISBN: 978 0 85784 282 4 (pdf)
Also available for Kindle.

For my grandchildren Paul, David, Uaan and Ty.
This is a book for their future.
And for Burwell, for putting up.

In memory of Hendrik Houbein (1796–1874)
grower of cabbages, carrots, onions and potatoes
in North-West Frisia
and
Uncle Wim Schild
who taught me about vegetables,
fruits and chickens in his magic
food garden at Laren,
North Holland.

Lolo feeding the chickens in Uncle Wim's garden.

'The earth is the origin of all things,
the root and garden of all life . . .'
Kuan Chung, Kuan Tzu, 330 BCE

'Produce locally what is consumed locally.'
E. F. Schumacher

'I have never read of any Roman supper that
seemed to me equal to a dinner of my own vegetables;
when everything on the table is the product of my own labor . . .
It is strange what a taste you suddenly have
for things you never liked before.'
Charles Dudley Warner

Contents

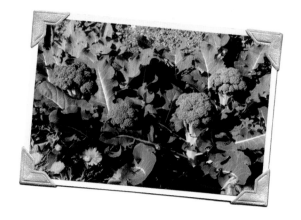

PART TWO: Toward Food Self-Sufficiency 73

PART THREE: Tips & Tricks 115

PART FOUR: Descriptions of Food Plants 225

Abbreviations

For quick reference write these on sturdy paper and fold into a bookmark.

B&B = blood & bone.

CM = compost topped with mulch.

CMC = composted manure with a topping of compost.

CLS = compost and liquid seaweed.

COF = compost and organic fertiliser.

LS = liquid seaweed.

OF = organic fertiliser.

Half a square = one square metre divided lengthwise or diagonally.

Half row = half a metre.

Plot = the same as square, a one square-metre plot.

Plugs = plants plugged in.

Quarters = a square metre divided into four equal squares or triangles.

Row = 1 m long, i.e. one side of the square.

Season = either **spring/summer** or **autumn/winter**, spring and autumn being sowing seasons and summer and winter growing seasons.

Singles = single seeds.

Square = one square metre or 100 x 100 cm.

How to Use this Book

To start growing your own food without delay, put down this book, go out in the garden and select a spot in the sun. Dig over one square metre with a garden fork and remove all the weeds by hand. If digging up lawn, cut out the sods with a spade, roots and all, and stack them upside down under a tree as mulch.

Come inside again and thoroughly wash your hands and clean your nails, as you must always do after working with soil. Pick up this book and in Part One select what you want to grow in your first Salad Plot. Make a list and go out to buy seedlings or seeds for your chosen vegetables and one small bag of blood and bone (B&B), since you don't yet have compost and composted manure. If you dug a square hole in the lawn, you may need to fill it with a bag of potting soil and plan to put in deep edgings to keep the grass roots out. There must be something you can recycle!

Return home to read descriptions of the vegetables you have bought in the **List of Common Vegetables** in Part Four. Put a bookmark at every vegetable you would like to grow. It's easy to grow your own spuds. No more lugging home 10 kg bags – lug manure instead. Love corn on the cob? They're easy too. So are artichokes, asparagus and rhubarb.

Go outside again and rake a few handfuls of B&B through the square, loosening the soil to a depth of 15 cm. Water it in. Now plant your seeds and seedlings according to your chosen Salad Plot plan. Water again. Go indoors to scrub your hands and nails as a surgeon would.

You are now a food gardener!

This book presents plot designs graded from the easiest and most robust to the complex and tender, starting with four plans for salads and leading you in easy stages to the degree of food self-sufficiency you decide on. The sequence presented takes care of crop rotation to keep the soil healthy. However, you can grow plots in a different sequence by feeding plants regularly.

Having done the hard work, sit back and read this chapter and any two chapters in Part Two and Part Three that interest you, gathering ideas for your own little food paradise. Also read **Seeds & Seedlings** in Part Three. Make notes on the back of an envelope. Don't make it more complex than need be! If you never go beyond the Salad Plots, but maintain your square through the seasons by practising crop rotation with peas or broadbeans in winter, you could double your good health and wellbeing.

Each plot has suggestions for follow-up crops to avoid plant diseases, building up from growing the same vegetables season after season. Follow the plots list to become familiar with growing a variety of vegetables over several seasons on just one square metre. If you grow all plots in succession, as presented in Part One, your square will remain healthy and productive. Or choose a Stir-Fry Plot, Pasta/Pizza Plot or Soup Plot, then grow green or bean crops in between. See Part One. And if some vegetables fail to produce, there are many things to blame: climate change, freak weather, a scorcher, snap-freezes, dud seeds or the neighbour's cat. It's not your fault. Flops happen to the experts. They just don't publicise them!

When the season and the spirit is upon you check out other plot plans in Part One, dip into relevant chapters in Part Three, and roam through the lists of common vegetables, herbs and easy-care fruit trees in Part Four.

Use this book as a guide to grow salad vegetables all year round, or two squares of salad greens with pasta and pizza tomatoes, peppers and aubergines. Or, start that way and season by season extend the squares until you provide most vegetables for your table. Or, stay with one or two squares to grow gourmet vegetables. Learn how to grow and prepare them unconventionally while extending their productivity.

Reading all of Part Two on a rainy weekend will clarify your hopes and desires. Maybe you settle for gourmet vegetables, or expensive delectables such as artichokes, asparagus, baby squash, garlic or salad onions. Easy and rewarding.

Some plots are sown like a jungle with mixed seeds, such as the Horta Plot for lovers of wild herbs and vegetables. Horta can be sown any season. You could make it your first plot as it grows fast, provides variety, and can be resown on one quarter each season thereafter.

Of course you can't be self-sufficient in cabbages on one square metre; the big drumheads feel crowded at four to a square. But you can be self-sufficient in one vegetable or another on one square. Plant compact Hispi cabbages four to a quarter, with another four on a quarter not adjoining. That's eight cabbages for coleslaw, with two quarters for lettuce, carrots, radish and a tomato. Check out mini cauliflowers.

Such density does not suit rambling pumpkin vines, but drape two cucumber plants over an old chair, trellis or wire tower on a quarter. Go vertical with peas, beans and mini pumpkins draped over the edge. With trellises on two sides you are in clover, but in summer don't place them against hot fences or walls. But in winter a plot dug close to a fence or wall benefits from reflected warmth.

Water your plot once a day without fail and when vegetables start coming up read some more in Part Three, depending on what you want your food garden to be this year.

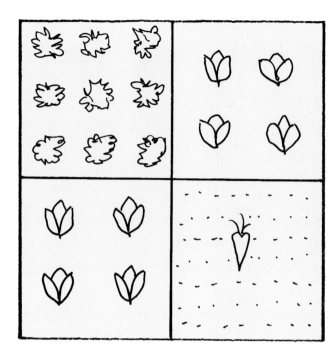

9 lettuces

8 Hispi cabbages

1/4 square carrots

Everyone likes salads. Supermarket lettuces – too big for singles and couples – are often crisp from overwatering but not always tasty. Yet one square metre of soil makes you self-sufficient for months in pick-and-come-again salad greens, up in six weeks. Grow half a dozen varieties of non-hearting lettuces and radicchio close together, with chives and radishes in between, and cucumber and giant red mustard hanging around on the corner of the block. Such a bed keeps going if you plug in more seed. If meanwhile you prepare another square, you will have salad greens all year on two square metres. For soil health, grow a bonus of beans in summer and peas or broadbeans in winter on the finished plot. What is two square metres in a British back garden in return for daily fresh salads and seasonally fresh peas and beans?

Do you love garlic, nature's antibiotic that adds such a kick to pastas and

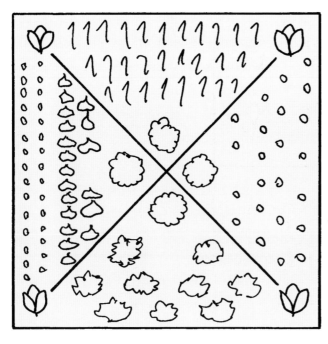

corners: 4 Hispi cabbages
centre: 4 mini cauliflowers
north: spring onions
east: 20+ beets
south: 9 lettuces
west: 30+ radish, 20+ garlic

soups, salads and stir-fries? It is no longer a cheap knob because it takes the better part of a year to mature, tying up the commercial producer's soil longer than other crops. Most shop-bought garlic is now imported – cheap from China. Yet, if you deep dig one square, or one quarter of reasonable soil in a corner of the backyard, fork in composted animal manure, plant the cloves of garlic bulbs, and mulch thickly, you will have the joy of seeing green sprigs turn into edible straps until drying tops announce that new bulbs are ready for harvest. Plant plenty for cooking, pickling and replanting. Enjoy the luxury of whole roasted garlic knobs, artichoke hearts in garlic sauce, or baby squash with garlic butter. Present a trio of knobs plaited together to your best friends, who wouldn't be your best friends unless they also loved garlic!

Each plot is charted to start in the season best suited to the vegetables it grows, then carries through the year with other options for crop rotation. You can therefore start your square at any time of the year. Many vegetables are sown repeatedly through summer, while others are harvested to be replaced by cool-weather plants in autumn. The majority of plots grow a multiplicity of vegetables, so intercropping occurs naturally. Companion-planting principles and nitrogen-fixing plantings govern the plot designs.

To recapitulate:
- Choose your first plot from Part One on the Contents page.
- Read the section on your chosen plot.
- Choose which vegetables and herbs to grow.
- Read up on the vegetables and herbs of your choice in Part Four. If you don't see a vegetable in the first list, it may be a herb.
- Read two chapters in Part Three, choosing those of immediate concern.
- Prepare soil as described for your chosen plot.
- Read **Seeds & Seedlings** to decide which to use.
- Plant seedlings and sow seeds, water in well and daily.

Should there be the faintest possibility that you will continue to extend your food garden, it would be advantageous now to go straight to Part Two and Part Three, put up your feet while the lettuces germinate, and read some chapters with practical ideas. *There are certain things you will want to know before you turn your second square, even if your are going to lay out that food garden in annual increments over 10 years.*

It's so easy to make mistakes that may be long regretted. One vital ingredient of a food garden is your choice of watering system. This should determine the layout of the beds, not the other way around. Read **Water & Watering** in

Part Three.

Another point to consider is the garden's aspect. Where does the sun strike, the wind blow, the shade fall? Where is the garden bordered by walls, fences, trees or buildings that function as windbreaks or heat reflectors? Think infrastructure and make a sketch.

Jot down ideas you will need to start doing what you want to do, be that a perpetual Salad Plot, just growing gourmet food, or following the sequence of seasonal plots in Part One.

If you are developing an entire garden, either because you haven't done so before and the backyard is an abandoned football field, or because you have moved into a new housing estate, read the whole of Part Three. Sketch a plan on the back of a large envelope. Jot down a shopping list for seeds, B&B etc. on the front of the envelope.

Now sift your desires and visions splendid, clarify your aims and postpone a few ideas. By the end of Part Three you will know just what you want and be able to find any description you need through the Contents page or Index.

Read through Part Two in order to grasp the philosophy of taking control of your food supply. Imagine the flavour of organic food grown the peasant way. Know that you are doing something for yourself as well as the planet's biodiversity.

No week, month or year is ever the same in the food garden. Use the alphabetical lists in Part Four to make choices for each season, read up on favourite food plants, observe as they grow, and keep adjusting compost, mulch, manure, water, fleece and companion plants until you get incredible results. You can become an expert in growing your chosen vegetable in one year, because you are doing it on such a small scale!

Not all vegetables need so many adjustments, but a few minutes attention can mean the difference between a puny cauliflower and a snowy head. Placing wood or a tile under a pumpkin to prevent rot takes little effort. So does placing a small cloche over seedlings or lettuces.

By reading Parts One and Three while your Salad Plot grows, you grasp how a number of closed cycles benefit an organic garden and figure out your own cycles and how they operate. You become an authority on your chosen vegetables, a chef in your own kitchen and a healthier, fitter human bean.

A Salad Plot showing six varieties of pick-and-come-again lettuces, cucumber on the fence, tomatoes, and a broccoli seedling and shallots around an onion setting seed.
A dozen new lettuce seedlings have been plugged in between with fresh compost.

PART ONE
The Magic Square Metre Plots

The square-metre plots are graded according to the ease with which the plants grow in parts of Britain. Salad Plots start the list because lettuces, chives and radishes are quick and easy to grow. These are followed by the Broadbean Plot in autumn to give copious results for little work, while putting nitrogen back into the soil. Gradually the plots get a little more complex and varied. Please yourself to add or delete vegetables as you go.

If you have any outdoor space, a few boxes on the balcony or patio will allow you to plant most plots in this book on an even smaller scale. A square-metre plot translates into approximately 4–5 boxes. Boxes dry out quickly so push them together and pack wet towels or newspapers around their sunny side in hot weather. Or put a water tray under the plants during days of blazing sunshine to ensure a healthy harvest of fresh greens.

While your Salad Plot is growing, read **How to Use this Book** if you skipped it and make yourself familiar with the essential list of abbreviations.

The Salad Plots

All mentioned salad vegetables and herbs are discussed individually in the **List of Common Vegetables** and the **List of Common Herbs** in Part Four. Varieties of lettuce are discussed under Lettuce; Radicchio and Endive have separate entries; see also Salad Greens.

Salad Plots are discussed in detail, because they are probably the ones you grow most often. Almost all green leaf vegetables mentioned are pick-and-come-again plants until they bolt to seed. If you want the easiest of all salad plots, buy a packet of mesclun seed, a mixture of up to a dozen salad greens. Sow half the packet, rake in and water well. Sow pinches of seed through the season as space becomes available.

Home-grown salads can contain a dozen vegetables without a leaf of lettuce. Leaves of amaranth, beetroot, endive, giant red mustard, yellow mustard, radicchio, rocket, sorrel, spinach, bok choy and mizuna, as well as cucumber, peas, swedes, nasturtium leaves and flowers, carrot, radish, salad onion, tomato, chives, bronze fennel, cauliflower and broccoli florets, borage, marigold, and courgettes, all mix in the salad bowl. If fresh dandelion grows in your garden, use the leaves to add a delicious bitter twang and lots of nutriments. Then there are beans, beetroot (raw, boiled or pickled) and cabbage for coleslaw. These take a little longer to grow.

Try adding sprouting mung beans (which take up to a week to sprout depending on temperatures), or succulent brown or lima beans to add bulk to winter salads. Or toast croutons with crushed garlic and olive oil in a skillet and toss over the greens.

Herby salads are achieved by adding basil, chives, coriander, fennel, mints, marigold petals, pennyroyal, salad burnet, and tarragon. Look around a herb nursery and sniff the leaves. Small leafy herbs, e.g. coriander, basil, dill and caraway, grow well between vegetables. Make a separate plot for herbs that sprawl – e.g. rocket – in a border or under a tree with at least half a day's sun. Later in the season take cuttings or seed from there to grow on as companion plants for vegetables, in the ground or in mobile pots.

A square-metre plot can produce enough to provide 3–4 people with a small daily salad if you feed and water it well and keep plugging in seeds or seedlings. If artistically inclined, you could even paint with your vegetables by dividing the plot into triangles and growing different coloured vegetables in each with a marigold in the centre.

Read the chapter **Seeds & Seedlings** on raising seedlings and the unexpected benefits of toilet rolls. And don't forget about seed-saving.

Seed-saving: Let one of each variety go to seed. Stake tall plants.

'Goldrush' courgettes produce reliably in Paul Zabukovec's seaside garden, here flanked by jalapeño chillies.

Salad Plot A

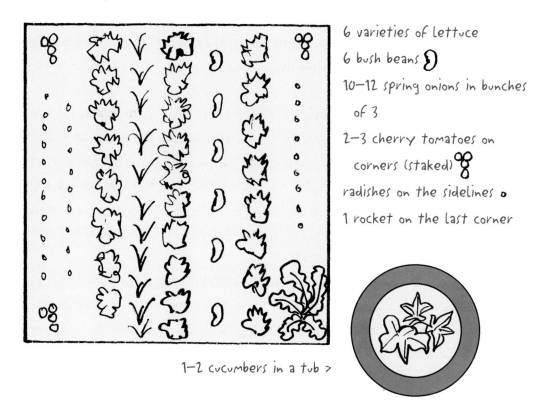

6 varieties of lettuce

6 bush beans

10–12 spring onions in bunches of 3

2–3 cherry tomatoes on corners (staked)

radishes on the sidelines

1 rocket on the last corner

1–2 cucumbers in a tub >

In mid winter, dig the square with well-rotted manure and compost. In late winter rake in B&B and lime if soil is acidic. Mix six pinches of lettuce seed varieties in a cup (cos, butter head, green oakleaf, red Lollo, mignonette, chicory). No need to keep these separate. Sow a row. If the weather is vile, or you want to protect seedlings from wildlife, sow in a deep box – e.g. a wine casket with a few drainage holes – that can be kept in a protected place until plants are large enough to be planted out. Sow 1–2 rocket seeds in one corner of the square.

Sow 2–3 cherry tomato seeds and 12 spring onion seeds in separate seed trays (a seed tray can be a margarine tub with drainage holes). Plant six bush beans in toilet rolls stacked in a tub, and two cucumber seeds in two toilet rolls standing in between seed trays. Choose dependable Lebanese, striped or heat-tolerant Chinese cucumber. Place all in a warm, protected place. Water daily, twice if temperatures rise above 30 degrees, and thrice if it gets awful. Seedlings should never dry out.

When seedlings are 5 cm high, transplant lettuces 10 cm apart, in three short rows 20 cm apart. When soil has warmed up and all danger of frost is over, plant tomato seedlings on the corners where they can be staked. Plant spring onions in bunches of three, between lettuces. Plant bush beans between the lettuce rows. Plug in a dozen radish seeds here and there. When cucumber plants have four leaves, replant them in a large pot with plenty of CMC, next to the square where they can sprawl.

As plants grow, plug in compost where there is space. Pick outside leaves of lettuces regularly. Pick onion greens when young and they will keep growing. Pick rocket all the time and, when it grows large, use leaves in stir-fries. Tomatoes take longer to ripen, so start picking as soon as the fruit gets a blush and ripen it on a sunny window sill. Late, unripe tomatoes can still ripen inside or make green chutney. Freeze cherry tomatoes for sauce. Pick cucumbers young to keep plants producing.

Salad Plot B

LATE WINTER, SPRING & SUMMER

1 endive on one corner

3 lettuce varieties (oakleaf, butterhead, red Lollo)

12+ garlic on two sides

2 x 6 bush beans in two plantings

10 beetroot

2-4 mizuna on two corners

1 courgette in a tub >

In mid winter, dig the square with well-rotted manure and compost. In late winter rake in B&B. Mix three pinches of lettuce seed varieties in a cup (butterhead, red Lollo, green oakleaf). Sow as in Salad Plot A, setting rows 20 cm apart. Sprinkle a few endive seeds in one corner and some mizuna seeds in an opposite corner. Break one knob of garlic into cloves and plant 8 cm apart on two sides of the square. Sow 10 beetroot seeds 9 cm apart in one row. Beetroot seedlings produce more than one bulb and don't like being transplanted. Beans

14

are best raised in toilet rolls, or plugged straight into the soil but protected from rodents – see **Pests & Predators**. Raise 1–2 courgette seeds in a pot in a warm position, or directly in a tub with plenty of CMC. When lettuces are 5 cm high, transplant 10 cm apart in alternate rows, parallel to the beetroot. When the weather has warmed beyond danger of frost, plant 2 x 3 bush beans as in Plot A. Plug in compost as mulch where there is space. As plants grow, pick young garlic greens for salads. One month after planting first beans, plug in six bush bean seeds where there is space. Protect – see **Hardware in the Food Garden**. Repeat once more before mid January.

Pick young beetroot leaves for salads, leaving plenty of crown leaves to feed the bulb. Pick endive and mizuna leaves as soon as plants grow vigorously. Pick courgettes young, as courgettes, to encourage continued production. Feed and water well.

Courgettes, when growing well, should be picked just as the flower shrivels; very large courgettes are less tasty. Courgette flowers can be fried in batter or shredded in salads.

Salad Plot C

LATE WINTER, SPRING & SUMMER

2–3 pak choy on one corner

2 lettuce varieties (butterhead, red Lollo)

onions in a diagonal row

carrots in two rows along
   onions

mustard between lettuces

1 perennial spinach on other
   corner

1 patti pan in a tub >

In mid winter, dig the square with well-rotted manure and compost and set up a large pot for pattin pan. In late winter rake in B&B and sow two pinches of lettuce seed as in Salad Plot A. Sow a few pak choy seeds and a few perennial spinach seeds in two opposite corners. Make three diagonal drills connecting the other two corners, sowing the middle one with onion seeds 5 cm apart, and the other two with carrot seeds every 2 cm. Don't get the ruler out, just sprinkle between finger and thumb. Cover with 2 mm of soil, tamp down with a flat hand. Sow two patti pan seeds in a pot and raise in a protected position – the kitchen sill is fine – until all danger of frost is over and plants can go into the stack or large pots.

When lettuces are 5 cm high, plant out as in Salad Plot A. Plug in compost as mulch between plants. Plug in a dozen mustard seeds between plants. Pick outer leaves of lettuces, pak choy leaves and flowers, and spinach. Pick mustard leaves from the bottom up, also use in soups and stir-fries. Pick some onion greens and the biggest tufted carrots.

Mustard can be picked young for adding to salads, for stir-fries when bigger, dug in for green manure before flowering, or grown on for mustard seed production.

Salad Plot D

SUMMER SALADS

endive	bok choy	chicory green	cucumber
fenugreek	mignonette	cos lettuce	chives
mibuna	radicchio red	oakleaf lettuce	mizuna
rocket	sorrel	radishes	tomato

3 bok choy

1 chicory, green

chives, thin sprinkling of seed

1 cos lettuce

1 cucumber on a corner

1 endive on a corner

fenugreek, thin sprinkling
   of seed

5 mibuna, pick early

4 mignonette lettuces

mizuna, sprinkle 10+ seeds,
   pick early

1 oakleaf lettuce

4 radicchio (red)

20–25 radishes

1 rocket on a corner

1 sorrel

1 tomato, staked

+ nasturtiums, 3 seeds
   in a tub >

In mid winter, dig the square with manure and compost. On the first day of spring rake in B&B, then sow a cucumber seed and a tomato seed in toilet rolls. The other varieties are to be sown in open ground. Divide the square into 16 squares of 25 x 25 cm. Next, sow or plant a different vegetable in each small square, e.g. four small lettuces or radicchios, a sprinkling each of seeds for fenugreek, mibuna, mizuna, small radishes, and three bok choy seeds. Sow large-leaved spinach and sorrel on corners. Grow rocket on an edge so it can flop outside the square. This is a basic salad plot and it is pretty full. If you like more solid salads you can leave out some leafy greens and plug in green or butter beans or swedes. Once plants are 5 cm high, add compost as mulch.

When the danger of frost is over, plant cucumber and tomato on two corners kept free, where they can be staked. And the plus? A large pot with nasturtium seeds, placed next to the square to provide peppery leaves, edible flowers and fake capers to pickle for the salad bowl. While harvesting plants from summer salad plots, plug in bush beans until mid-July. Water daily. And do save seed!

A Salad Plot ready to go to seed but still providing plenty of pickings: endive in the background, four kinds of lettuce in the foreground, tomato on the right and chicory on the left.

Salad Plot E

WINTER SALADS WITH A DIFFERENCE

endive	baby carrots	mizuna	daikon radish
Coriander	Shallots	Chinese radish	Corn Salad
Snow peas	tatsoy	onions	parsley
Spinach	winter lettuces		rocket

baby carrots, light sprinkling of seed

9 Chinese swedes

coriander, light sprinkling of seed

5 corn salad

1 mooli radish, on a corner

1 endive, on a corner

mizuna, sprinkle 10+ seeds, pick early

16 onions

parsley, light sprinkling of seed

1 rocket, on a corner

25 shallots

4 snow peas, on a 4-stick tepee

spinach, 1 perennial or sprinkle seed

1 tatsoy

6 winter lettuces on two small squares

+ 1 salad burnet in a large pot ^

+ 3 new potatoes in a tub 7

Divide the square into 16 smaller ones as in the previous plot. Sow one of each of the vegetables from the above list. Once the plants are 5 cm high, plug in compost as mulch.

There are two extras to try. Place a tub beside the square with new potatoes cut into 5 cm pieces – see Potato in Part Four – for that firm potato salad with fresh coriander. Also place a large pot in front of the tub, sown with a pinch of salad burnet seed – see **List of Common Herbs** – to lend a touch of colour as well as grace the salad bowl.

If the parsley takes off and you make tabouli, remember that a renowned Lebanese chef said that tabouli needs spices, especially five-spice.

One quarter of a Salad Plot showing beetroot seedlings, coriander, oakleaf lettuce, new leaf beets and young nettle.

SALAD DRESSINGS

Many a salad can be elevated to gourmet food by an imaginative dressing. But as taste is such a personal thing, the last word will never be written. You can hardly go wrong with a plain vinaigrette. Invest in good virgin olive oil and balsamic or wine vinegar; add pepper and salt to taste.

Try rice wine vinegar and the pleasantly acidic pulp of tamarind from the Asian grocer. Make herb vinegars by steeping any of the following in a small bottle of white vinegar for a month: thyme, oregano, rosemary, lemongrass, sage, juniper berries, lemon balm, lemon and/or orange zest, Persian catmint, bergamot, nasturtium leaves and flowers, elderberry flowers or marigolds.

Visit an Asian grocery for sauces: Japanese, Chinese, Vietnamese, Thai, Indian, Balti, Korean and more. Check out your local grocery. Read the names and if your tastebuds start to salivate, read the label of the bottle that did it. If there are no objectionable ingredients (e.g. MSG, aspartame sweetener, or genetically modified ingredients), buy that bottle. Organic soy sauce, garlic chilli sauce and mustard are a compatible trio. A few drops of sesame oil add a nutty flavour to any dressing.

Rudjak is an Indonesian salad, made with either fruit or vegetables, with a unique sauce. For vegetable rudjak parboil (for just a minute) florets of cauliflower, broccoli, sliced carrot and green beans. Cube cucumber and drain. Add frozen peas after draining. This is a basic version and you can add whatever you grow, including courgettes. If you want more filling, add marinated tofu. For a fruit rudjak, chop bananas, papaya, canteloupe, apple, pear and anything not too juicy – even sweet cucumber.

For the sauce, mix half a jar (a whole one if feeding a tribe) of crunchy organic peanut butter with 2 tbsp of white vinegar, lemon juice or tamarind.

Mix in 1–2 tsp of chilli paste (sambal oelek) and 1–2 tbsp of dark brown or palm sugar. These measurements are but a guide – add more of one or the other ingredient until you find the taste irresistible! If the dressing is too stiff, add coconut milk by the teaspoon, stirring vigorously until it is the consistency of a thick mayonnaise. The fruit or vegetable juices will thin it down further. Carefully fold the mixed fruit or vegetables into the sauce with two implements. Serve in a blue bowl, garnished with cucumber slices. Take this to a party to reap compliments.

For a more authentic rudjak sauce, fry onions and garlic in oil, adding chillies, shrimp paste, coconut cream and crushed peanuts. Keep stirring before adding more coconut cream, lemon juice and pinches of salt and sugar. This is also a thick sauce. Thin it down for a green leaf salad.

Another great stand-by for anything from a garden salad to a parboiled salad with cooked beans or a plain potato salad, is a yoghurt-based dressing. Use plain or Greek yoghurt. Crush several cloves of garlic and add thoroughly mashed coriander seeds, cumin and black peppercorns. Add a good shake of olive oil, and dashes of sesame oil and orange essence to finish.

One of the simplest dressings is freshly squeezed orange juice, with or without a touch of lemon. Delicious on textured salads of apple, grated carrot and courgette or on plain garden salads or grated carrot with fresh coriander.

There is no end to the varieties of vegetables and herbs that can make a salad, nor to unique dressings. There is no excuse for an iceberg with mayonnaise from a jar. And if you live in wild parts, you may find additions in field and forest. Eating wild green leaves is the peasant's way and we lost much more than a pleasant ramble through the fields when we started to live in big cities.

The Broadbean Plot
AUTUMN & WINTER

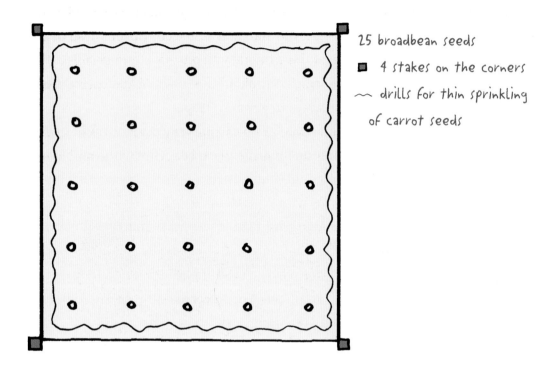

25 broadbean seeds

■ 4 stakes on the corners

~ drills for thin sprinkling of carrot seeds

This plot follows the Salad Plots to return nitrogen to the soil, as all beans do. The broadbean is the only bean that will grow through winter. Should there still be lettuces and seed-producing plants in the square, just plant broadbeans in between and harvest the others by cutting their stems so as not to disturb bean roots. Add compost and OF.

Leaving a 10 cm edge, push single bean seeds 3 cm into the soil at 20 cm distance, five across both ways. This gives 25 plants per square. Dense planting avoids stems breaking. If you have night prowlers, protect each seed with a plastic protector, either rings of PVC pipe or bottomless yoghurt tubs. Push a piece of netting or pot scrubbers into these. Alternatively, place wire cages or dish racks all over the plot. See **Hardware in the Food Garden**.

Make shallow drills around the edges and thinly sprinkle carrot seed. Cover with 2 mm of soil and pat with a flat hand. Water well. Cover these drills with strips of old tea towel, held on the corners with stones, to aid germination of carrot seed and prevent ants eating it. Peek after a week. When carrot seedlings are 2 cm high, remove strips, wash, dry and keep.

Once the broadbeans have four strong leaves, remove protectors and spread CMC between plants but not along carrot drills. Soon beautiful white and black

Only 16 broadbeans were planted in plastic rings with netting pushed in to prevent rats digging up germinating seed. Four stakes for roping in growing bean stalks. A denser planting of 25 would have provided better protection against wind.

flowers appear. Might the white cabbage butterfly with its black wing dots mistake these flowers for competitors? Try growing cabbages on an adjoining plot.

Place four supports on the corners of the square and run baling twine or rope around the plot. As they grow, repeat this higher up to prevent outer plants breaking in the wind. Plants can reach 2 m high. While the top is still developing flowers, finger-length beans appear near the base. Start eating the young ones whole. Picking helps the plant put energy into newer pods. Plants produce multiple pods. Pull baby carrots to thin out and serve with young broadbeans.

When there are no more finger-length pods to eat whole, begin eating podded beans twice a week. They also freeze beautifully, tasting as fresh as the day they were picked if frozen minutes after picking – a connoisseur's food out of season.

When harvest is over and seed beans have dried, cut stalks at ground level, leaving the roots with nitrogen-fixing nodules in the ground. It may be too late in the season to sow summer vegetables needing 5–6 months to mature. But in this nitrogen-enriched soil you can plant green-leaved vegetables, of which there are more varieties than supermarket shelves reveal.

Seed-saving: As pods grow bigger, choose the largest for seed. At 4–5 seeds per pod, tie red wool around 8–10 pods. Let these dry on the stalk. But beware, during a hot spell they could dry to a sudden pitch black which may cook the seed. Dried pods should be dried but not dead.

The Anti-Oxidants Plot

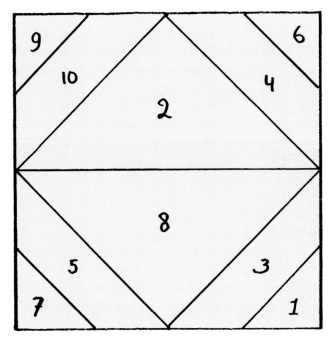

1. Amaranth
2. Chinese broccoli
3. Endive
4. Mizuna
5. Mustard
6. Pea shoots
7. Rocket
8. Chard
9. Spinach, perennial
10. Turnip greens

In winter swap some of the above for beetroot, bok choy, broccoli, cabbage, or kale.

If you never grew anything else but this plot and picked three meals a week, the benefits to your health would be without measure. Anti-oxidants are essential to fight damaging free radicals in our bodies and help delay the onset of degenerative diseases. Fortunately, anti-oxidants in the form of green-leaved vegetables grow easily, tall and fast.

If you grew broadbeans last season, cut stalks at soil level, fork in B&B, cover the plot with a thick layer of CMC and water in well. Choose up to 10 vegetables from the above list to try.

All brassica leaves are edible: pick lower leaves of cabbage, cauliflower, broccoli, Brussels sprouts and kale, and also the leaves of swedes, turnips and Asian greens. Stir-fry or steam a weekly mixed bunch with some onion, ginger, garlic and a little spice.

For a spring planting, don't choose beetroot, bok choy or kale, but plug these in during early autumn if you want to keep this plot going through winter. Raise broccoli in toilet rolls. All the others can be sown directly. Perennial spinach comes up in spring and grows throughout the year.

Pea shoots are young pea plants, picked at 10 cm for stir-fries. They only shoot once and are cut above ground. Sow a handful or harvest pea shoots from pea straw.

For easy germination plant seeds in a handful of potting soil pushed into the compost layer. Ten different vegetables grow at different rates, but soon you should be eating raw greens in vinaigrette, or steam up concoctions of 10 different leaves for a taste sensation.

Whether you plug in winter greens or not, this plot is bound to continue into winter. So for your next plot you might just take out the garden fork and prepare another square metre. Two plots will make you doubly self-sufficient in vegetables this coming winter.

The Curry Plots
AUTUMN & WINTER

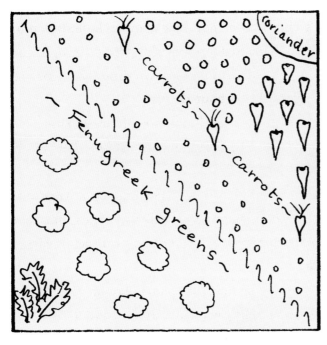

Curry Plot A

From bottom left to top right:

3 Russian kale/broccoli or
  6 bok choy
7 mini cauliflowers
fenugreek
red or brown onions on
  the diagonal
double rows of peas
carrots
20 swedes
8 mooli, pull young
coriander

In spring/summer grow aubergines instead of cauliflower.

+ garlic (in a pot) <<
+ potatoes (in a tub) <

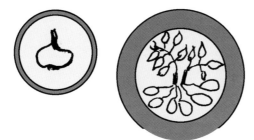

While camping in Northern India my travel companions and I ate a basic
curry of cauliflower, carrots, potatoes, onions and peas almost every day.
If the curry spice is a good mix this is a most satisfying feed. Autumn and

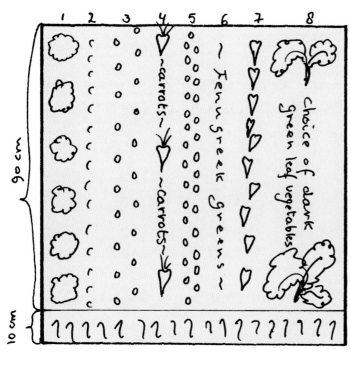

90 cm

10 cm

carrots~ ~carrots~ ~carrots~

~ Fenugreek Greens ~

choice of dank green leaf vegetables

Curry Plot B

1. 6 mini cauliflowers
2. 15 coriander seeds
3. 20 peas in a double row
4. 50 carrots
5. 30 swedes
6. Fenugreek, sprinkle thickly
7. 10 mooli radish, pull young
8. 9 bok choy or 3 broccoli or
   3 Russian kale

Fertilise with compost and LS.
Only manure rows 1 and 8 for
cauliflower, bok choy, broccoli
and kale.

+ garlic (in a pot) <<
+ potatoes (in a tub) <

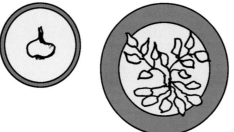

winter are good times to grow these vegetables. To avoid water-logging and
ground frosts, grow potatoes on a little hillock or in a large tub. Because
caulie and carrots take time, grow a row of fast, succulent Japanese swedes
as well. Mooli, the monster white radish, does well in curry and makes good
use of small spaces. If your soil is a bit impenetrable, grow mooli in a deep

box or large tub. If you like more green additions, no need to stay Indian. Bok choy loves winter, as do quick-growing kale, broccoli, fresh fenugreek and coriander. Add garlic for greens.

To grow gross feeders such as the cabbage family as well as root crops in Curry Plot A, divide the square diagonally. Fertilise the gross feeders half with COF plus B&B. Dust the other half with B&B and add a layer of compost. Dust the whole with a little lime and water well.

Sow broccoli and cauliflowers in toilet rolls. All others can be sown directly three weeks after soil preparation. On the gross feeders side, plant cauliflowers with your choice of bok choy, broccoli, or Russian kale, and a row of fenugreek. On the diagonal line, sow red or brown onions, on the other half carrots, coriander, mooli, peas and swedes. Plant salad or other small potatoes in a tub or hillock, and garlic cloves in a big pot. Curry Plot B suggests an alternative pattern of 90 cm rows with a metre row of onions.

Read up on how to grow all these in Part Four. Douse seedlings with LS once a week and again after planting out for several weeks until they take off. Throughout the season apply OF or B&B monthly.

Meanwhile, grind your own curry powder, just in case the blackbirds eat your fenugreek sprouts. All curry cooks have their own favourite combinations, so try the basic recipe for garam masala in the chapter **Cupboard Self-Sufficiency** in Part Two, and vary it gradually by adding a bit more of one or another spice. With fresh garam masala, add the diced vegetables starting with the most solid, keeping the tender stuff till last. Add vegetable stock. Serve curries with rice and a plain yoghurt dish garnished with cucumber, coriander, lemon juice and pepper.

In the beginning pick leaves of bok choy, broccoli, coriander, fenugreek, kale, onion and swedes to go with cooked chickpeas or sprouted mung beans.

Later there will be baby carrots and swedes, peas in the pod and broccoli florets, after that cauliflowers, peas, mooli to grate, early potatoes, bigger swedes and carrots. You either have to buy onion and garlic for curry day or do with the greens, as bulbs won't be ready till summer.

Other combinations of vegetables, such as beans, parsnips and celery, are tasty, but the more absorbent a vegetable the better it blends in a curry. Cumin leaves, lemongrass or mint can be added, or fresh ginger and turmeric. In summer the Curry Plot could grow versatile aubergines and tomatoes.

Seed-saving: Come spring, let coriander and fenugreek go to seed to dry for next year and make garam masala. Bok choy, carrots, cauliflower, mooli, peas and swedes are gradually harvested. All that will be left are onions, garlic and either kale or broccoli in one corner. These latter two produce edible flower heads and seed to save.

Broccoli and cauliflower absorb curry flavours well.

The Beans Plot

SPRING & SUMMER

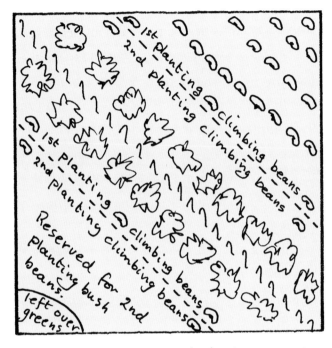

This plot follows Curry Plot A with its diagonal row of onions still maturing.

plant lettuces on either side of onions

set up trellises either side of lettuces

2 x 9 climbing beans on trellises, 1st planting

18 bush beans, top right corner, 1st planting

later in the season: 2 x 9 climbing beans on other side of trellises, 2nd planting

18 bush beans, bottom left corner, 2nd planting after removal of winter greens

+ garlic (in a pot) <

Here we are in fantasy land in the realm of Jack and his bean stalk. You will remember this when your climbing beans grow beyond the farthest reach of your bean poles and when suddenly, one morning, there hangs a whole handful of beans where you had not noticed anything yesterday. Beans like to surprise you.

If you have flogged your square for two seasons, it is time again for a nitrogen fix. Grow early bush beans and slower climbing beans with under plantings of green and brown lettuces. Serve succulent garlic beans for dinner; make bean salads with radishes and almonds. Do remember that the scarlet runner bean likes cooler weather.

We are taking a risk here if last season you grew the Curry Plot and are left with that onion row on the diagonal and either kale or broccoli in one corner. Onions and beans are supposed to be incompatible. Test this, for there are gardeners who claim this companion plant ruling is rubbish. When it's warm enough to plant beans – they don't even like chilly nights – start harvesting onions so that the acquaintance is kept brief. And if you grew Curry Plot B, where onions grow along one side of the square only, plant lettuces between them and the beans. Your garlic pot is still going.

Begin by raking in a light sprinkling of B&B on both halves. Cover with compost and water in well. Make shallow drills either side of the onions and thinly sprinkle mixed lettuce seeds, cover with 2 mm of soil and tamp down with a flat hand. Water with LS.

Indoors, set up six containers with six toilet rolls each. Sow three trays with bush beans and three with climbing beans. Here we enter fantasy land again, because choosing beans is pure myth. If you have joined the Garden Organic Network (see **Useful Addresses**) you will know that people make claims for their beans that border on the fantastic. Yet by trying them out you will find that some claims are true – all things such as soil, weather etc. being equal.

The Painted lady and scarlet runner bean sport bright-red flowers. Others make do with mauve, purple, yellow and white. Resolve to try them all out over the coming years, sticking to one bush bean and one climbing bean per year and learn to grow these well. If you are a bean lover – health be upon you – grow them every summer to revive a winter plot. Spend an hour rigging up a wire or bamboo trellis across the lettuces for the climbers, or poke in tall twigs.

When all danger of frost is over, plant out beans with at least four leaves, in their rolls, roots already hanging out. Dig deep holes, fill with water, drain and push toilet rolls into the mud, firming the soil around them. Plant nine climbing beans between each row of lettuce and the trellises, totalling 18 beans. Plant 18 bush beans in the triangle not retaining winter greens. Water well and apply LS.

After one week, place CMC between rows. Set up the second sowing of 18 bush beans and 18 climbing beans in 36 toilet rolls. Or, if you do not have enough trellis, do 36 bush beans. Nurture these until big enough for bare ground. Plant 2 x 9 climbing beans on the outer sides of trellises and plant 18 bush beans in vacant triangle after removing remnant winter greens. Place small cloches where necessary. Treat like first planting.

Plant out germinated beans until mid July for a continuous supply. Keep harvesting lettuce leaves. Yes, they are in a slightly inconvenient spot between two trellises, but as they enjoy dappled shade they'll be succulent and won't bolt to seed too soon.

Harvest last season's garlic – see Garlic in Part Four. Replant some in fresh soil, dry some and pickle some. When bean plants are definitely finished, cut stems at soil level, leaving nitrogen nodules in the ground. May you have had your fill of beans!

Seed-saving: Tie red wool on as many bean pods as you will need next year and some to give to friends. Especially if growing heritage beans, ask friends to grow some on so that the variety gains a foothold. Let one of each variety of lettuce go to seed. Some lettuce leaves are still quite edible when the plant is setting seed.

The Stir-Fry Plots

Use up end of summer greens, beans and roots in a tasty stir-fry.

Stir-fries are a wonderful way of using up summer's last greens, beans and roots, old carrots and celery stalks that mash in the wok with onion, garlic, ginger and soy sauce. That's your basic stir-fry when the seasons flow into one another in your food plot. Serve with a bowl of rice, noodles, or roasted potatoes and pumpkin. If you grew the previous plot, autumn is waving its gentle wand. Cut old bean plants at soil level, cover the plot with a layer of CMC or COF and water in well.

Winter Stir-Fry Plot

AUTUMN & WINTER

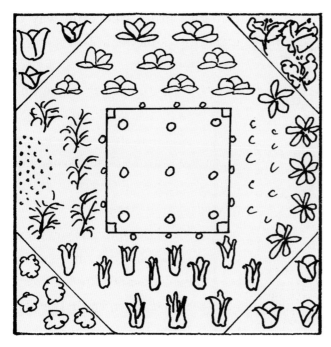

Centre:

4 stakes surrounded with twine

9 broadbeans

4 x 3 snow peas under the twine

Corners:

3 flowering broccoli, 3 cabbages

5 mini cauliflowers, 3 cabbages

Field:

North — 9 bok choy

East — 5 tatsoy + 10 coriander

South — 9 brassica juncea

West — 5 mizuna + pea shoots

Raise three flowering broccoli raab, six cabbages and five mini cauliflowers in toilet rolls. Plant nine broadbeans in a 3 x 3 bean square in the centre, placing four stakes around them, tied with twine to prevent stems breaking in high winds. Plant 4 x 3 snow peas under the twine to climb up.

When seedlings have several sets of leaves with roots hanging out, plant broccoli, cauliflowers and cabbages in the corners. Sow directly the spaces between centre and corners with bok choy, mizuna, brassica juncea, tatsoy, coriander and pea shoots. Rake in seed and tamp down. Pea shoots grow from thickly sown peas cut as shoots at 10 cm, or collect seed from pea straw.

When all are growing, scatter B&B. Water in well. By mid winter apply CMC and fortnightly douse with LS. Now put that wok on the stove twice a week for the pickings.

Summer Stir-Fry Plot
SPRING & SUMMER

Central tepee of twigs:
12 sugar snap peas on tepee
1 marigold in centre of tepee

Field:
North — carrots, sprinkle thinly
East — 10 flowering broccoli
South — giant red mustard
  3 mizuna or mibuna, thinly
West — 10 Chinese leaves

Borders:
spring onions, sprinkle thinly

Since these plantings have different requirements, don't do anything to the soil except sprinkling lime around the four edges for spring onions and in the central circle for peas. Then cover the square with fresh compost.

Sow the following in individual toilet rolls: 12 climbing sugar snap peas, 10 flowering broccoli raab and 10 Chinese leaves. Raise them on LS. Sow a whole packet of spring onion seed into two seed trays. The other vegetables are sown directly.

Build a tepee of tall twigs or bamboo (e.g. from old blinds) in a circle of 35 cm diameter. This is a small tepee, so push twigs well into the soil and tie tops firmly so that it doesn't keel over in a wind gust. Plant marigold seed in the centre.

Reserve an 8 cm edge all around the square for spring onions. Divide the remainder of the square from inner edge to outer circle into four diagonal sections.

Sow carrots in one section and cover with wet tea towels. In another section sow mizuna and/or mibuna with a few giant red mustard. The remaining sections take flowering broccoli raab and Chinese leaves when seedlings have 4–6 leaves and roots are showing.

The peas may grow quickly. Cram 12 in a circle around the tepee. Spring onions are planted out along the four edges when 6–8 cm high, covering white parts with soil, for they are modest and shy.

Since no manure was applied, make seedlings tick over with LS. Apply B&B to broccoli and cabbage monthly. Gradually pick one vegetable after another until your summer stir-fry contains the full complement.

Seed-saving: Before you devour it all, remember seed-saving. Tie red wool on one tall carrot plant, one each of mizuna, mibuna, mustard, broccoli and a handful of pea pods. When the seed peas have dried on the vine, cut plants at soil level. Enjoy the coming and going of happy insects buzzing around beautiful vegetable flowers setting seed.

The Root Crop Plot

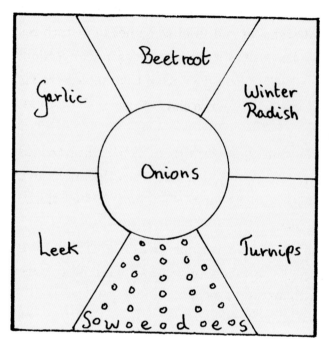

1 seed tray onions in centre

1 seed tray leek, lower west

2–3 knobs of garlic, upper west

Sow seed of beetroot, winter radish, turnips and swedes in rows radiating from the centre (see swedes, south) at distances appropriate for the size of the root vegetables.

If you grew the Summer Stir-Fry Plot there will be many plants still going to seed. This is a good opportunity to plug root vegetables in between. Root crops quietly mature in the earth while rain and wind lash taller plants. They mature at different times, so eat those that are ready. Leave out carrots if they grew here the previous season.

Sow one seed tray of onion seed (red, brown or white) and one of leek. Prepare square with a light sprinkling of lime. In soils that are poor to start with, root crops can't get ahead on nutriment left after a previous crop. So if your soil is poor, add a modest sprinkling of B&B; overdo it and you reap more leaf than root.

Mark out a circle in the centre of your square for the onions. Divide the rest of the square into six sections. Sow around last season's seed-bearing plants and when these are finished, cut stems at soil level so as not to disturb root crops. Sow winter radish, turnips, beetroot and winter swedes in four sections. In order to mulch for winter, sow in short rows radiating from the centre and mulch in between. Break enough garlic knobs into cloves to plant the fifth section and cover thickly with straw.

When onions and leeks are 6–8 cm high, plant them in the circle and last section respectively. Mulch between rows with CM. As the other vegetables come up, mulch them also with CM. Once the plot is up and growing, douse it once with LS. That should be enough.

You can eat the leaves of onions, garlic, turnips, swedes and beetroot as well as young radish leaves, but don't rob a plant of its crown. Pick lower leaves gradually for a weekly feed before pulling the roots.

Seed-saving: Tie red wool on your best plants. Save one leek, beetroot, swede and turnip and three onions (plait together to avoid flopping). Let garlic tops die down, pull, then tie in a bunch or plait, after storing a few knobs in a dark cupboard for replanting in autumn. To let one winter radish go to seed brings a glory of mauvy-pink flowers, but it is a big plant. Choose a radish on the edge of the plot and gently guide it to flop sideways, for it can take as long as the garlic for the pods to dry. Pick young radish seed pods to pickle in vinegar with olive oil. Should you produce big beets, pickle a few sliced into jars and add to your home-grown food store.

The Pasta/Pizza Plots

These are the favourite plots of many a busy cook because bland pasta is so amenable to being married to these pronounced flavours for a quick and healthy meal.

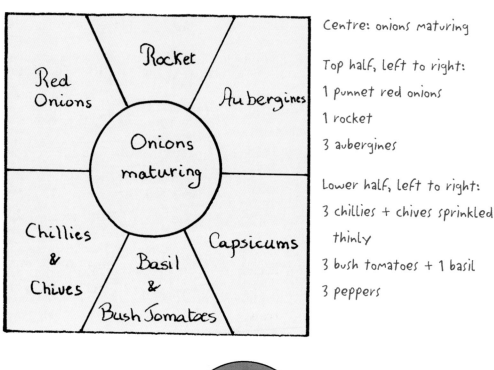

Centre: onions maturing

Top half, left to right:
1 punnet red onions
1 rocket
3 aubergines

Lower half, left to right:
3 chillies + chives sprinkled
   thinly
3 bush tomatoes + 1 basil
3 peppers

+ 3 salad potatoes in a tub or
   hillock <

Pasta/Pizza Plot A

SPRING & SUMMER

There are half a dozen plants going to seed in all directions of your square. As these plants dry off they don't use nutriments, so you can plant around them or harvest what seed there is and pull them out. Avoid watering the onions in the centre when the tops are drying off. Alternatively, prepare a new square for pasta/pizza vegetables and herbs and sow a summer Bean Plot in the old Root Crop Plot.

In spring, sow three seeds each of aubergine, pepper, chilli and bush tomato in toilet rolls. Sprinkle a pinch of basil seed in a pot and red onion seed in a seed tray. As none like frost, keep damp and warm under glass or indoors. If you don't want to raise basil from seed, wait till the weather warms up to buy a plant.

As previous seasons have used up any goodness you put into the soil, prepare your plot as for gross feeders. Apply CMC plus OF or B&B. Preserve the division in six sections.

Sow rocket directly and early – it likes cool nights but may bolt to seed in summer. Chives are sown direct. Prepare a big tub or hillock and plant potatoes, mulch with compost and straw.

When the weather warms up plant out red onion seedlings. As nights grow warm plant aubergines, peppers, chillies and tomatoes – protect with plastic if in doubt (see **Hardware in the Food Garden**). Plant basil between tomatoes. Douse all except last season's onions with LS. As plants grow up, push in mulch to preserve moisture as these plants hate drying out.

This plot can be used in so many ways, apart from roasting the fleshy vegetables. A mushroom and potato pizza with chives, rocket and goat's cheese goes down really well. You can cut aubergine slices and vine-ripened tomatoes to sun-dry on a tray under muslin. Peppers can be dried, or preserved in glass. Basil can be frozen. Make tomato sauce.

If cold weather sets in, dig up aubergines, basil, peppers and chillies with root balls, pot them up and bring indoors. Feed with LS. Rather than design a new plan to follow this Pasta/Pizza Plot, continue to sow where there is space for a winter plot.

Pasta/Pizza Plot B
AUTUMN & WINTER

Rake in some B&B between still-growing plants. If you grew the Stir-Fry Plot the onions have now been harvested. Flop one rocket plant over the edge to produce seed.

Around the old rocket sow lots of coriander for Thai dishes. Plant garlic where no onions grew previously – this is where a garden notebook comes in handy! Sow Asian greens and giant red mustard in all other spaces. Apply compost. Plug in a few Swiss chard seeds for ricotta torte and vegetarian lasagne.

Those who love asparagus with pasta or pizzas should dig a separate permanent plot, because asparagus are perennial plants, producing for decades. See Asparagus in Part Four and plant roots in autumn, applying thick CMC.

The Horta Plot

This is a made-to-measure crop for a food garden developed one square metre at a time. The Greeks have since ancient times gathered horta by climbing rocky mountains after autumn rains to pick a multitude of edible wild greens for the pot. If your environment does not have such abundance – few British landscapes do, hedgerows notwithstanding – you can sow a Horta Plot. Until you know how much horta you will consume, prepare one square and divide it into four quarters with a trowel. Sow one quarter every 2–3 months, choosing seasonal varieties.

Go to the spice cupboard with a deep bowl. Put into the bowl a teaspoon each of yellow mustard and coriander seed, and add generous pinches of buckwheat, caraway, dill, fenugreek and any whole spice seed you have. From your seed collection add 3–4 seeds each of bok choy, brassica juncea, Chinese leaves, kale, mizuna, giant red mustard, rocket, Swiss chard, tatsoy and any other fast-growing greens, plus a sprinkling of chive seeds. Go outside, mix seeds and rake lightly into one quarter of your plot. Water in well. The mustard will be up in a week, shading the others. By the time you start picking this plot, seed the next quarter. Pick leaves and tops of mustard, lots of rocket, Chinese greens from the bottom up, and stems of spicy greens, leaving the roots to shoot again.

Enter the kitchen with a bowl heaped with greens. If your natural environment sports edible greens like dandelion, nettle or milkweed, add these. Greek cooks put it all in a pot of boiling water to simmer for five minutes before they drain and fry it. A lot of the goodness remains in the water, which women take as a health drink.[1] I prefer to wash, drain and roughly cut the lot and throw it half wet into the wok to quickly stir-fry with a dash of olive oil, and onion and garlic to taste. Or steam the horta. The volume goes down rapidly. You get two small heaps of dark greens with a powerful yet velvety, spicy taste. Combine horta with bland sweet potato, tofu or omelette. Eat horta the Greek way with chunky fresh buttered bread and olives. I would have put the horta plot at the head of the list, because it is my mainstay in a new garden with unimproved soil. While other vegetables took time, we were eating horta six weeks after moving in, almost as soon as radishes. Through winter I add shredded cabbage leaves. At any time I add anything green to the horta fry-up.

The Greeks also serve horta cold. Boil greens a few minutes in water with salt, tough ones first, tender ones last. Drain, then rinse in cold water. Swing them dry in a tea towel before chopping finely and serve on a flat dish. Sprinkle with salt, pepper, olive oil and lemon juice. Or go Greek–Korean, using oil, chilli salt, rice vinegar and toasted sesame seeds.

Although this is intense companion planting, pick the plot clean seasonally to grow peas or beans followed by a root crop for rotation purposes. Set one square aside for next year's horta. Quickly grown food carried straight from the garden to the kitchen and eaten within the hour is as good as it gets! You and those you feed will burst with health after a year on horta. They fed Olympians on it!

Seed-saving: Let one of each kind of green go to seed so that the plot becomes self-perpetuating.

The Aztec Plot

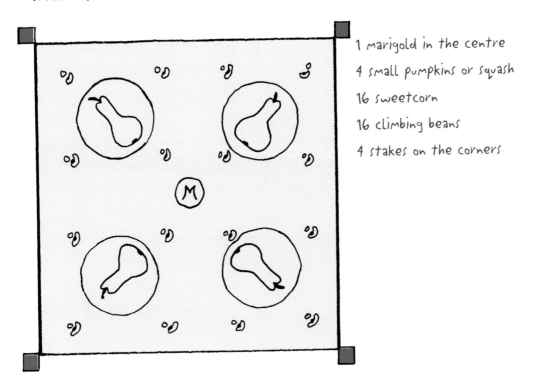

1 marigold in the centre

4 small pumpkins or squash

16 sweetcorn

16 climbing beans

4 stakes on the corners

The healthy diet of the Aztecs was based on companion planting. Aztec staples were corn, beans and pumpkin or squash, all shallow-rooted plants. The beans climb up the corn stalks, shaded by its broad leaves, and the pumpkin or squash vines ramble underneath keeping everyone's roots cool. Read up on these in Part Four.

After so much crop rotation on one square, why not let the horta grow on into summer, and if you have not done so yet dig up another square for a new experiment. The Aztec combination can also grow after a winter's Broadbean

Plot. But it is not a pick-and-come-again plot. You will pick beans first, corn late summer and squash in autumn. So consider sowing a Salad Plot as well, or plug seeds into the Horta Plot.

What still succeeds in Mexico's climate may not flourish where you are. None of these plants stand frost, but some varieties take cold nights better than others. Instead of sowing all seeds simultaneously, plant squashes first, sweetcorn next and lastly beans when spring warms up. Use a plastic roof, or re-seed if plants fail.

Three weeks before planting, prepare the soil as for gross feeders with CMC and a sprinkling of lime to please the beans. As you do for broadbeans, pound stakes on the corners to rope corn stalks in when 50 cm tall.

4-year-old Emile's accidental Aztec Plot: sweetcorn, courgettes, bean.

Fill four toilet rolls with potting soil, plant four pumpkin or squash seeds, germinate under glass or indoors. Raise with LS. If rodents are a problem, also raise 16 sweetcorns and 16 climbing beans in toilet rolls indoors until 8–10 cm with a good set of leaves. Plant out when the danger of frost is over. Raising plants before that date gives you a head start.

If you prefer to sow direct when all danger of frost is over, push 16 sweet-corn seeds 2 cm deep in four rows of four. Plant 16 climbing bean seeds next to each sweetcorn. Place PVC rings or bottomless yoghurt tubs over both, preferably with netting (see **Hardware in the Food Garden**). Place four rings with pumpkin or squash seeds equidistant between the sweetcorn and put a marigold in the centre because you can't have enough of them. Sprinkle organic fertiliser between rings and water in well. Douse with LS. When all plants are up and away, top dress with CM. The Aztec Plot supports a lot of growth, so rotate LS, B&B and OF fortnightly.

Expect several pounds of beans depending on variety, 32 corn cobs and 10–20 squashes depending on how well the bees pollinate the flowers. If you have any doubt about bees, hand pollinate by picking a male flower (the one without the swollen base at the stem) and pushing it full onto a just-opened female flower (with the swollen base at the stem), rubbing them well together. That's getting physical, and it works.

Seed-saving: Tie red wool around your best cob and best beans. Let them dry on the stalk. Leave one pumpkin or squash drying on the vine, scrape out seeds, rinse well, and leave to dry in a dark place. Sweetcorn seed does not remain viable for long – use it next spring.

The Pea Plot
AUTUMN, WINTER & SPRING

My second job was in Australia pea picking in late winter. Those were bush-podding peas, whereas now we have tender snow peas and sugar snaps, which tend to grow well in early spring. Generally peas don't fancy hot summers, but if you live in cool or snowy regions you may have to plant peas in early spring for a summer harvest. Know your own mini-climate or experiment with seasonal sowings of pea varieties until you learn what does well when, where you are.

Peas are as exciting a crop as beans. Flowers of white and pretty colours climb high or huddle demurely, bush style. Lime your plot. If you don't have rodents sow direct three weeks later. Otherwise sow seed in toilet rolls. Protect with wire, racks, or cages until plants are 8 cm high. Plant bush peas densely, six across the square, 36 plants in all. For climbers, push a tepee, wire trellis or tower into the ground – see **Hardware in the Food Garden**.

When plants are up and away, apply B&B or OF and douse with LS. This should be enough to keep them developing. To add to pea dishes, plant mint in a pot and place on a stone to stop roots sinking in. In case of overproduction, snap-freeze peas.

The Melon Plot

I used to sprinkle melon seeds in a corner during the busy spring planting season, to discover by midsummer that nothing had come of them. One year I decided to pay attention to melon seed, raising six seedlings of Hale's Best and Amish melons in toilet rolls in a cold frame. I prepared the bed with manure covered with compost. When the weather was warm enough I planted the seedlings and applied B&B.

I watered daily and deep. 'See,' I grinned to myself, 'the other seeds must have been taken by the birds.' By July the vines sported a few dozen melons the size of tennis balls. In August they all died.

Canteloupes need to ripen until the leaves dry off.

So I tried again, using Percy's plastic roof (see **Hardware in the Food Garden**) to keep seedlings warm during spring, feeding them pig compost. Edible melons were almost mine, but when they ripened the wildlife ate them!

Next year I'll dig a ditch in a sunny spot, layer it with manure, B&B, compost and straw and drench it, to imitate the Turfan Depression. I may experiment by sticking water-filled plastic bottles with drip holes in the caps upside down in the soil to irrigate, applying compost, LS and OF, and pinching out the tips of the vines when the melons have set. The sight of melons in your own garden is worth all that.

For watermelons I am tempted to try the same method, but I also know they love to spread their roots through undisturbed compost heaps that get watered. Don't come to me with tales of people who just spit out a few seeds from the veranda and eat melons all summer! They aren't telling where they spat. As for not sharing my melons with the wildlife, I'll try a cage held down with bricks to keep those rats out. Best of luck to us.

Canteloupes have been known to ripen outdoors in Britain, as have watermelons, but they have generally been grown on a hot bed and/or in a sheltered spot, with fleece to keep them warm at night. They represent a real challenge to the home gardener.

If you want success, it's far better to grow in a greenhouse, possibly on top of a hot bed.

The Herb Plot

Bay laurel, marjoram, mint, oregano, parsley, rosemary, tarragon, thyme, wild celery. Sow dill, coriander and cumin in autumn. All these culinary herbs will grow in one plot semi-permanently, so dig a separate circle in a sunny spot, or make herb beds around small fruit trees in full sun for mutual benefit – see **List of Common Herbs** for companions. Plant borage, marigold and nasturtiums among any vegetables as companion plants.

Prepare soil with CMC. Plant the bay laurel in the centre – unless there is a fruit tree – and divide the circle into six segments. Bay laurels become big trees in wet places – keep yours small in a large pot. Plant mint in a pot placed on a paver to prevent it sinking roots everywhere. Arrange the other herbs around the tree. Rosemary is a large herb that can be pruned frequently and dried for tea, baking bread and cakes, adding to pastas and roasted spuds, sweet potato or pumpkin. Do all that with thyme as well.

Woody herbs need less water than vegetables. But do mulch plots to preserve moisture. Herbs like to be picked regularly. Prune when leggy. Dry leaves for mixed herbal tea – excepting bay laurel and wild celery. Use bay laurel leaf only for flavouring in cooking, do not ingest but fish it out.

Get herb-wise and add other fragrant plants to the circle when space allows. Read up on herbs in Part Four, as some herbs are better planted in pots, as a hedge, or in shady places.

The Soup Plot

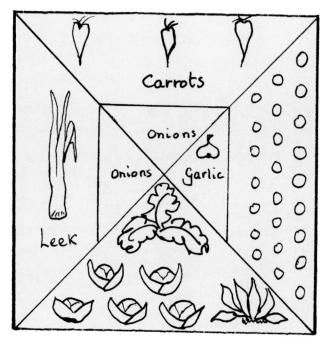

Centre: 1 seed tray of onions in two triangles

1–2 knobs of garlic

1–2 Russian kale

North: carrots, sprinkle lightly

East: 20–24 beetroots

South: 1 sorrel and 5 drumhead cabbages

West: 1 seed tray of leek

+ potatoes in a tub or hillock

Also recommended are herbs from the Herb Plot. Three weeks before planting rake lime into the square. Divide into four quarters. Prepare one quarter for gross feeders with CMC and B&B.

Sow five drumhead cabbage seeds in toilet rolls. Sow one tray each of leeks and onions. Plant potatoes in big tub or hillock, mulch with straw. Sow beetroot, carrots, garlic and Russian kale direct. See Plan opposite. Plant out leeks and onions in shallow ditches as explained in Part Four under Leeks and Onions. Plant one sorrel plant, or a few seeds in a corner of the cabbage quarter. When plants are up and away, douse with LS to give them a boost. The cabbages are planted tightly, so pick outer leaves as they swell.

You are still eating pumpkin soup from the freezer compartment, blended from summer's last pumpkins. Soups are meals par excellence to freeze and pull out in a hurry, served with bread, cheese and salad. Your cupboard holds lentils for lentil soup. Make a hearty blend with lentils, pumpkin and cumin. Maybe you grew celery and are a bit sick of celery soup from those leafy heads. A little celery goes a long way, and it's great for your health if organically grown. There are still pickings in the square for a mixed vegetable soup. Once all that is gone we are into winter soups, one-pot meals that do not need a dollop of fattening cream on top, because that would mask the good taste of vegetables grown especially for winter. Serve with fresh buttered bread. Garnish with fresh herbs. Apart from making soup, you can also eat the greens of beet, kale and sorrel, and fry cabbage with garlic and onion greens.

The vegetable stock used in the following recipes can be made in bulk and frozen in meal-size portions. Roughly cut carrots, celery and onions to simmer in water until soft. Cool, blend, store and freeze. For clear stock drain first and use vegetables as puree. Alternatively, save vegetable off cuts (roots, peel, onion skins, pods, herb stems etc.) and freeze until there's enough to boil a pot of stock – add fresh herbs.

A bouquet garni that will enhance any soup is made with a bay leaf, sprigs of parsley, two cloves, half a teaspoon of cumin seed and some peppercorns tied in a square of muslin for easy removal. Or tie other combinations of parsley sprigs, rosemary, sage and thyme in a bunch. These bouquets can be used fresh, made ahead of time and frozen, or dried in a dust-free place.

WINTER SOUPS

Borscht

Sauté raw, grated beets with sliced leek, onions, celery, shredded cabbage and garlic. Stir frequently until vegetables are reduced. Add vegetable stock. Boil for several hours. Traditionally served with sour cream added just before serving, so put a dollop on top with a sprig of dill. Also excellent served chilled with plain yoghurt, dill and diced cucumber.

Cabbage Soup

This soup is famous in European novels for leaving a nauseating stink hanging in the stairwells of crowded tenements. Let's start anew with this noble vegetable that has saved many people from starvation, and was the mainstay of my hardy ancestors.

In the midst of the Dutch famine in the 1940s a compassionate enemy soldier gave me a large green cabbage. It was so heavy that, as a 10 year old, I could not carry the bag but had to drag it two kilometres through the snow during curfew hours. I could have been shot for this cabbage but I got it home and it fed us for a week. Unforgettable things happen in wars.

Finely shred a quarter drumhead. Sprinkle with half a cup of wine, cover and set aside. Grate 2–3 potatoes, sprinkle with a splash of vinegar, cover and set aside. Sauté a big diced onion in olive oil. Add half a litre of vegetable stock, grated potato and a flat teaspoon of caraway seeds. Simmer 20 minutes. Whisk until smooth. Add salt and crushed black pepper. Add shredded cabbage and bring back to the boil. Simmer until cabbage goes limp, but is still al-dente. Serve with sesame bread sticks.

French Onion Soup (ditch those packets!)

Chop onions into rings and sauté until translucent. Add black pepper and vegetable stock. Turn on the oven. Cut a French loaf or two baguettes into slices and toast one side under the grill. Place half the bread in an ovenproof pot and grate hard cheese over it. Pour in the hot soup. Cover with the rest of the bread and more cheese. Brown a little in a hot oven before serving this French lunch.

Another recipe starts the same, with sautéed onions. Stir in a few spoons of flour, add enough hot milk for a soup, then pepper and salt. Cook and stir. In a separate bowl beat some egg yolks and add soup one spoon at a time until it is fifty-fifty. Then pour the egg and soup mix into the soup while whisking. Reheat without letting it come to the boil. Serve with fried bread.

Garlic Soup

Contrary to the powerful sensation the name of this soup brings to the taste buds, it is a gentle soup. Crush half to one dozen cloves of garlic and boil in vegetable stock with as varied a bouquet garni as the garden provides: parsley, bay laurel, tarragon, thyme, oregano, fennel and rosemary are good. Boil for an hour to extract flavours. Add salt and pepper. Beat one egg, slowly pour into soup while whisking, but don't boil. Serve with cheese sandwiches, fried, grilled or plain.

Leek & Potato Soup with Sorrel

Slice leeks and potatoes. Boil until soft. Cool and blend soup while adding salt, black pepper and a pinch of fenugreek powder. To serve, reheat. Meanwhile, lightly sauté a handful of chopped sorrel in a tablespoon of olive oil and stir into the soup just before ladling it into bowls. Serve with boiled egg slices on crackers.

Russian kale Soup

Coarsely chop leaves of Russian kale and simmer with one chopped onion and garlic cloves until soft. Cool and blend. For a punch, blend the onion raw. Add soy sauce to taste. Reheat this delicious green soup and serve with cheesy dreams, cheese sandwiches fried on both sides.

SUMMER SOUPS

Cucumber & Yoghurt Soup

A lovely soup for late summer gluts of cucumber. Cook cucumber in water, cool and blend. Mix in plain yoghurt. Serve chilled with dill or rocket and a dusting of cumin or ground coriander. Make this soup also with courgette.

Gazpacho

A famous Spanish dish and a main meal. Mix a few slices of bread with olive oil, a little vinegar, garlic and a litre of stock. Add chopped tomatoes, cucumber, pepper and onion. Blend or mix well, carefully adding cayenne pepper. Add salt and chilli to taste. Serve cold with chives. Adding crushed walnuts tastes good, though maybe not very Spanish.

The Pick-&-Come-Again Plot

SPRING & SUMMER

By now you may have a collection of seed packets for all sorts of pick-and-come-again greens. Check which can be planted in spring and summer. Since you may have grown onions, garlic and leeks for the soup plot and these continue into early summer, plug in seeds of Asian and other summer greens while harvesting the older vegetables as time goes by. Plug in non-heading lettuces and raise one cucumber plant and 1–2 cherry tomato bushes in toilet rolls. Scratch B&B between plants and douse seedlings with LS. This plot will give you ingredients for stir-fries, soups, quiches and salads, if your way of cooking and composing meals takes into account what grows at a particular time. This is all you can do while the *Allium* family is drying off. But nothing stops you from digging up a new square if you haven't done so yet, to grow your favourite starchy staples. And if you have done so, there should be space available.

Endive and perennial spinach take up one sixth of a square,
yet provide interesting greens for most of the year.

The Starchy Staples Plot
SPRING & SUMMER

Sweetcorn grows well after a winter crop of broadbeans – leave the stakes in place – or after crops that were well fed. If the plot is new, treat with CMC or COF. Plant seeds in a square grid 20 cm apart, denser than for the Aztec Plot – 5 x 5 seeds may yield 30–50 cobs if you feed and water plants well. Use plaited baling twine or pantyhose to tie around stakes to keep stalks standing in high winds. Apply B&B when cobs start forming and keep up the watering. Harvest when the 'hair' dries off. Should rats eat ripening cobs, cut waxed paper plates once to the centre, place one under each cob upside down, staple the cut section and wind a strip of sheeting around the stem to keep the plate in place. Or, cover each cob with an orange net bag. Cobs can be frozen. Dry the best cob on the stalk for seed and use within a year.

Potatoes are prolific croppers. One plant can produce up to 2 kg of potatoes, depending on the variety and soil fertility. You will get much more from one square than from the tub we've used to grow new potatoes for salads and pizzas. Choose a bigger potato this time. *Whereas broadbeans and sweetcorn can be alternated for a few years, never grow potatoes in the same place for more than five years, to avoid root rot.* Apply manure and straw.

Sweet potatoes grow mostly in tropical to subtropical climates, but in temperate regions try sprouting a tuber indoors, then plant it in a sheltered, sunny spot. Water daily but assure good drainage. If the plant produces plenty of vines above ground, you can pick leaves and crunchy fry them for a delicious green vegetable. Apply a thick cover of CM after planting. Read more in Part Four.

The Rotating Mono Crops Plot

Many people take pride in growing one prolific crop really well each season, rather than bother about diversity. As long as you can buy a range of locally grown organic vegetables, your square can grow the fillers.

Begin in spring with a plot of sweetcorn. Follow this in autumn with broadbeans. Follow this the next spring with potatoes, and the following autumn with peas. Read up on their cultivation in Part Four or in previous plot plans. After harvesting, snip bean and pea plants at ground level, chopping up and digging in the plants as green manure. Such a sequence returns some of the nutrients the crops take out, but in the fifth season it is best to grow a grain or a green crop like mustard to dig in. Or, cover the square thickly with CMC and B&B and grow shallow-rooted lettuces, Asian greens or horta through summer and winter, before returning the plot to the sequence starting with sweetcorn in the fourth spring, but omitting potatoes for another four years.

The Onion & Garlic Plot
AUTUMN & WINTER

If you grew starchy staples and peas there ought to be enough nutriments left to grow a root crop. Maybe you are too busy this year to pay attention to the food garden. But you can save much money without spending much time by setting out an onion and garlic plot. Decide how much garlic you want and how many onions. Clean the soil and draw a dividing line. Divide a packet of onion seed over two seed trays and break knobs of garlic into cloves. Buy a handful of shallots to plant direct and triple in volume.

To save maintenance time, plant garlic in rows and transplant onions in straight drills when 8–10 cm high. Mulch thickly on top of the garlic and between onion drills. Douse with LC. The only work left to do is weed the onion plot while seedlings are struggling up. They look like grass but they don't feel like grass between the fingers, much less smell like grass. This once-only weeding job cannot be avoided. Do it when straps are 12–15 cm above ground, then cover soil between rows thickly with CM.

Water the square if it's dry weather and douse with LS once a month. You can harvest onion and garlic straps to flavour many a meal. You are having a winter off from food gardening, yet saving money and eating home-grown. Plan to have more variety next season!

The Anti-Cancer Plots

Kids object to strong-tasting vegetables. So do some adults. Brussels sprouts and broccoli used to taste bitter, but this has been bred out to make these vegetables more palatable. The old bitter taste was caused by glucosinates that helped the plants ward off pests, and also helped the human immune system ward off the formation of tumours. That is how the brassica family, especially broccoli, became known as cancer-fighting vegetables. There is evidence that modern vegetables have less vitamin and mineral content than old varieties. The epidemic of cancer in a bewildering variety of forms has been blamed on an equally bewildering number of possible causes. But since the maintenance of our bodies and immune systems relies largely on what we ingest, we should perhaps take note of these findings.[2]

It seems that by altering vegetables for modern tastes or for longer shelf lives the plants' innate protection mechanism has been reduced. Subsequently, genetically modified crops have been bred to make them pesticide resistant so they can be sprayed against pests. Waste no time, but return to the old varieties available from seed banks (see **Useful Addresses**).

Anti-Cancer Plot A

SPRING & SUMMER

For a spring and summer Anti-Cancer Plot, plant Chinese flowering broccoli, green summer cabbage and kale. Raise broccoli and cabbage in toilet rolls while preparing soil with CMC, OF and lime. Plant broccoli and cabbage 20 cm apart. That's crowded, but you'll pick outer leaves for stir-fries. Sow seed for several kale plants to make green soup – see the Soup Plot. Douse all plants with LS.

Russian purple kale.

Also eat yellow/orange vegetables to bolster the immune system. Read up on carrots, pumpkins and squashes in Part Four. Sow carrots direct as instructed, raise pumpkins and squashes in toilet rolls as in previous plot plans. Plant out when danger of frost is over.

Feed monthly with B&B, OF and LS in rotation. If there's space, plug in seed of summer-loving Asian brassicas – see **An A–Z of Vegetable Groups** in Part Four.

Anti-Cancer Plot B

WINTER

In mid summer raise half a dozen Brussels sprouts in toilet rolls to grow on into winter. Sow seed for new kales, winter broccoli (slice the thick stems and cook with florets), cabbages and Asian brassicas preferring cool weather. Grow winter or all-season carrots and mooli radishes (see recipes under Mooli in Part Four). Sow a row of beetroot, for all red vegetables and fruits are cancer fighters.

Apart from eating brassica vegetables 3–4 times a week, make meals with one green and one yellow/orange vegetable and add red fruits and vegetables whenever you can. Prepare these foods in several ways – fresh, steamed, in soups or salads – so the body gets a steady supply of disease-fighting nutrients. Do not discard outer cabbage leaves, but wash and simmer with onion, garlic and caraway seed. These leaves are the best of the cabbage. Make cabbage rolls with grated mooli, fresh coriander or fenugreek and marinated tofu. Steam beetroot greens. Use all stems of kale, broccoli and cabbage for juicing, adding apple, carrot, or ginger for flavour. Blend beetroot juice with carrot. Health!

Carrots, our main orange vegetable.

Berry Plots & Hedges
AUTUMN & WINTER

All berries prefer cool weather. For growing notes see the **List of Easy-Care Fruit Trees & Berries** in Part Four. *Appropriate netting not dangerous to wildlife may be necessary, therefore plant hedges that can be reached from both sides.* Berries are superior foods providing immunity boosters, disease-fighting and health-restoring minerals and vitamins. Red and blue berries are cancer-fighting fruits.

Presently blueberries top the list of anti-cancer fruits, followed by blackberries, a disappearing species due to spraying by landholders. If you have a stand of blackberries on your land, and you can keep a goat, let her prune it after fruiting. Goats know what's good for them. The bushes grow back to fruit copiously. Dig out seedlings where you don't want them. The main reason for the spread of blackberry seedlings is neglect of unattended land, of which there is still some in the UK. If they get into your garden, either dig them out or cut them down continually. Regular very hard pruning for three years eradicates them. Should you have acres of blackberry bushes on your new country block, mend your fences and get another goat. But don't contaminate the neighbourhood and waterways by widespread spraying.

A thornless blackberry is available from nurseries. It grows like topsy on a support and can be pruned into shape.

Also consider raspberries and other brambles such as youngberries. Youngberries bear large juicy fruit and will grow vigorously on lower wires between espaliered fruit trees. They tolerate part shade, especially if they get shade in the heat of day. Water during dry spells.

Raspberries need a string support between stakes. Train new shoots espalier fashion for easy picking.

Berry bushes with thorns are best kept away from vegetables. Plant bushes so you can cultivate the soil around them. Or plant a freestanding berry hedge, spacing bushes according to their labels. Include one or two of each variety, let them fight it out and pick your three-berry mix straight from the bushes. My partner grew up in North America. One day, picking over a large wild blueberry bush, he sensed someone else was picking the other side. Peeking around the bush he came face to face with a large brown bear! The bear was more interested in the berries than in other pickers, so that expedition ended well. See Part Four for blueberry requirements.

Gooseberries are delightful if ripened on the bush. They are thorny and perennial.

Strawberries live the low life in semi-permanent beds. As they need netting, make a bed the size of your cage or netting. It's a nice idea to plant strawberry borders, but long borders are hard to protect from birds. Even under netting, millipedes and mice come for dessert. Read up in Part Four for important directions.

Consider strawberries in their natural environment of dappled light in forests and hedgerows, partially shaded in richly mulched, well-draining soil, surrounded by nutritious weeds. Hard to imitate. Commercial strawberries grow in open fields, through slits in black plastic sheeting on rows of heaped-up earth made weed-free with chemicals. They need to be fed and watered heavily to produce the three large annual crops that make them commercially viable. They keep every latest wave of human immigrants in part-time work, picking, packing and cultivating.

Mulch strawberries with pine or other needles to improve the flavour.

The Pumpkin Plot
SPRING & SUMMER

The pumpkin takes an important place in our diet. It used to be the sloppy yellow one you had to have alongside your greens. With luck it was baked pumpkin. As innovative cuisines gained popularity the pumpkin took off in the form of a golden soup, adorned with herbs, spices, cream and chives, whose popularity has not waned. Roast pumpkin turns up in convenience foods – baguettes, tarts, pizzas – and chef's gourmet creations.

Now that the seed of many old-fashioned varieties is procurable, everyone can find a favourite pumpkin, although the Queensland blue and the Chianti-bottle-shaped butternut will deservedly remain favourites for their sturdy flesh and keeping qualities.

The ideal growing medium for pumpkins is the compost heap. Question is, how to leave a compost heap undisturbed for half a year to allow pumpkins their place in the sun? Compost heaps provide a variety of nutriments and preserve moisture with good drainage. All these the pumpkin vine appreciates. Pumpkins have been known to grow in long-term heaps, those you throw the rough stuff on.

Present climate changes leading to hotter summers must be taken into account. Planting three pumpkin seeds in a hillock and pulling out the two weaker seedlings may still work in cooler and wetter parts. But anywhere with sandy soil in a dry part of the country, grow pumpkins in a thickly composted and manured bed, or try growing them in a ditch.

Cutting three 1 m ditches side by side gives a compact situation, where all water expended is kept in the family, whereas one long ditch of 3 m tends to dry out on both sides. In the three-ditch square the middle ditch may do best. Dig 30 cm deep. In late winter fill ditches with layers of soft weeds or green leaves and stalks, manure, compost, OF or B&B and straw mulch. The green matter decomposes quickly; all layers will mash to form the feeding ground, with applications of LS or OF as pumpkins are forming.

Start off one variety only of pumpkin seedlings in nine toilet rolls as described in the Aztec Plot, three plants per ditch. Of course they will clamber all over each other and sprawl beyond the square. But as long as you place straw, planks or tiles under forming fruit it should not matter. When there are several fruits on a vine, pinch out the tips. This tells the vine to stop having babies and put its energy into the ones it already has. Steam the tips and young leaves, flowers and all, in coconut cream and serve as a vegetable.

In very hot weather, without shade, pumpkins may suffer, but generally, with sufficient water and mulched to keep the soil moist, they will perk up again in the cool of the night time.

Don't pick pumpkins too early. When stems start drying out and are obviously unable to feed the fruit any longer, cut pumpkins with a 5 cm stem. Place on a table or bench in an airy place outside, to harden off. Blend immature pumpkins for soup and freeze. Immature pumpkins have an immature taste, but mixed with lentils, herbs and spices give edible results.

Seed-saving: From the best one – the biggest and most mature – wash the seed, dry it for several weeks out of sunlight, and store in a mouse-resistant container.

The Perennials

Read up on these vegetables in Part Four for more details. Perennial vegetables are ideal for the busy person who often does not see the garden in daylight until the weekend. These vegetables can look after themselves better than annual vegetables. Make sure you want them where you plant them, because they mean to stay more or less forever. *They do not fit into the pattern of rotating vegetable plots.* Here are a few indications of how little work is involved.

Artichokes are an underrated, decorative and easy crop to grow along a sunny fence. A perennial vegetable, the plants can be divided each year to establish a hedge.

Artichoke is easily grown from seed in late summer, or offsets from a nursery. The plants make a great hedge, but after harvesting – spring to summer – they must be cut to the ground to rise again. They are not choosy about soil, although better soil breeds better chokes. Mostly they require mulch and an application of CMC and B&B in late winter, before they fruit in spring. Give weekly waterings in summer as they grow back. When new plants form at the base, these can be cut off with a spade and planted out. One packet of seed gives a good hedge, and that hedge will give you another hedge in time. And so on to the neighbours! For seed, let one choke turn into a thistle-blue flower and don't cut down till it is dried on the stalk.

Asparagus is for the patient gardener, but worth every juicy bite. Dig soil a spade deep. Grow from seed sown in autumn, or plant crowns and cover with CMC and thick mulch. Do not eat any spears for two years, and then only a few, before picking meals in the fourth year. Cut ferns only when yellow, as they feed the plant. One annual big feed will do.

Perennial spinach and sorrel, both spinaches, can be grouped together and cooked together. Both grow through all seasons, both survive on a twice-yearly feed and watering in dry times, and both increase by division or dropping seeds. Cut seed stems if not needed. They are a great stand-by.

Rhubarb grows from crowns and one or two plants are enough for most families. As the (toxic) leaves grow big, two plants take up half a square, so it is advisable to plant rhubarb out in the garden to look decorative. Rhubarb also needs a good feed before the growing season and a rich mulch.

The Spice Companions
AUTUMN, WINTER & SPRING

The adventure of a Spice Plot is that you would never have seen some of these plants, even if you cook with spices. A Spice Plot does not have to fill a whole square; a quarter will do, or even a handy strip by the kitchen door.

Just as you grow coriander and fenugreek from seeds bought in the grocery, so with other spices. Rake seeds into the soil in small patches or tiny rows and stick in name tags, as they tend to look alike.

Caraway, cumin and dill look similar when young. Like coriander and fenugreek, these green herbs are all great seed producers. Fennel grows enormous, so plant just one, and separately. Don't let seed spread to the neighbourhood – cut off seed heads before seed drops. Mustard soon towers over others and is better grown among vegetables. Buy kalonji or 'onion seed' (visibly related to love-in-a-mist) from the Indian shop.

Duck into shops of various cultures for seeds in little packets. Ask what they are used for. Try them out in the kitchen and plant a few. Some, being tropical, may not respond, but other fresh spice greens make delicious additions to small meals of a few vegetables, noodles, roasted pumpkin, salads, blender soups, or bread sprinkled with olive oil and cheese. Gourmet eating made easy.

PART TWO
Toward Food Self-Sufficiency

Chard, lettuces and cauliflowers occupy a bean bed during spring, before
summer beans are planted.

The Terrifying Importance of Growing Food

This book has been inspired by the chaotic times we live in. It aims to put you in control of the production of at least part of the food you need. Food economists say it is now urgent that consumers start growing some of their own food, before shortages become the norm and prices hit the roof.

The book starts with one square metre of soil to grow your chosen vegetables, providing about one tenth of your food needs. One food producer acknowledged on radio in 2004 that periodically world food reserves in storage drop to less than one month's supply. Another expert revealed that more fish is fed to fish in aquaculture than comes on the market, and that oceans will get fished out in the foreseeable future. In 'first world' countries, more grain is fed to animals – those we eat, those that work and those that run the races – than is consumed by humans.

Although the world population keeps increasing, food production is decreasing. Only about two per cent of Britons, Americans and Australians are food producers. Countries at war cannot produce sufficient food or invest in agriculture. Their resources are destroyed or used to feed non-productive armies.

The global farming industry continues to dictate competition by lowering prices in supermarkets and raising shareholders' profits.

74

During 1944 and 1945 I endured a famine and, at 175 centimetres tall, was reduced to 34 kilograms of bone and sinew. I carry an abiding memory of my hometown, Hilversum (population 80,000 in the 1940s), breaking down as war action cut off the region. All trees became firewood, as did doors, cupboards, furniture and fences. Cats, dogs, and rabbits disappeared. I starved rather than eat our rabbit Trudy. Mice, rats and birds went into the pot. Rivers were fished out. We ate sugar beet, which was normally pig fodder, and tulip bulbs which made me ill. I dug for grass roots under the snow to steady my stomach.

Now I witness the world's food-producing regions decline again through wars, landmines and farmers' deaths. All famines are caused by war. In peace-time, crop failures through natural calamities, usually local and short-term, can be met by rapid food aid.

Some people still believe that genetically modified (GM) foods will feed the world. But GM food has not been discussed enough, nor is it supported by long-term testing. Meanwhile, the better policy is to foster food plant diversity, preserve the inherently good qualities of reproducible food plants, and maintain extensive seed banks in case of regional crop failures due to war, weather or new space-age weevils. See **Useful Addresses** for seed sources and seed banks.

Professor Julian Cribb of the University of Technology in Sydney foresees growing populations needing to increase food production by 110 per cent over the next four decades while facing decreasing resources of water, farm land and soil fertility, and a global decline in agricultural research.[4] Even aquaculture – meant to feed us as the oceans get fished out – is in trouble due to contamination from the land. Frequent droughts are to be expected as the norm and some countries will grow more biofuel crops than food crops. Professor Cribb regards adapting to greenhouse conditions as urgent, but not nearly as urgent as working toward doubling world harvests with fewer resources.

During half a lifetime of food gardening, in four locations with different soils and climates, I found that books with illustrations of perfect aspects, lush black earth, plentiful water and beauty-parlour vegetables did not match my own experience. Hence my illustrations of vegetable jungles and cabbages with holey leaves. But I learned that healthy food can be grown anywhere. Food will grow where *you* are. Some of our best agricultural land is being covered by suburbs; therefore we should grow our food in the suburbs.

Scientists calculate that if food crops are consumed by people instead of being fed to livestock, one person can in theory live on the produce of 100 square metres.[5] That is 10 x 10 m per person, intensively cultivated. A family of four would need four such plots, covering 20 x 20 m (not counting paths) with one rotating plot growing grain, and another peas and beans to dry and freeze.

A one-square-metre garden gives you a fair idea how far you want to go. The labour required is minimal and pleasurable because you don't start off with a big project only to find you have overreached yourself, throwing the garden fork away and running to the supermarket for half a sprayed cauliflower and two pale tomatoes.

In the year 1500, the globe supported approximately 400 million people of whom some 80 million lived in the Americas. Of these, Mexico had 25 million people who were fed on corn, beans and squash. In 1999 the populations of the United States (258,233,000), Argentina (33,778,000), Chile (13,813,000) and Puerto Rico (3,620,000) alone totalled just over 400 million.[6] In 500 years the world population has risen to approximately 6.3 billion, taking up all arable land for sustenance, and is expected to increase to approximately 10 billion by the middle of the 21st century.

Important reasons for growing your own food keep mounting. The same multinational corporations that gave us global warming – by using fossil fuels in industry and cutting forests around the globe, robbing millions of people of self-sufficiency and causing man-made disasters that force untold millions to lose their land, homes and belongings, if not their lives, through floods, droughts and climate change – are now bringing us genetically modified foods because they profess to have a new mission 'to feed a hungry world'.

The corporations are as compassionate about hungry humanity as giant pharmaceutical companies are about poor children with AIDS or malaria. These corporations have switched from mining, logging and manufacturing to seed and food production because these are globally consumed commodities they don't yet control. Moreover, it's time to get out of manufacturing cigarettes and logging. They will want to get out of oil before it runs out.

Genetically modified foods are unknown quantities because manufacturers do not want to label them correctly, which would allow consumers to check contents, make informed choices, avoid substances that may cause allergies, or give the foods a miss altogether. Governments buckle at the knees because these food companies are also major investors in raw materials – from mining to wood pulping – and are potential investors in our mining, railways and armament industries. That's why they won't legislate for adequate labelling. No long-term safety trials have been done either, so we don't even know how GM and genetically engineered (GE) foods will affect our future health.

The best way to feed a hungry world is to return to poor people the security of an average plot of land with a water source and control over their own seeds, enabling them to grow their own food and sell the surplus in local markets. But corporations want to control the world's seeds in order to insert terminator genes, meaning the next generation of seeds will be unable to germinate. The company can then sell farmers and gardeners new seeds every year, combined with the fertiliser and herbicides needed by these hybrids. Thus they protect their investment in the 'improved' seeds, which came from a farmer in the first place and whose ancestors saved them over centuries. Selling seeds has been identified as having a vast, as yet untapped, global market.

You and I are fortunate to have private plots of soil, however small, and should not waste a day to get stuck into these and avail ourselves of earth's bounty. Nature will surprise us by conducting its own biodiversity maintenance as long as we feed, mulch and water. It's that simple. We only play at being conductors of a green symphony composed at the beginning of time on earth. The music starts slowly to end in a crescendo of delectable tones, tastes and colours.

People who do not currently regard themselves as poor, who can afford to buy fruit and vegetables, are increasingly finding some becoming luxury items. Farmers have to pass on their increased costs to the consumer. Corporations are always 'improving' seeds and want to be paid handsomely for their efforts – more handsomely than any farmer ever is – and water restrictions, droughts and climate changes are making food crops scarcer and more expensive.

UK food prices have risen 12% in real terms over the last five years taking us back to 1997 in terms of cost of food relative to other goods. During 2001, the hottest summer in 95 years in South Australia, courgettes and cucumbers doubled in price, tomatoes and celery almost doubled and potatoes went up by a third.

In the recent past people grew their own vegetables to avoid toxic sprays on their food, to get that lovely freshness and superb taste of a sun-ripened tomato, and because it saved a little money. Now it's becoming more serious.

DEFRA's Pesticides Residue Committee concluded in 2013 that the common foods with multiple pesticides in them were: tomatoes, parsnips, cucumber, carrots, lettuce, beans in a pod, peas in a pod, sweet potatoes and courgettes.[7] The Australian Government Analytical Laboratory reported organically grown vegetables can contain an average of up to 10 times more nutrients than chemically fertilised vegetables.[8] These facts are disturbing, but pale compared with other major forces that threaten our food supplies. We must start taking responsibility for producing some of our daily food.

Hunger is caused less by failure of food production then by failure of distribution, interruption from wars and regional conflicts, political chicanery, robbery or plain apathy. Now distribution is being interrupted by the withholding of viable, reproducible seeds and exacerbated by years of drought. It would be foolish to think that a famine periodically happens somewhere else and could not happen where we live.

In the UK, changes to our land are apparent. Underground water resources are being overused and rivers have stopped flowing. Alarmingly our wildernesses have shrunk and our forests are still being axed.

However, there is one place that can still be a biodiverse wilderness. That is our garden. Not just the garden – that utility area for bins, barbecues, dogs, kids and the washing – but the front garden, side garden and the strip along the driveway: all are private domains. Privacy and wilderness are important to you. To almost walk into a giant spider web hung with dew on a path between two shrubs, to see brilliantly coloured beetles at work, to find stick insects, butterflies, frogs and tiny birds skating between plants you have given the freedom to reach for the sun, is hugely satisfying and elevates the spirit. The only wilderness you can access daily, whose gates do not keep you out or charge a fee, is your garden. Make it beautiful. Make it a place of increase.

Your own wilderness can feed your body and soul.

As urban food growing becomes a necessity instead of a hobby, it's good to know we have so many urban and suburban growing spaces in the UK. Imagine squares of green edibles in every backyard that doesn't grow vegetables yet! Globally, more than half of all people now live in urban areas and urban food farming is bound to increase.

Naturalist Sir David Attenborough said in his television series, *State of the Planet*, that the decisions we humans make in the next 50 to 100 years will determine what happens to all life on earth thereafter. Sadly, what happens to all life on earth hereafter may have little to do with decisions you and I make and more with decisions by our and other people's governments.

For decades small producers have gone out of business due to competition from government-subsidised agribusiness. Agribusiness, in the language of the World Trade Organisation (WTO), concerns soya bean, maize, rice, wheat and canola, some of which go into processed foods that sit on supermarket shelves for years without going bad, but most of which feeds animals raised for meat to feed the humans who can afford to buy it.

Moreover, just one company, Monsanto, is responsible for 94 per cent of all GM seeds planted across the globe. To have the world's staple food crops narrowed to so few varieties, and to have ownership of practically all commercial seed for these major crops in the hands of one corporation is an unprecedented and frightening situation – especially when you know that this company is also developing the technology for terminator seeds. The company wants the 1999 United Nations moratorium on this technology lifted. So do the US, Australian, New Zealand and Canadian governments. Can they all be wrong? You bet they can.

Crops can fail. When they are big crops, they are big failures, causing famines. Corporations can fail too – especially those that make huge mistakes incurring liability and causing the loss or disappearance of all assets. Meanwhile the pollen of crops with terminator seeds, once let loose, will cross with normal crops, endangering their seed-producing viability. There is no known method to prevent this. In time – no one knows how long or short a time – seed stocks could be perpetually compromised until self-replicating seeds are a thing of the past.

Therefore, what we can do in the coming years with our part of the globe has already been decided by those who went before – which is how things work of course. Or fail to work. The water shortages and hosepipe bans of recent years, the drying up of rivers and streams, the removal of trees and the erosion of topsoil – these and many local land issues caused by lack of good governing are going to determine what we can or can no longer do, never mind what we had wanted to do.

For the home gardener this means the garden becomes the last resource. As agricultural lands keep shrinking and water supplies dry up, it's a piece of land still fertile that, with care, can yield sustainable food production. The home garden will also increasingly be a place where biodiversity is preserved on a small scale.

As the best agricultural land around cities and towns is urbanised and put under concrete, it is an inescapable fact that the best land on which to grow our food lies at the backdoor. Even in a concrete jungle you can grow food with some care. There may be minerals waiting to be unlocked, and like all other worlds, the plant world is one of entrepreneurs waiting for opportunities; all they need is a hand-up.

Industrialised food is sometimes claimed to be cheap, but as India's food activist Vandana Shiva has pointed out, it uses 10 times more energy to be produced and 10 times more water than food grown in organically maintained soil. She includes in the cost the technologists, producers of pesticides and farm machinery, truck drivers, the cost of diseases contracted by mono crops, environmental destruction in the name of agricultural expansion, government subsidies, and the cost of wars fought over the indispensable oil that drives the food industry. What you produce behind your home is dirt cheap by comparison.

Jeanette Fitzsimons of the New Zealand Greens pointed out that our present civilisation is the only one ever to be based on oil and the only one that ever will be.[9] Having used up in one century half of all oil resources – the half-way point, or peak oil, was reputedly reached in 2006, earlier than even the pessimists expected – we will now have to scale back our usage. Oil has given rise to previously unimaginable mining of resources from rivers, forests, seas and soils, and the shipping of these resources around the globe. As a result, the carbon dioxide level of Planet Earth's atmosphere has increased more than a third since the start of the industrial revolution.

It is now inescapable that every individual must scale down their oil consumption. By growing your own food you save not only the petrol for driving to the supermarket, but also the oil the industry uses to place food on supermarket shelves.

There are times when really cheap food is on offer, just as the multinational corporations promised. But we ought to investigate the true cost of 'cheap food'. It may be a dumping. We posed this question at the start of this century during outbreaks of mad cow and foot-and-mouth disease. Both spread far beyond what would normally have been contained locally due to the globalisation of trade and transport, the centralisation of abattoirs, and a variety of animal husbandry measures intended to drive production up and prices down. Once the diseases broke out and spread rapidly, entire herds were destroyed, businesses went broke, and families became destitute. Now many people live under a death sentence from diseases formerly unknown to affect humans. Add that to the cost of your cheap food. Something similar could happen with vegetables and fruit.

There is no free lunch. There is no cheap food. The cheapest and best food is the food you grow yourself – food that does not accumulate added costs for transport from other states or continents, needs no refrigeration because you pick it minutes before preparing it, does not add to pollution because it only travels from garden to backdoor, is free of costly chemicals, and needs no packaging. Consider the real cost of a cucumber in a plastic jacket, grown in a temperature-controlled poly tunnel, refrigerated, put in the jacket, transported a great distance, and displayed in an air-conditioned supermarket under burning lights. The cucumber you grow yourself just has to be fresher, tastier and healthier than that, doesn't it?

By growing your own organic vegetables you make unnecessary all the spraying, heating, cooling, and transport – from state to state and continent to continent – needed to stock greengrocers and supermarkets. Heed the warnings of outspoken oil experts. Without oil, transporting food over vast distances becomes prohibitive. We ought to start shortening as much as possible the distance between our fork and the farm.

All it takes on your part is a seasonal pick-up of a packet of straw and some organic fertiliser or manure. If you don't have a car, buy compressed straw cubes and organic fertilisers in small bags that fit in your shopping trolley. If the garden centre doesn't have what you need, persuade them to order it in. Buy seed as you do other shopping, or by mail order – see **Useful Addresses**. Find a hand trowel and fork. Yes, there is some transport involved, but the reduction is enormous.

As your food ripens a few steps from the backdoor, the environment is spared clouds of toxic fumes and run-off because you turned a sod one Saturday and wielded a watering can as you watched the sunrise. You are doing Planet Earth a service, as well as yourself and those you provide for. More so if you frequent local growers' markets for what you cannot grow yourself.

As part of this process we simply have to change our expectations of how vegetables ought to look. The horticultural industry achieves those sleek good looks by toxic means. With your own plot, you will eat vegetables and fruit in season and adjust menu planning to what the garden offers. Whereas a shopper muses, 'Shall we have cauliflower or green beans?', the gardener lifts up leaves and discovers that it is bean day, or cauliflower day, or a courgette emergency. If there's nothing but chard and tomatoes in quantities, it may be a stir-fry day with small pickings: beans, broccoli, a small squash, the biggest swede, or maybe two carrots and an Asian radish. Add a handful of cut-and-come-again greens and herbs and you will still have a feast of flavours!

Therein lies an enormous plus for the home grower. The selection in shops is limited to varieties that have shelf life. If a shop provides vegetables with short shelf life, you pay a price that has quick wastage calculated into it (plastic bags of mixed salad greens for example). So grow a dozen salad greens on one square, pick daily and grow them for months. You can grow 50 varieties of fresh beans and peas in your garden if you so choose, but buy only two at the shop. You can experiment with pumpkins in all colours and patterns, grow exotic cucumbers or a dozen different chillies and black tomatoes. There are many vegetables that never even reach the shops, not even the markets, so read a catalogue of organic non-hybrid seeds and let your imagination take flight.

An experimental summer delivered the good keeper Queensland blue pumpkin, Japanese pumpkins and some prolific yellow squashes.

Climate, Weather & Microclimates

Scientists are constantly readjusting predictions for the effects of human pollution on the world's climates. As gardeners we must grapple with global warming, global dimming, evaporation rates, less or more rain and ultraviolet rays. Where you live it may become cooler and dimmer due to increased pollution fall-out. You may experience less or more rain, storms, droughts or periodic floods. May you live in interesting times, so goes the Chinese curse.

Scientist Dr Tim Flannery has confirmed that in less years than my lifetime, world temperatures have risen by an average of six per cent. One model, since superseded, forecasts a more humid climate for south-western Australia, presently mostly desert. That would be offset by the number of days over 35 degrees doubling over the next 60 years, which seems to be happening already. He predicts the melting of a major Antarctic iceshelf by 2010 that will raise sea levels by a metre. And of course there are other iceshelves. There is already a water crisis and a fauna and flora extinction crisis (that may rise to 50 per cent of species), and can expect biodiversity collapse in southern Australia's near future.[10]

More than half the world's ecosystems are about to collapse. Then there is the under-reported fact that the global female population has declined to 10 per cent less than the male population through the termination of girl-baby pregnancies, female infanticide, and starvation of girl children in some countries. Females are food growers and nurturers.

So much for the bad news. There is a little good news named 'microclimate'. As food gardeners we rely on our understanding of regional and local climates. Your macroclimate may still be unpredictable temperate, with or without El Niño, but your microclimate is something else. After adding the peculiarities of your location – elevation, river, forest or seaside – the interesting phenomenon is that any number of gardens in the same macroclimate region may have different microclimates, and therefore different growing climates, depending on their surrounding gardens, built structures, trees and aspects. A garden in a suburb near sea level with all its built structures and trees may be easier to grow food in or more complex, depending on the ratio of trees to concrete. Gardens bordered by a park or reserve will have a different microclimate from the next street.

The beauty of a microclimate is that you can control some of it, whereas all you can do about your general location is plant trees with the neighbours and protest against logging. Anything you do to slow down global warming, climate change and the effects of El Niño weather patterns is worth doing for future generations, but won't have much bearing on your food garden now. So before you plant half the garden with trees, consider that some trees should not be grown close to homes. There are many beautiful trees of medium size, including fruit trees, that can give shade, flowers, fruit and even leaf mould for the food garden. In the natives vs exotics debate, we consistently overlook that we ourselves are the exotics, as are our fruit trees and food plants. Few Britons survive on foraging alone. Life is a compromise.

You can influence your microclimate by manipulating details. When transplanting plug chillies into pots, create a favourable climate by doing it under a broad-brimmed hat to shade the little devils. Garden umbrellas save bean crops on scorching days. A length of shade netting can be pulled over the greenhouse to protect a crop about to suffer sunstroke. In a cold snap, pack straw around root crops, broadbeans, cabbages and citrus trees. To protect against wind, erect a fence, screen, trellis, or a fast-growing hedge of elderberry, artichokes or bee-loving shrubs.

A body of water, however small, adds interest and a cool area. At least fill up the birdbaths. A minute's watering of the food plot makes a difference. Naturally, microclimate is firstly determined by the lie of the land, structures that block or tunnel sun and wind, and whether there are trees and shrubs to provide shelter and shade.

Observe your microclimate before laying out the food plot. If you locate the plot south of a row of newly planted trees, their roots will absorb water and soil nutrients, while dense shade can reduce your crops and prevent insects visiting for fertilisation and pest control. On a sunny day feel the heat bouncing off walls and fences, heat that could be a bonus to plants a metre away, but a killer to anything hard up against it. On windy days test where the wind tunnels are in your garden and don't plant your plot in their paths. But, all plants need moving air, so utilise gentle breezes. Observe how much full sun, morning sun, or afternoon sun the area receives, remembering the sun is lowest in the sky in mid winter, right overhead in mid summer, and between these extremes in spring and autumn when you put in young vegetables.

Plan to create a more beneficial microclimate. Plant flowering shrubs for windbreaks and bird havens; they don't have to grow high to benefit vegetables. A shaded or netting cloche or plastic tunnel not only houses delicate plants and seedlings, but provides four new possibilities. Grow heat-loving plants on the south side, lettuce on the north side, honeysuckle and pot herbs around an eastern entrance, and protect the west from ferocious winds with a hedge of strong plants: elderberry, hazel hedge, large daisies, wild plums, or golden rod.

Any strong plant will do, but those with other uses are best.

Be aware that whatever you place in the garden – be it a tepee, birdbath, or table and chairs – changes the path of the wind, casts shade and attracts perching birds. Your major success in creating a microclimate, beneficial to all types of fruit and vegetables, will come from how you plant your boundaries against the worst of weathers.

Just as you reshape your microclimate, so Planet Earth constantly re-shapes the macroclimate. Coastal climates are moderated by warm ocean streams. Mountain ranges stop rain or provide snow melt. Volcanic activity destroys vegetation before creating new fertility. Wind and water constantly wear down the highest mountains and redistribute minerals across the valleys or carry them afar via creeks and rivers. Deserts march up or retreat. The whole amazing global fertility show is constantly shedding and adjusting to maintain some golden mean, which may well be what lies between those once prolific tropical rainforests either side of the equator and the two poles. Vast weather patterns do not stop at borders, a change of season or hemisphere, until they have worked off their energy. When the Northern Hemisphere has a severe winter it may be preceded or followed by a wet one in the Southern Hemisphere. If one hemisphere has a drought, the other is often sure to follow.

Climate is one thing, weather is another. We used to think of climate as constant and weather as erratic. A weather pattern can afflict half the globe in one season. We see global droughts, floods and regional phenomena like El Niño and La Niña, and know we will be in for unusual weather events, although we may live far from the source. Continental weather of storms and rain patterns affects neighbouring continents or islands. Eventually, when certain weather patterns become regular features, they turn into climate, that supposedly predictable phenomenon that rules our lives. Yet over a long time, climates can change considerably.

When summers turn cold or dry, food gardeners need to be stubborn. Fruit may not set, pumpkins hardly flower, tomato plants huddle. Even if you assiduously add manure, compost, water and mulch, nothing grows well. Wildlife becomes desperate. Birds scratch mulches, slugs eat unripe tomatoes, mice dig for roots, and some unidentified creature removes hundreds of newly sown onion seeds, earning a tummy ache as well as bad breath! Rabbits may nibble suburban lawns. In such years the harvest is miserable and even courgettes fail to keep you supplied. Chard becomes the Great Stand-by, with kale, picked young.

You get one debacle or another, or two ganging up, but usually not all at once. But as times are unpredictable, it is wise to grow a variety of foods. One cold summer we had good cabbages, quinces and pears. The next spring came after a sunny dry winter with frosts. When good spring rains arrived the remaining cabbages, broccoli and cauliflowers cried: 'What's this? Rain? Never heard of it!' They took up the moisture alright, but soon one in every 10 plants had a head full of aphids. Those were the weakest plants, out-competed for water and food by their relatives. Whereas I claim elsewhere that even the smallest brassica can suddenly decide to become a real cabbage, when it is aphid time it's the runts that are attacked.

So you cannot wholly rely on charts telling you what you can grow in your climate. These are rough guidelines only. By becoming a food gardener now, you can make adjustments and invent methods that create a microclimate in which to survive the future. Macroclimate, microclimate, seasonal weather patterns and your adjustments plait something unique together. This is where food gardening becomes as exciting as competitive sport – it's about having the edge on the odds.

Never garden in a mood of wanting to control everything. Observe nature's ways. Don't be quick to interfere when things grow in unexpected ways – there may be reasons. Patient gardeners discover out-of-season surprises, such as ripe pumpkins in winter. Fruit tree seedlings may spring up from the compost. Wait a year or so, and perhaps they'll become disease-resistant plants that bear unexpectedly good fruit true to type. Let nature take over a little – become her assistant. Feed and mulch where soil looks exhausted and hand water to stay in touch with what grows where.

In a circular bed made with plastic water bottles, a tepee of wooden slats provides shade and shelter from wind for climbing beans and other vegetables.

Inspirations & Credentials

My understanding of food gardening comes from long ago. My great-great-grandfather was an estate gardener in Fryslân, the Netherlands, where Friesian cows hail from. In later life he was registered as a *kooltjer*, a grower of four main vegetable crops: potatoes, cabbages, carrots and onions. Maybe he became a market gardener because socioeconomic changes caused people to give up growing the family's food in favour of working for wages. Food had to be purchased and someone else had to grow it. His son operated a vegetable shop

Lolo feeding the chickens in Uncle Wim's garden.

as well as teaching school, and his grandson, my grandfather, owned a vegetable shop and wholesale business. One of my grandfather's sons, my uncle, grew oranges in California. On mother's side, Uncle Wim took me for walks from the time I toddled through his pride-and-joy food garden in Laren, North Holland. The first garden I ever grew food in was in Australia. My daughter, son and grandson grow herbs, fruit and vegetables. Yet I know people with no food-growing history whatsoever who produce impressive vegetables at first try!

A childhood dream was to surround myself with a garden that would be a treasure trove of resources. This dream was realised by living in an Adelaide Hills forest at 500 m altitude – a garden surrounded by a living ecosystem full of helpful predators who kept plants bug-free. No sooner did I construct plots and a greenhouse than in trooped frogs, lizards, skinks, praying mantises, beetles, ladybirds, spiders, birds and other flying wonders. Attracted by dam water sprayed on plants, and interesting things in manure, compost and mulch, they also came for a change of diet. Soon snakes and lizards ate strawberries for dessert and birds claimed their share of fruit. Animals, birds and insects are garden helpers as well as food entrepreneurs, making a living as best they can, and to some extent we should share our produce with them.

Our next garden was surrounded by native trees and open fields, with greater variations between hot and cold. We planted hundreds of trees, flowering plants, and a food garden on good river clay with compost made from prunings. Around the existing henhouse we designed a netted, espaliered orchard which chickens, ducks and geese kept bug-free.

Having experimented with as many as 65 varieties of food crops in one season in my first garden, in the second garden I focused on what grew best, raising more of fewer varieties, especially broccoli, cabbage, cauliflower and

Asian brassicas. Emerging from the garden with a bucket of produce gave me a sense of security. Even in lean times the garden provided meals, flowers, pots of herbal tea and wood for an evening fire.

In some ways I like scarcity – roaming through an autumn garden picking the last beans, a little kale, late onions or leek, the last shoots of a long-serving broccoli, an underdeveloped squash, or a handful of delicious kumquats eaten skin and all. No food garden is complete without a few fruit trees.

During the worst drought in a hundred years we moved to our third garden only to find soil that had been paddock for a century and was so nutrient poor and acidic that seedlings stopped growing at ankle height. On this 500 m high ridge winds blew from several directions simultaneously and rain came horizontally. The first year was heartbreak – we had to buy vegetables! In the second year we started eating piecemeal from the garden. New fruit trees were espaliered and hens, geese and ducks grazed the orchard, but three trees died and we ate a lot of tough chard. It took time to turn this one around – time, it turned out, I was not to have before we moved again.

My fourth food garden – Adelaide Hills, elevation 460 m – was hurriedly laid out atop rough grass to beat the oncoming winter, on layers of wet newspaper, straw and potting soil. We actually ate from it daily, but grass roots infiltrated and we had to rebuild the plot the following autumn with deeper edgings. So now you may profit from my mistakes.

From Garden to Table

One great delight in my circle of friends is the 'peasant lunch', a term we adopted to cover all probabilities and eventualities when serving an entirely home-grown meal. We had sat around camp fires in the earlier years, eating revolting communal stews concocted from tinned food brought by members of the archaeological team we worked with. No wonder we became foodies in later years, savouring the purest of foods, slowly and carefully prepared.

My early peasant lunches consisted of whatever vegetables and fruits were in season and dishes made with goose, duck or chicken eggs. I might have bought cheese and cream, or added olives from a crate bought at the market and pickled annually.

Gradually peasant lunches translated into meals from other cultures, using authentic recipes. Over the years we have savoured flavours from China (soy, spring rolls), India (chai, paneer, *laddhu*), Tibet (*tsampa*, *momos*, butter tea), Bali (chilli, coriander), Korea (pickles, roasted sesame seed), and the Middle East (salted lemons, almond mousse). Everyone contributes, often with no more organisation than each person bringing a different course. Sometimes a meal consists of starters, soup, salad, side dish and dessert, omitting a main dish. And we have a wish list of countries whose cuisines we are yet to try in our super-mature years, when excellent food becomes the primary joy of life.

Fortunately all great cuisines are based on peasant food and home-grown and farmers'-market produce. We found that Korean cuisine uses the same seeds, spices, sesame oil and rice vinegar for almost every vegetable, yet each dish tastes different. In Malaysia, just about everything is made with rice flour.

For some cuisines we buy new ingredients, but mostly we rely on our gardens and markets to travel the world at our table. Needless to say, the drinks are local, although we went to some lengths to make Tibetan butter tea and Indian chai.

For everyday cooking I lean on recipe books for the volume of green-leaf vegetables I dish up. Books can be found that deal mainly with anti-oxidant open-leaf vegetables, those that help fight cancer and heart disease, and which include many of the brassica family. Instead of using greens as a garnish, a gesture, or a display bed for meat and fish, such recipes feature green vegetables as the main ingredient. In many cultures, most parts of the vegetable are used to make tasty salads, soups and mains. One advocate for home growing, Mark Bittman, points out in his book that leafy greens are easier to grow, have fewer pests than other vegetables, can be started earlier, will last longer and many will grow throughout the year in temperate climates.

Have I mentioned pride? Well, no. Pride in produce is ultimately due as praise for Planet Earth, for providing the raw ingredients for us to grow and place the very finest food on our table. Humble food is undeniably the best tasting food. Bon appétit.

How to Find Time to Grow Food

One major hang-up people have about growing their own food is not having the time. They look from their garden to magazine pictures of gardens covered from fence to fence with productive beds and throw up their hands.

Do not do this to yourself! *Small is truly beautiful.* No matter how overgrown your garden is, you can weed one square metre, plant it and keep it tidy. It may lead on to two square metres or even a block of four – that is up to you. But be kind to yourself. Start with one magic square for the plot of your choosing.

At present your problem is that you don't have time. You are overworked and a little stressed. You don't get much opportunity to relax and when you do you'd rather . . . whatever. You worry weekly about the bills or the amount of fast food consumed. You may be depressed and unable to appreciate the good things in life. You are always busy – yet bored, not stimulated, and you don't get enough exercise but hate jogging, the gym, hitting a ball – all those purposeless remedial activities.

If any one of these conditions depict your life, change it instantly by digging up one square metre. It won't take much time or work, as it is only 100 x 100 cm, one stride by one stride. But it will relax and delight you, make you feel a long-forgotten feeling, and put you in touch with your wild side without leaving home! In a short time it will provide you with fresh food. Your depressive moods will evaporate when you tend your magic square, and you'll discover other micro worlds than the world you thought you lived in. Boredom will subside and you will do a daily three minutes bending-and-stretching routine, without being aware of it. Hand watering the square will become your meditation.

Where to find these minutes? Time is a gift from nature's own lovely chaos. So many books on growing vegetables show photographs of neat, weed-free rows of carrots and beans with not a shrivelled leaf in sight, bed after bed in similar order. These are ready-made free dinners for hordes of insects that can identify whole rows of their favourite food from the sky. Control your urban yearning for straight rows! Grow vegetable varieties in minute little plots within your square, interspersed with companion plants, self-seeding herbs and marigolds – the hordes will fly over and the weeds will find no space.

You will argue this won't be enough to feed a family and you'll be forced to dig up more squares once your loved ones are hooked on garden produce. But in Part Four you'll find tips to grow vegetables other than shop produce, so that you get by with a few broccoli, kale, come-again lettuces and Asian greens for months of picking. Grow carrots closely and pull as needed, making space for the remainder to grow. Plant chard in a dense drift and pick it tender for several seasons. One square of sweetcorn can yield 50 cobs, or 20 fresh broad-bean portions and another 20 for the freezer compartment. Potatoes, beetroot, swedes, tomatoes, beans, cucumbers and anti-oxidant greens are all high yielders in small spaces.

Less time spent on shopping for vegetables provides time to tie up the beans and plug in a few seeds. Bend, reach, turn, stretch and take deep breaths of fresh air, so you don't need to go to the gym, saving time and money and escaping conversations that go nowhere. Move beyond one square and you won't need to go jogging either. Forego boring club meetings with the excuse that you have to get stuck into the food garden (don't say 'veggie patch' lest someone tosses corny jokes). A food garden will soon acquire status. Be subversive in controlled green silence. Food gardening is the most intelligent adult endeavour on earth and ought to be understood by anyone who eats.

More time can be found by working according to methods that suit you. Let method be your mentor. 'Small is beautiful' also means not saying 'Oh, it's a mess, I must clean up the plot and weed that path'. Instead pick over a quarter, plant seedlings, sow seeds, water them and call it a day, satisfied. Another day remove spent plants from a productive corner and manure and water that, ready for replanting.

Work in time increments. Ten minutes of mulching. Time yourself. Don't cry: 'Oh Mother of Cabbages, I have no time for all that today!' Look at one aspect, like staking three tomato plants before dinner. On your weekend afternoon in the garden, the very worst you can do is cast eyes over a four-square food garden and wonder how in heaven you can do all you want to do by evening. The whole vision can be depressing. Deny the greater picture, go for the detail. Most plants and plots can wait another week, but there may be one thing that is urgent. Do that!

List small tasks, decide priorities and do one of these only:
- weed and mulch one corner and feel good.
- string up flopping beans.
- prune broccoli and pumpkin vines to increase productivity.
- free up two tiny plots for sowing next week and manure now.
- spray the whole plot with liquid seaweed and feel virtuous.

These jobs take from five to 50 minutes, depending on how long you linger, so there's also time for a break with a drink in the shade to admire your work.

Enjoy your garden. Don't despair of an overgrown plot after being away, big rains, or plain neglect. Think of how the wildlife enjoys it. Don't abandon it, but do a corner, a bit or a border. In no time things will be back on track. You will experience abundant satisfaction.

Just like abandoning straight rows for sweet chaos, so composting can be simple, see Part Three. If you prefer to process kitchen scraps instantly, read about worm farming in **Compost Compositions**. Some plants lend themselves to self-mulching. Decaying leaves of artichokes, leaf beet, cabbages, squashes and pumpkins can be cut and folded at the base of plants to return their nutriments to the soil. The leaves soon decay or can be covered with straw.

Consider livestock to help you in the garden. In urban areas roosters may not be welcome, but hens are usually allowed. Maintaining a feathered flock creates an almost closed cycle – you need to buy or construct a coop and run, buy straw for bedding, and distribute a handful of grain before sunset. The fowl mix their manure with soil, straw and vegetable remains into ready-made compost. Pure chicken manure needs composting with other ingredients before going on garden beds, but I spade out composted black earth from the run several times a year to use straight on vegetable plots. Bedding straw goes as mulch on unused plots to break down further, before I make ditches to fill with compost. Outer leaves of vegetables, fallen fruit and other plant debris provide food for the flock to turn into eggs. *Try achieving closed cycles in what you do in the garden to save time and money.* Read the chapter on **Permaculture** to save time in the long term. Plan for later if you can't do it now.

In your second year as a food gardener, you will have found so many personal time-saving tricks that you will want to write a food growers' guide to tell others who are still in denial. Do it!

Gardening with Attitude

To some a garden is a combination graveyard for deceased cars and stalled machinery and a playground to plant a barbecue and basketball pole. Or it may be your spacing-out secret place, or a display the neighbours judge you by. If you fall in between, why not put up a sign near the gate announcing 'Work In Progress', to tell visitors what not to expect and stop yourself apologising.

A work in progress allows freedom to refrain from interfering, an important activity that takes place in the mind and consumes no real time. It happens when you see a new green shoot not far from an old plant, or in an unexpected place, and contemplate what it might be. If you have an anti-weed attitude and pull it up, you will never know. Why not watch it for a few weeks until it declares itself? In this way I gained good self-sown fruit trees, herbs and vegetables. One memorable nectarine seedling bore delicious fruit.

You are now a food gardener, although still burdened with society's attitudes. Step back from these to notice and give gratitude for a giving garden. You know how much edible vegetable matter is wasted in retail outlets: outer leaves of cabbage and cauliflower, tops of celery, beetroot and carrot, and of broccoli only the heads are being sold. Only big vegetables reach the supermarket, except in country towns where local growers sell surplus through the local shop. There is nothing wrong with small beans, carrots and cabbages. There is food value in outer leaves and tops.

Your supermarket-shopper attitude may turn around 180 degrees. In shops we expect perfect looks to make up for lack of taste. In the garden a cabbage with holes in its socks is still a great tasting cabbage. The holes prove it was organically raised. Shopping for vegetables and fruit makes people choosy, rejecting broccoli with yellowing tips, limp greens and discoloured fruit. But if you have backyard fruit trees you do not throw away half your crop because some fruit has spots, bumps or bird bites. You treasure home-grown fruit enough to sort the good from the not so good, and clean up damaged fruit for juicing, stewing and freezing.

When growing your own, you proudly bring in a broccoli head, enough to feed the whole family, but remember not to rip out the plant, as it will continue producing shoots for months. These shoots, as nutritious as the head, are never seen in shops as they cost too much to harvest and have a short shelf life. Under-size late tomatoes are almost as good in the kitchen as big early ones. A tender leaf with a hole cooks up just as well as a sprayed shop leaf, and is better for you.

Broccoli plants can grow closely together. Pick half the outer leaves for stir-fries or hens to preserve plants' energy.

Cabbage is a wonder food. Those outer leaves the greengrocer lops off, leaving only the pale inner cabbage, can be utilised in your kitchen if grown organically and not filmed over with insecticide. You can eat broccoli leaves stir-fried with garlic and soy sauce, dark green and delicious. First cut out the fat ribs and then juice these with carrot or apple for an energy boosting drink. You can also juice kale and cauliflower ribs. Steam the tops of organically grown beetroot, swedes, turnips, and mustard. Make green tomato chutney. Sauté baby carrots. Weave baskets with sweetcorn leaves. Cut and dry herbs every few months for herbal tea. You can do so much with the produce of your magic square that you could never buy in shops.

Trade in perfect looks for good taste and high nutrients – a recipe for a good marriage – and build up a relationship with your food plot that satisfies stomach and tastebuds, but also your spirits.

As a child I used to help my mother sort vegetables. They came from the greengrocer, but as all vegetables were organically grown we floated each batch in a bowl of water to inspect the leaves one by one. Beans often carried caterpillars and spinach came in bunches cut with seeding stalks that had to be removed. Cleaning and washing vegetables was normal then. Ironically, it went out when insecticides and herbicides came in, delivering clean-looking vegetables that carry invisible toxicity instead. Cultivate vegetable attitude. Pick over your own vegetables rather than chopping up something from the shop without even rinsing, as so many cooks do.

The most important attitude for the food gardener is to *eat what is in season*. Vegetables and fruit are at their best when ripened in season. Eat them then and do not desire them too early or too late. Grow early, middle and late varieties, but go without sometimes to experience the joy of a transient food coming into season. You waited half a year, now the moment has arrived. You know you are eating the best when you pick your first artichoke, strawberry or baby squash.

Essential Utensils

Any vegetable can be cooked on the stovetop and many can be eaten raw, but with a few gadgets you can get a lot more out of home-grown produce. Food gardens have times of overproduction. With a blender, a juicer and a wok you manage these times without waste. Buy during the sales and save dollars, or buy a combined blender-juicer, a cheap little machine giving years of service.

A blender enables you to make delicious soups, chutneys and sauces with vegetables, fruits and herbs. Experiment with blended, spiced-up cold cucumber or courgette soups, apple and rosemary chutney, and fresh tomato sauce – simple additions to meals that you will not be without once tried.

A juicer is terrific when fruit ripens in the span of two weeks. Store un-blemished apples and quinces on newspaper, in a dark, cool place. Bruised ones are best steamed, sauced and juiced. I love that time of year when we drink glasses of fresh juice, concentrated goodness toning up the body.

People with cancer and those with digestive problems are often advised to drink vegetable juices. Why wait until you are ill? My favourite summer vegetable juice recipe is Cabbage Ribs & Co. Pick six big cabbage leaves, stripping the greenery for a stir-fry or chicken food. Cut lengthwise one large carrot and half a courgette. Push ribs, carrot and courgette through the juicer with a knob of fresh ginger and a quartered apple. Or add lemon or orange. You can use overproducing courgettes at the rate of one every two days just by juicing.

The wok is a splendid invention from China, where it sits in a hole atop a brick stove. To use it on gas or electric stoves, buy a wok ring to steady it. Woks are for stir-fries and stir-fries are for times of overproduction or underproduction, when a little of everything is enjoyed with rice or pasta, chutney or sauce.

Take a bowl and go for a walk around your magic square (or squares). Pick bits of everything, plus onion greens and a handful of mixed herbs. In the kitchen wash, strip, chop and divide all into bowls according to firmness. Assuming you have garlic and fresh ginger on hand, sauté these with onion in olive oil over fairly high heat. Pour in a little water or vegetable stock to create a steam cloud. Add the firmest vegetable, toss one minute, then the next firmest, toss, and so on, leaving tender greens till last. Add a squirt of soy sauce. Add chutney, sauces, grated cheese or spices, and either cooked rice or pasta, for a very repeatable meal.

A spice grinder is another handy kitchen utensil, so useful for home-grown seeds of coriander, fennel, fenugreek and dill – oh, the aroma! Or get a cheap mortar and pestle from the Asian grocer and use elbow grease. Save brown paper bags and old pillowslips to dry spice seeds before threshing and grinding. Bring fragrance back into your life.

Wok time: young broccoli, giant red mustard, beans and courgettes.

Shopping for Roots & Seeds

While shopping for gadgets and utensils, keep an eye peeled for roots in Asian groceries. Unless your knowledge of Asian horticulture is academic, buy good-looking roots, cook half to see whether you like them, then plant the rest. Some rot, some die, but some may grow.

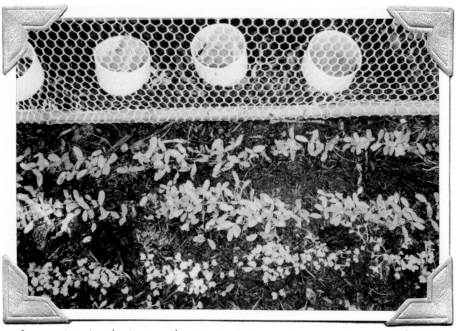

Fenugreek and coriander seedlings. In the background are broadbean seeds in PVC rings, protected further by a bamboo netted cage.

Multiplier onions can still be found in farmers' markets. Pounce on them, propagate, and share them with friends to grow on as they are quite rare. Look for slim bunching onions, Egyptian onions that produce tiny pickling bulbs at the top instead of underground, and other old onion varieties. Make space for these hardy varieties so you'll always have onion material for the pot, be it tops or bottoms.

Buy lemongrass with a bit of root left and plant in a warm spot. Look for other vegetables to grow on. Just as potato pieces with an 'eye' will grow a plant producing potatoes, so will sweet potato if grown in a warm place. Experiment.

Although growing food and buying local products is preferable, there are imported food items that make life interesting. Spices are bought more economically in Asian and continental groceries. Store cinnamon, five spice, ground coriander and cumin, ginger, mustard, turmeric and paprika in glass jars on a dark shelf. Lay in a store of 'whole' spices which keep their aromas better: aniseed, cardamom, coriander, caraway, cumin, fennel, fenugreek, mustard and peppercorns. Buy whole nutmegs and grate as needed. Buy sesame seeds and roast a spoonful in a dry pan to add to salads, rice or pumpkin, or grind as needed. Keep the jars in a dark cupboard to keep seeds viable for growing. You can enhance all you bake or cook with spices.

You are now ready to sow some spice companions such as dill, cumin and coriander – see Part One. Pick the green leaves of spice plants to create gourmet dishes.

Cupboard Self-Sufficiency

Cupboard self-sufficiency is a natural companion to self-sufficiency from your square plot. By combining the produce of your square with the contents of a dry-foods cupboard, you will find it easy to prepare tasty meals of high nutritional value. We currently enjoy the luxury of having a choice of imported and local grains, pulses, spices and dried foods. Buy dry foods each time you shop. In the not-so-long run you save money. You could stay at home for a month and never visit a shop for anything. And you can plant bought seeds and beans to grow and eat fresh, then dry the surplus.

Easy Party Dip

Cook chickpeas or orange lentils till soft, drain and mash. Chop a large onion into a juicy pulp and stir through pulses. Mix in a tablespoon of paprika, taste and add more as needed. Thin down with yoghurt. Serve with corn chips.

Garam Masala

For Indian curries, buy ready-made garam masala or mix your own from ground cardamom, coriander, cumin, cinnamon, cloves, nutmeg, ginger, fennel, fenugreek, black or white pepper, turmeric and dried chillies. Store in a jar. For fresh garam masala, dry-fry seeds of cardamom, coriander, cumin, fennel, fenugreek and mustard until they pop. Keep the lid on the pan. Mash in a mortar with drizzled oil, adding the other ground spices. Use fresh.

Chai Tea

Make your own chai, spicy Indian tea. In a glass jar stir 3 tbsp of cinnamon, a tablespoon each of ground coriander and ginger, a teaspoon of ground cardamom, and half a teaspoon each of five spice and turmeric. Vary by using aniseed, clove, fennel or nutmeg. In India tea is boiled with milk, sugar, and a heaped spoon of this mixture, but you can just add a teaspoon to the pot with the usual amount of tea and pour on boiling water. Good to chase away a headache.

Mushrooms

Mushrooms are a healthy addition to any meal. Grow them yourself in a commercial mushroom box, buy fresh, or go for affordable dried mushrooms. Try varieties in small packets, as some can cause havoc with your personal plumbing. When you know which suit you, buy a humongous pack at a lower price. To use, boil 15–20 minutes, then slice and fry.

Shiitake mushrooms – also known as winter mushrooms or *dong gwoo* in Cantonese – recommended for people with cancer, are available dried, looking like small potatoes bursting out of their skins. Soak them for 10 minutes in warm water, slice and cook with vegetables. If you worry about what is in meat these days, replace it with small amounts of tofu, mushrooms and beans. *Freeze tofu overnight before use, as this opens the pores to other flavours.*

Pulses

The food value of peas, beans and lentils is so great that if you make it a habit to add them to meals three times a week you'll soon find yourself turning away from less nutritious foodstuffs and saving money. Beans come in all colours and consistencies. The softest are lima beans, which are good with homemade tomato sauce, but most brown and red beans will cook soft after a soak. Brown lentils go with almost anything. Fry small orange lentils raw until crisp before adding to pasta and rice.

The versatile chickpea – supplying protein, iron and vitamin C – makes great patties, hummus, dips and fill for soups and stir-fries. Soak chickpeas overnight, cook until soft, and make delicious chickpea salad with a blended sauce of garlic, olive oil, lemon juice, and a crumbed slice of bread. Add rocket, parsley, mint and ground rosemary, and top with sliced tomatoes.

An unripe pumpkin harvested with its last desperate flower after the vine shrivelled up. It made a decent pumpkin soup with lentils and spices.

Buy dried broadbeans to make your own falafel if you can't grow enough. The hardest beans to cook are soybeans. After overnight soaking in just-boiled water, they need a long cooking time in fresh water. But plant them and you harvest fresh green soybeans called *edamame*, as gourmet as young broadbeans and delivering all the benefits of soy. Bought soy products should be labelled as to whether they are GM-free or not.

Invest in a batch of fermented black beans to use sparingly in stir-fries or rice dishes. No cooking needed and they keep well.

Reduce cooking time of beans and pulses by placing them in the freezer for a day. After soaking beans overnight, drain and rinse, boil vigorously in fresh water for 10 minutes, then simmer till soft. Add pinches of aniseed, caraway or fennel to the water to counteract flatulence.

Green mung beans sprout easily. Sprouted beans multiply their food value a hundredfold and can take the place of vegetables when your square is bare. Steep 1–2 tbsp of mung beans in hot water and soak overnight, then rinse, pour into a glass jar, and cover with cheesecloth and a rubber band. Keep near the kitchen tap. Rinse and drain through the cloth several times a day. Soon the beans begin to sprout. Kids love to rinse and watch them. After a few days start adding them to salads, soups, stir-fries, pastas and rice. Use as a sandwich filling with chutney or tahini for a fresh, crunchy snack. Start a new batch for a continuous supply. Try sprouting other beans and seeds: alfalfa, buckwheat, or fenugreek for curried sprouts.

Tasty Dhal

Rice and pulses combined are more nutritious than if eaten separately. One billion Indians can't be wrong eating rice, dhal and vegetables daily. The incomplete protein of pulses becomes complete when combined with a grain.

For a tasty dhal fry a cup of orange lentils in oil until lightly browned. Add 3 cups of water and bring to the boil. Chop garlic and onion to simmer along.

Separately dry-fry on low heat pinches of seeds of cardamom, coriander, cumin, fennel, fenugreek and mustard until they stop popping under the lid. Pound spices. Fry chopped ginger, chilli and ground turmeric and add to the lentils. When dhal is soft, add fried spices. Serve with rice, vegetables and sliced cucumber in yoghurt.

Oma's Haybox

My Oma (grandmother) cooked in a haybox to save on gas. A haybox cooks rice, beans and stews while you do other things. I have a lidded wooden box, painted ochre to double service as a rustic table or cushioned seat. It measures 55 x 55 x 42 cm. If you have a lidded box, fill six pillowslips with hay, padding bottom and sides, keeping one to place on the cooking pot. Spread newspaper on the table or floor. Bring beans, rice or stew to the boil on the stove. With rice, wait until there is only water in the dimples of the rice. Whip the boiling pot onto the newspaper, wrap tightly, place in haybox and cover with hay pillow. Close the lid and don't look for three hours. It keeps it hot for longer, even all day. You can also cook in bed! Place the pot in newspaper wrappings in a bed and pile pillows and blankets on top.

Flours

On the flour shelf you will find gram, or chickpea flour, suitable for people on a gluten-free diet. It tastes nutty and is used for all floury purposes; for the self-raising kind just add a pinch of bicarbonate of soda or baking powder. Use it for sauces, tempura and dumpling batter or mix with rice flour (great for cakes) for a tasty pancake. In Indian cooking, gram is used in homemade sweets. Making *laddhu*, my very favourite confectionery, takes time, stirring continuously for 15 minutes, but lets you meditate on the amazing properties of chickpea flour as it metamorphoses spectacularly under your spellbound gaze.

112

For Italian dinners, buy polenta. Boil in water or vegetable stock, stirring constantly. Make it thick (2 cups of liquid to 1 cup of polenta) to set in a foil-lined form. Cool and turn out as a loaf, then cut in slices to grill or bake with olive oil. Serve with goat's cheese, olives and rocket, or with casseroles of tomato, peppers and mushrooms. The ways of serving polenta are as numerous as cooks. You can do the same sort of things with couscous. Consult Moroccan recipes for combinations.

Sago is your next purchase. I knew a sago expert in Papua New Guinea and am ashamed to admit I laughed on hearing he was off to a sago conference in Manila. How ignorant I was. Sago is the staple food for millions of people in South-East Asia and Melanesia. I have eaten it fried as crisp pancakes, cooked with vegetables, and smoked in bamboo over a coconut-shell fire. All most satisfying. Sago has little flavour, but plenty of texture to combine with strong flavours. A friend recently revived the recipe for lemon sago. So simple it hardly needs a recipe, it became our favourite palate-cleansing dessert.

Lemon Sago

Sago swells to many times its dry state, so be prudent! Soak overnight half a cup of sago balls in 3 cups cold water with the zest of one lemon. Keep the lemon in the fridge. Next day bring sago to the boil. Add the juice of the lemon, or 2–3 lemons depending on how strong you like it. Aim for a consistency of thick porridge. Add small amounts of water if needed. When sago balls turn glassy, taste. When soft enough to chew, add half a cup of white sugar and stir to dissolve, but don't drown the lemon tang in sugar. Pour into a bowl rinsed with cold water, cool and then refrigerate. A marvellous dessert for people on diets. You can repeat this recipe using oranges.

Grains

Buy brown and basmati rice in large bags. They taste nutty. Rice is a wetland grass which we import from Asia, Italy and America. If your home is not mouse-proof, buy strong plastic, lidded buckets, or use a new rubbish bin. Also stock up on noodles. Rice noodles for the no-wheat lobby. Thick, thin and hair-thin.

Pearl barley is a fine filler for vegetable soups and making barley water for upset tummies. At one time no kitchen cupboard was without pearl barley, but pre-cooked grains sent it into exile. Roast organic barley in the oven and grind it to make *tsampa*, a staple food of Himalayan mountain people. Brew strong black Chinese tea with salt and butter or ghee, and stir into a bowl of roasted barley. A truly exceptional taste experience, and so sustaining. Grow your own organic barley on several square metres.

Somewhere near the barley you should find coconut milk powder, for stir-fries and curries. Small luxuries go a long way. Also look for a packet of miso for nourishing soups. Miso is commonly made from soybeans or rice. Miso bouillon with finely cut herbs and onion greens is delicious.

Stock up on dried fruit and nuts for snacks, pilavs, cakes, and breads. Sultanas, figs, dates, walnuts and almonds can change plain dishes into festive food.

Have a wonderful time shopping the slow food way! The slowest of dry foods has to be soaked the night before – half a minute's work. Next morning rinse off and pop in the fridge until you get home that night ready to cook. The quickest dry food is putting some almonds through a grinder, or toasting sesame seeds to sprinkle over freshly roasted vegetables. Your dry foods supply waits in the cupboard for when you need it. Open the door and invent new combinations.

PART THREE
Tips & Tricks

The following chapters contain information that can prevent mistakes and failures in the vital first years of growing your own food. With beginners' luck on your side as well, success is virtually guaranteed.

Compost making at dawn.

Water & Watering

In the management of water, the home grower has the same problems as the ordinary farmer. Water is a precious resource and no matter where your water comes from, we must all harvest it and use it wisely.

David Holmgren of permaculture fame has provided figures showing that every pound's worth of fruit and vegetables has needed 183 litres of water to mature. Every equivalent pound's worth of home-grown food uses only 35 litres.[11]

For healthy development vegetables need water regularly. Water restrictions are an advantage because vegetables grow best when hand watered at the roots, rather than with sprinklers. On hot days, when you may have to water seedlings more than once, fill a watering can in the morning to see tender plants through days of hot weather and drying winds. Use shade netting – see **Hardware in the Food Garden**.

Hand Watering

While hand watering, note what every plant needs. More mulch here, plant food there, a cloche or a stake. Onions are drying off when tomatoes and carrots need extra water. Hosing lets you discover a big cucumber under the leaves. Douse individual plants after a dry day to assist leaves in taking up moisture and nutriments from the air. This daily attention to the food plot, whether it is one square metre or 10, creates a bond between grower and plants that leads to wonderful results.

Consider doing away with sprinklers altogether. Instead, reduce the need for water where possible with mulches or try to cover the soil with vegetation so that evaporation is reduced. The old days of letting a sprinkler on a pike dump water on a vast area for hours are gone forever. Sprinklers water indiscriminately and sometimes plants miss out, dying before you notice.

Be careful not to over-water. Deliver water only where needed and no more than is necessary. Gels that swell or crushed rock can increase the water-holding capacity of the soil. Mulch vegetables with compost and/or straw, even those in part shade, and try skipping a watering occasionally.

Although an established garden benefits from seep hoses under mulch, I will have nothing but a hose in the food garden where planting patterns change week to week. I like the interlude in my days, sauntering along, watering and selecting the next meal.

Start small, think hose and watering can. It puts you in control and you get a daily thrill from the plants' efforts.

Nozzles

You need control at the tap: wide open, half open or drizzling. You also need control at the nozzle: fine spray, wide spray, or a narrow jet to hit one spot or hose off aphids. Select a nozzle that will do a fine mist as well as a squirt. It's a myth that spraying plants on hot days causes leaf burn. Rain doesn't burn plants, does it? Leaf burn results from lack of water at the roots.

Position

Where you position your plants is also important. It is drier nearest a wall, and parts of the garden can be hotter because of paving or gravel. Some plants like lettuces prefer semi-shade rather than full sun, whereas root crops don't mind full sun.

Shade

Provide shade by temporary means and observe shade patterns before installing anything permanent, remembering that during winter plants need more light.

Don't plant a grapevine, as the birds will paint your vegetables white! Passion vines or climbing vegetables can benefit ground dwellers.

A.M. or P.M.

Debates whether to water early mornings or evenings pass you buy if you are a working person. You are unlikely to do it in the heat of day. In summer, water before breakfast if possible, as evening moisture attracts snails and slugs.

If your plot is densely planted and mulched, there should be little evaporation after morning waterings. In dense plantings any evaporation is likely to benefit the plants. Seedlings and young plants need daily watering in hot weather and twice a day if there is a sustained drought. If these conditions are predictable, avoid having seedlings at those times.

How Long to Water

Impossible to answer. It depends on microclimate, soil, mulch, compost and the plants. Water must get to the roots, so stick your finger in beside plants to test how deep it goes. Wait a few days to see how plants cope before watering again. Generally spaced-out deep watering is better than daily shallow watering, but many vegetables have shallow roots and grow fast in summer, so water daily then if possible. It takes five minutes to hose a 25-square-metre food plot.

Water Storage

If you are on mains water and don't have a water barrel, consider installing one or several now. They come in a variety of materials, sizes, shapes and colours to fit every situation, and rainwater is a saving grace for vegetables if mains water has impurities, is chlorinated, or if you're on a meter and want to save your money. By using rainwater on seedlings and young vegetables, more survive than if they have to battle salt, chlorine or competitive organisms.

Tanks fill up quickly from the average house roof after a few downpours and even dew raises a tank's level. Install gutters on your shed to harvest more water. Consider installing gutter guards for cleaner water. Some water companies give rebates for collecting rainwater, contact them to find out their conditions.

If the water is from a reservoir you may face periods of brackishness as the water level drops mid summer, just when you douse vegetables daily.

I have learned which vegetables can survive on brackish water, although none do terribly well. These include:
  – globe artichoke
  – cabbage family, including hardier Asian greens
  – onions, garlic, chives and leek
  – leaf beet, perennial spinach
  – asparagus, lettuce, chicory, endive, salsify, scorzonera
  – most herbs survived, especially *Artemisia* species
  – grey plants such as succulents and lavender.

Other Water Saving & Delivery Systems

Drip irrigation under mulch saves water, but is inconvenient in small plots.

Composting toilets need no flushing and will gain in popularity as water bills increase. They provide compost and will become almost maintenance free as technology improves.

Grey water systems benefit the surrounding garden where the household water ends up, freeing up water for the food garden if you rely on tanks.

Waterwise planting Vegetables in densely planted, well composted and mulched plots need less water per plant than those standing solitary in bare soil in rows wide apart. Dense plantings don't wilt easily on hot days as the plants shade each other's roots, and the compost and mulch holds moisture.

Raised beds and trenches Raised beds dry out fast along the sides. Those made from sleepers are better than those of bricks that hold heat. Pack the sides with straw before filling with soil, and push more straw in periodically.

The method of planting vegetables in raised beds or mounds is appropriate for the UK where it rains a lot, soil seldom dries out and roots rot. If you expect months of rain, make hilled-up rows.

But faced with having to grow food in rocky sub-clay in a dry climate, remember the Israeli desert kibbutz where pumpkin seedlings were planted in trenches, the very opposite of a hill. Hack a trench in 'concrete' clay, fill it with manure and compost and plant pumpkins. They will produce beyond expectation.

Is your soil water retaining, does it drain excessively, or does it not hold water at all? How long between rains? Is your wet season long enough to rot roots? *Between these variables you decide whether to mound, dig a trench, or grow on the flat.* When living in a hill's village where I had to call the landlord to pump water for the tank, I grew vegetables on flat soil, each in its own earth saucer. I watered with cup and bucket each evening and they did alright. On one square metre that takes one minute. Earth saucers work especially in impervious soil.

Soil Secrets

Over 50 per cent of the world's population with back gardens going spare. Back-yards may have suffered less of the contaminations caused by the agricultural revolution, although Bill Mollison, the founder of permaculture, believes the opposite. Gardeners do buy a lot of toxic sprays, but look in any shed and they sit there mostly unused as many never bother to use them.

There are still soil secrets in suburbia. Micro-organisms do have a life in gardens. Without micro-organisms in the soil, plants cannot take up nutri-ments and good soil structure is not maintained. Compost and mulch add to soil structure, keep soil moist, protect from UV rays and so help micro-organisms to work. Seasonal small applications of calcium-containing lime help if the soil is acidic. Rather than turning soil over, put on layers of manure, compost and mulch. *Don't walk on garden plots.*

I wish I'd been paid a fiver for every person who told me: 'Oh, you can't grow anything in my soil/your soil/that soil, it's no good!' Wholesale condemnation of soil is just an excuse to get out of gardening. Soil can be made by 'industry and art', as the Shakers said. The chapters on compost and mulch tell you how. The first year you have a vegetable plot you may resort to buying bags of potting soil to start plants off, but in the second year you'll have your own compost.

Before tarmaced roads and refrigerated transport brought food from fara-way places to rural areas, the people grew vegetables and fruit in what soils they had, adding wood-fire ashes and animal manure and watering with pure soapy washing water. Now they too can choose from seven long-life vegetables and pay a pound for an orange.

The subsoil in my forest garden in the Adelaide Hills was tens of thousands of years old, studded with ancient rocks releasing prehistoric smells. We pick axed planting holes to fill with potting soil, mulching the surface. We pruned native shrubs to bulk up compost and backfilled. Plants did not curl up stunted when roots filled the holes, but took off as if they'd hit the jackpot! This happened in the second or third year. The secret was good drainage due to all those rocks and minerals unlocked by moisture and mulch. We used manures and compost, but minimum fertilisers.

In our alluvial clay garden we could grow anything as long as animal manures, compost and mulches kept the top from drying out to a hardpan surface. We used gypsum and mulch on 'concrete' plots. Had the clay been stickier we would have had to double dig once to work in organic material, but mostly it responded to top dressing. Holes for fruit trees received compost and gypsum. The only snag with clay soils is that they must be made to drain well. Compost mixed with gravel can improve drainage.

Our ridge garden seemed to have easy soil, but nothing grew beyond adolescence due to a pH of 4.3 which is very acidic (7 being neutral). This soil required lime, dolomite and gypsum as there was hardpan clay underlying the sandy soil at a depth of 25 cm. After repeat applications of compost, manure and mulch, vegetables grew to edible size. This soil, looking easy on the surface, turned out the hardest to raise vegetables on, although by the third summer we had small amounts of broccoli, cabbage, cucumber, garlic, kale, lettuce, onions, pumpkin, chard, spinach, squash, tomatoes, courgettes and herbs. All over the world, from the West of Ireland to the Andes, people cultivate food in soils that are less than ideal. If they can do it, so can you.

Do pH test your soil – simple test kits are available from garden centres. Adjust acidic soil with lime. If your soil is too alkaline – above 7 – adjust with a mulch of acidic material like eucalyptus leaves, dust with sulphur, or sprinkle with a cup of vinegar per bucket of water.

If your soil grows a bounty of different weeds, it is probably fertile and well drained. Weeds protect soil from baking in sunlight and many have deep roots that aerate the soil, while decaying weeds leave a beneficial layer of humus. Weed-supporting soil is often crumbly and friable; just keep weeds down with mulch where you plant vegetables.

If you are starting out new on rocky soil you'll have good drainage. Plant trees whose roots can find their way deep down to where the nutriments are. Within two years they will form a windbreak for your food garden and provide leaves for compost.

If your soil is totally bare the question is: why does nothing grow here? Has the soil been chemically contaminated? Try to find out your plot's history. Have cars driven up and down here, or leaking lawn mowers? Stick a spade or fork into the soil. Can it be rehabilitated by forking, adding gypsum to break it up, a wetting agent to make it take up water, or digging in compost and mulching? Most probably. One instructor with whom I taught a vegetable-growing course grew carrots in his driveway!

Soils range from pure clay to pure sand. Many gardens have something in between, a loam of sorts. Experiment with pots containing the same soil, adjusting the pH in one, adding gypsum to another, fertiliser to a third, all three in a fourth, then grow lettuces in all pots and see what does best. Some UK soils are on the acidic side, when a light dusting of lime is in order.

Clay Soil Working Bee

You can easily prepare one or two square metres on a weekend morning. Have a soup-and-sandwich Saturday to free up time to bake a soil cake in the garden!

During the week pick up:

— a bag of mushroom or other compost.

— a bag of organic potting soil.

— a bale or pack of straw.

— a bag of animal manure. Available from garden centres. Horse manure from roadside paddocks is probably safer than from racing stables, as hobby horses are less full of antibiotics. Chop manure with a spade before spreading. (Note the horse manure caution on Abbreviations page.)

— a small bag of gypsum for clay soil.

— a tiny bag of lime for acidic soil.

— organic fertiliser pellets or liquid seaweed fertiliser.

Many of these are available in small packages you can sit on the backseat, cradle in your arms, or put in your shopping trolley.

That was hard work and quite an outlay of money, but you'll get it back with interest. Some supplies will last years. If unable to lift bales and bags, ask the garden centre people to deliver, or lift them in the boot of your car – then ask a neighbour to help you unload. Open a bag of manure inside the boot and spade the contents into buckets. Wear garden gloves and do the same with the potting soil, gypsum and fertiliser. Borrow a wheelbarrow and sweep up a heap of fallen leaves or grass clippings. Collect seeds and/or seedlings.

From here on it is as easy as making a layered no-cooking cake!

Firstly aerate the soil by pushing a garden fork in many places and wiggling it. Pull out any clumps of weeds and rake in gypsum, following directions on the packet. Add lime if acidic. Rake in chopped manure to compost in situ.

Cardboard, compost from municipal waste recycling and baled straw are good mulches and vary in price. Baled straw usually peels off in 'biscuits'. Cover your plot entirely with straw biscuits. If tightly packed, tease them out and fluff them up. Most gardeners who settle for straw end up with beautiful soil.

Water well to settle the 'cake'.

Leave for three weeks if you limed. Draw a planting plan, start off seedlings and remove weeds around the plot while waiting. Read other relevant chapters.

Then, open pockets in the straw and fill with potting soil and water. This is easiest on the junctions where biscuits meet, but for small plants make more pockets by pulling straw apart. Plant seedlings, sprinkle organic fertiliser, spray with diluted seaweed and water in well. When planting seeds, sprinkle fertiliser after plants emerge.

All done! Water daily. No weeds. Soon you'll eat!

Sandy Soil Work-Out

If you have pure sand that runs through your fingers, it may not retain water and could be magnesium deficient, causing yellowing of leaves. Add magnesium by mixing a spoon of Epsom salts in a bucket of water. To make the soil hold water make a thickly layered plot on top of the sandy soil. Hold layers in with rows of half-buried, water-filled plastic flagons, planks or sleepers. If you can obtain a bucket of clay, make a clay slurry (one spade to a bucket of water, stir well and pour onto raked sandy soil). Do this several times to increase water retention. Put down layers of wet newspaper over animal manure to attract earthworms, and layers of straw in which you will make pockets for potting soil to plant in. Keep mulching as the season progresses and add all the organic matter you can find: leaves, seaweed, broad leaved weeds (without seeds), seedless grass clippings, small twigs.

Both the pure clay gardener and the pure sand gardener have to start a compost heap at the beginning, for these soils need more organic matter than others. Prune and chop anything growing in your garden that will benefit from a haircut: daisies, privet or other hedges, ornamental shrubs. Mix with kitchen scraps, leaves, lawn clippings and manure.

On a nice loam, you still need compost to maintain fertility. So after planting your first square, read **Compost Compositions**. Start a compost heap now to be ready the following season. Get into the rhythm of the seasons, those realms they write music about!

Compost Compositions

Soil enriched by organic matter is the foundation of a healthy food garden that produces vegetables and fruit of high nutritional content. Compost gives plants the opportunity to graze about with their roots for what they need, just like chickens are healthier when able to scratch around an orchard for grass, worms and herbs than when they are fed a scientific formula.

Shaker Compost

The Shaker community in America, where the renowned Shaker furniture was produced, was almost totally self-sufficient. Shaker compost – now there's a concept worth exploring – was made from vegetable refuse and herb stalks with guano, gypsum, seaweed, fish waste, pond mud and ground-up bones. Shaker gardeners added this compost with animal manure to their shallow, rocky soil. Herb plots received as much as vegetables and fruit trees.

Their recipe – moderated by leaving out salt and adding extras – goes somewhat like this:

- One part mineral substances: wood ash, lime, sand or clay, gypsum or dolomite.
- Five parts organic matter: weeds, straw, leaves, roots, stalks, thin bark, sawdust (from untreated wood).
- Six parts animal manures (animal manures should be composted where possible before use to prevent E. Coli and other bacteria proliferating).

For a square-metre plot you can stir this up in a bucket! Decide whether your soil needs sand, clay or neither. Don't overdo the sawdust and balance it with a handful of lime.

Having acres of food gardens, the Shakers collected organic matter all year, piling it in layers to compost. When matured, they spread the compost at the rate of 40 oxcarts per acre, and became the best food gardeners in 19th-century America.

Making Compost

Compost is new earth made from old organic matter, including kitchen scraps, lawn clippings, ornamental garden prunings, leaves, twigs and anything organic that is locally available. It can really end up looking like that beautiful black stuff you see on TV. But even before it looks glamorous it will be useful.

There are a number of ways to make compost. Choose the one that gives you the least pain and most pleasure. Remember everything that is or was alive, and is subject to decay, will convert to compost. But don't add meat scraps and bones into your garden compost as they attract vermin, although you can pulverise the bones. Depending on matter and method you should have compost in a few weeks, months or years.

Hot or cold? Not everyone agrees. Hot composting destroys pathogens. Cool composting is now said to be better as the 'cooking' process uses up lots of nitrogen and carbon. No doubt the last word is still to be spoken.

Using bins The most gentle composting is done in bins. Keep two composting bins behind the shed and as you fill up the second, the first will be composting. Or if yours is a small operation, use two plastic laundry baskets lined with wet newspaper and covered with doormats held down by a brick (this may not be rodent-proof!). Or buy a tumbling bin on legs and turn it twice a day. You will need a covered storage bin for scraps while the bin is filled to capacity yet still composting. In the bins the material should be mainly kitchen scraps, lawn clippings, soft weeds, leaves, vegetable matter and soft prunings.

Put hard prunings in a heap at the back of the yard and don't look for a year – they will compost eventually. Gardeners working on a larger scale, or people with lots of ornamental garden prunings, will profit by building a composting area of straw bales. Throw it all in, as shredded as possible. When it's time to turn or take the compost out, simply remove one bale. Bales attract earthworms, which live underneath until the compost has cooled enough for them to work it, lacing the stuff with their castings.

Build a small compost heap using a round circle of chicken wire, a metre in diameter, pinned down with stakes. Line it with layers of wet newspaper and throw in organic matter. Sprinkle occasional handfuls of lime, straw and manure into the mix and water regularly. When the bin is full (it sinks constantly so this may test your patience!) Cover it with a piece of old carpet and set up another wire bin. When that is full, the first bin will have usable compost.

Turning compost There are those who do and those who don't, but turning speeds up the process. Build two adjoining square bins from corrugated iron or planks, no less then a cubic metre each, for it is mass that produces enough heat to make hot composting work and break down plant pathogens and weed seeds. In a wet climate, build bins with slats for air circulation.

If you have space, build three, four or five bins in a row by extending the back wall. The extra bins allow you to turn compost a second time from Bin 2 into Bin 3, to obtain that friable black and gold of TV pictures. Bin 4 can be a long-term composter for tough stuff such as wood thicker than your thumb, thorny rose prunings and shredded paper. A year later it will be compost without any turning at all. Bin 5 is for bad weeds, things you never want to see in the garden again. Leave them composting for a small eternity, or 'cook' them in plastic bags.

Using a Lawn Mower to Make Compost

Collect and spread where you will mow:

- prunings from the ornamental garden.
- weeds, except bad ones likely to regrow from pieces.
- leaves.
- very thin bark.
- a bag of animal manure.
- a small bag of lime. (You only need handfuls.)
- other organic matter, e.g. spoiled hay.
- fallen branches no thicker than your finger.

If you like, add onion material, citrus peel, nut husks, rhubarb and elderberry leaves, tea leaves and coffee grounds. Spread shredded paper and a layer of wet newspaper in the bottom of a bin.

Use two shredded yarrow leaves as a compost starter. There are commercial compost starters if you don't grow yarrow, or a cheap starter is urine, diluted with water and sprayed between layers – magic stuff. Or mow the lawn first – the clippings can also be used. Finally, make sure the mower's blades are sharp.

Wear goggles, earmuffs and steel-toe-capped boots!

Spread out the collected material and mix with a garden fork. If it's too wet, let it dry off. Spread out part of the material and mow across it several times until it is roughly shredded. It doesn't matter if there are small sticks in the mix.

To build a heap, spade in a 20 cm layer of shredded matter, a handful of lime, a shovel of manure, hay or straw, and add a compost starter. A dry heap won't compost fast, so water as you build. When the heap is finished, water the top long and hard, then cover with carpet (or other pervious material) and wet that also. The heap should start 'cooking' within hours.

To check whether the heap is brewing, lift up the carpet on day three, poke a hole in the top and watch steam rising! Cover up and water twice a week. When the heat subsides, worms will move in and accelerate the process. After one month, turn the heap with a garden fork. From Bin 2 or 3 it can be returned to garden plots. Your compost could be ready one month after turning, depending on your climate and what went in. If a handful looks like soil – albeit full of twigs and on the rough side – fill a wheelbarrow and spread it between the vegetables, worms and all. It will compost further in situ. If you want finer compost, turn it into Bin 3.

In-bed compost Should you have gone beyond a one-square food garden, you'll have spent vegetable plants by summer's end. After feeding your feathered flock and worm farm with greens, tops and fallen fruit, and after the backyard bins are full, you may still have heaps of decaying organic matter to clear away. Then do it in bed, as follows.

In autumn clear one plot to be a composting bed and spread manure. On this throw excess chard, courgette leaves, pumpkin vines, vegetables gone to seed and anything else that is reasonably soft. Shred big cabbage trunks first. When the bed is covered with 30 cm of organic matter, sprinkle with two shredded yarrow leaves and cover with 10 cm of compost, straw, or layers of wet newspaper held down with stones. When watering food plots, also water this bed.

Depending on the weather, the composting bed will be ready to grow cabbages or cauliflowers by late winter. Remove skeleton stalks to composting area. Some partly-decayed matter will continue to compost over time. You can fork the bed over or plant straight into the compost cover. If you used newspapers, peel these off carefully, guiding worms back to the soil, and place decaying newspaper in your compost bin or worm farm.

Commercial composters use a lot of cardboard and shredded office paper, but in backyard compost I find these a nuisance. You have to shred it fine and disperse it so it doesn't form lumps, and even then paper often shows up in the final compost as just what it is. Use it underneath compost instead.

Some seeds survive the composting process and once back on the plot will surprise you with vigorous seedlings. If they are vegetables, leave these where they are, they will turn out the best!

Scott Nearing, inspiration for The Good Life series of books written with partner Helen Nearing, built eight compost bins to grade material according to hardness. The hardest bin would not be used for several years, but eventually even thick branches decomposed.

Tree compost Harvest fallen debris from your trees – leaves and twigs will compost, branches can become fire wood, edgings, or brush fencing or be put in long-term compost. Nothing need go to waste; nothing should be burned.

Worms & Worm Farms

Worm farms can range from a size you can put on the balcony, to vast structures housing millions of the creatures – councils with foresight feed the district's organic rubbish into enormous worm troughs and sell the compost back to the public.

The balcony-size farm is a natty set of plastic trays that fit on top of each other and hold a worm population, kitchen scraps and weeds. The bottom tray with tap drains off the worm juice. The sets are rodent-proof. This is the ideal composting system if you live in a flat or unit and should produce enough castings and worm juice to keep several boxes with food plants in optimum health. Larger sizes are available for gardens.

Worm farms come with instruction booklets listing the addresses of where to buy **composting worms** (epigeic, smooth, several varieties), which apparently do like living in small apartments and will procreate in plastic trays. There is some controversy about whether composting worms will ever thrive in garden soil as earthworms do. They will, but only in the top layers where they compost leaves and sticks and become bird food. The earthworms that turn over deep soils are anecic worms, which wear a red band around their bodies. Cardboard boxes with 1000 worms that will breed in the box are recommended for worm farms. If your worms don't thrive despite regular feeding, seek advice from the supplier.

Worm juice is liquid fertiliser, a fine boost to young vegetables. Tap it regularly and dilute with water 1:10 before spraying on plants. The worms' main product is **castings** which is pure compost. When this matures, pick out any tardy worms and surprise your seedlings and vegetables.

Old bath tubs are popular as worm farms, with a wooden cover and old carpet to keep the worms cool. Collect the juice by placing a tray under the plughole, plunging your hand in the mass and pulling the plug.

Always place worm farms in the shade and cover with wet hessian, carpet, underfelt or towels. In winter a small farm may do better under cover, but if you put it in the shed, don't forget to bring food. The worms will let you go on holiday for up to a month if you leave them a big feed. Give them cores, stems and peelings, cut fine like you would for kids, as well as old manure, tea leaves, tea bags, coffee grounds, eggshells, fallen fruit, shredded wet cardboard and newspaper, old vegetables and mixed weeds. On special occasions, for instance when a worm has a significant birthday, throw a few lettuce leaves their way. They love rotten apples.

Plant Food & Soil Food

If you live on a valley bottom, surrounded by hillsides that for centuries have deposited topsoil and organic matter on your patch, the soil may contain all that your plants need for years to come. Gardens on flat ground may have lost nutriments to huge trees, or may have become deficient due to old age. Buddleia and elderberry survive in impoverished soils, but vegetables don't. The better you feed your soil, the better fed your vegetables are, and the better fed you are.

Plant & Soil Foods

Synthetic fertilisers sold as compounds of NPK (nitrogen, phosphorus and potassium) also contain salts harmful to soil microbes, depleting the soil which then needs more fertiliser. Chris Alenson found leafy green vegetables grown with synthetic fertilisers are in danger of having a high nitrate intake. His paper notes that vitamin C reduces in these green leaves as nitrogen increases.[12]

NPK are only three elements of about 15 needed for balanced plant health. For reasons of continuous fertility, run-off into waterways, and the high cost of fertilisers, organic growing – using compost and manure – is more sustainable.

Mineral soil improvers like gypsum break up clay, dolomite adds calcium, granite adds minerals, and volcanic rock dust has it all.

The food requirements of vegetables differ. It is a generally held view that root crops need little food, but that depends on how much nutrient was left by previous crops. At the other end of the scale are the gross feeders. What are gross feeders? Cabbage, cauliflower, broccoli and Brussels sprouts. Fork in CMC several weeks before planting, spray seedlings with LS, give them side dressings of B&B a week later, top up CM regularly, and fortnightly apply one or the other of these nutriments. Stop applying B&B when plants are well established.

Animal manures For health reasons, most organic standards require that applications of animal manures be followed by two green crops before growing vegetables.[13] Therefore it is quicker to compost manure. Chop it up and mix with other composting materials (see previous chapter) or, if you can obtain old dried pats of cow, horse, donkey, camel or elephant manure, use a shredder or lawn mower to turn it into fine manure dust. Only put manure on a bed you prepare several months before planting and always cover it with mulch, straw or compost to assist earthworms in breaking it down.

The major plant foods used when growing organic vegetables are animal manures and compost, as these contain the variety of nutriments plants need to access as they grow. If you can't use animal manure remember Scott and Helen Nearing, North America's gurus of the self-sufficiency movement. They didn't believe in exploiting animals so their food production was fed entirely on compost made from everything they weeded, pruned and swept from their own land. Fortunately they had tonnes of deciduous sugar maple leaves. They fed themselves and countless visitors for decades.

On a scale of manures, chicken and pigeon contain the most nitrogen, while pig poo is powerful and provides phosphorus. Sheep manure is an all-rounder. Horse and cow manure contribute potassium – cow is more acidic, so add some lime, while horse manure builds soil (but please see the note about horse manure on Abbreviations page). If you are in the country you can often buy roadside bags, or ask a farmer whether you may fill a bag or trailer in his paddock. Donkey manure takes time to break down, chop or mow it and dig it in during autumn to soften. When the circus comes to town people rush the elephant keeper with requests. No doubt big poo is a major soil builder, but being fresh it needs composting.

Blood & Bone (B&B) This widely used by-product of the meat industry has been observed to keep rabbits at bay when incorporated in seed-bomb trials in Australia. A seed bomb is a clay ball packed with selected tree seeds, which is thrown onto bare land at the start of the rainy season to germinate. If rabbits are put off by B&B inside seed balls, they are also likely to object to the stuff lying around their favourite vegetables. This may explain why some gardeners claim there are rabbits in the next paddock, yet they don't touch their vegetables. If you are plagued by bunnies, try it around seedlings. Organic B&B is widely available in the UK.

Clay has essential locked up nutriments. A bucket of clay, broken up carefully and mixed with gypsum, can be forked through sandy soil.

Dolomite/dolomite lime corrects acidic soils. Use when a plot is cleared for new crops. Provides lime, calcium and magnesium.

Green manures Plant barley, buckwheat, broadbeans, fenugreek, lupins, red clover, mustard, oats, peas or other legumes and dig in before they flower. If you have too many old vegetable seeds, plant some to grow vegetables and rake the excess through a bare plot. When the plants are 4–8 weeks old, fork them in, cover with CM and water. This makes soil structure and attracts earthworms. The patch will be ready for sowing a few weeks later.

Green crops can be sown in the heat of summer, when you can't plant seedlings, or during winter. Sow a green crop after harvesting a patch, even one quarter of your only square. For the one-square gardener, mustard is quick to grow and the seed widely available. Eat some, dig most in and let some produce seed.

Epsom salts provide magnesium sulphate for prematurely yellow leaves. Apply 1 tsp per watering can.

Gypsum Hardpan, sticky clay or compacted soils can be 'opened up' by forking in gypsum, starting in autumn and repeating in spring.

Hay Bale Spotted in a garden magazine, a most delightful photo of two tomato plants growing in a tiny hay bale still in its plastic wrap.[14] Make drainage holes in the bale and make holes for plants by taking out some hay and replacing it with soil. Soak plants in weak LS solution before planting. Water the bale thoroughly through the holes before planting. This is an elegant solution for small patios. Experiment with other vegetables in hay bales.

Humus is the soil nature makes unaided. Leave a heap of leaves, twigs and small branches alone for a year, then lift them up and scoop up the humus underneath.

Iron chelate Apply when plants have yellow leaves, are stunted, or bear rather small fruit.

Lime Supplies calcium to soils. Don't apply in dry weather to prevent it blowing away. As lime takes away nitrogen from manure in compost when it breaks down, apply three weeks before planting. Alternatively, add B&B three weeks after liming. Plants that don't like lime are amaranth, aubergine, blueberries, celery and potatoes.

Liquid manures Make these from potent herbs, e.g. stinging nettle or comfrey. Chop up plants, steep in plenty of water in a bin and cover. After 10–14 days, stir and apply the liquid around vegetables and seedlings, diluted with water 1:10. Brew up a smellier and even more potent manure by adding a variety of other soft-leaved weeds such as milk thistle, dock and dandelion, herbs and plants like borage, fennel, nasturtium, cosmos, and leaves of arum lilies and succulents. It is best to use rainwater as mains water may contain chlorine, which will attack the bacteria that breaks down the organic matter. If you have no water barrel, catch buckets of rainwater for a liquid manure experiment (then install a water butt!). Scoop off half a litre of liquid from the bucket per week, pour into an almost full watering can, and sprinkle around vegetables. Add more plants and water to the bin and repeat weekly.

Liquid seaweed (LS) If you won't have a smelly bin around, the commercial liquid manure of highest value is LS, used so greatly diluted that a container lasts a long time. Seeds, cuttings and uprooted plants can be soaked in a weak LS solution before planting to encourage root development. Spray any seedlings, young and maturing plants with LS, especially when they meet adverse conditions in soil or weather.

Seaweed is good for all stages of vegetable growth, but it is still necessary to prepare plots with manure, compost and mulch to create soil. Use LS as the icing on the cake – or the greening on the broccoli. Spray the whole plant, as LS is taken in through the foliage as well. LS improves soil structure and can be used to prevent plant diseases and treat soil where predators lurk, e.g. codling moth under apple, fig, pear and quince trees. Fresh seaweed put on the garden will contain sea salt.

Lupins are a green crop for poor sandy soils, adding calcium and fixing nitrogen.

Mineral rock dust Another mineral food for new plots, or to dig in with green crops.

Nitrogen is contained in the NPK synthetic fertilisers that organic gardeners avoid. Nitrogen produces huge leaf growth and has been overused in agriculture, in parks, on golf courses and in backyards.

In the decade 1980–1990, the amount of industrially-fixed nitrogen applied to global crops was evidently more than all industrial fertiliser spread in the whole of humanity's history prior to 1980. Moreover, a doubling of transferred nitrogen from the atmosphere takes place due to the way humans treat Planet Earth. When soil saturated with nitrogen goes into the waterways, it takes along calcium, magnesium and potassium, making soils acidic, killing fish in lakes and causing toxic blooms.[15] Yet nitrogen is a plant food. It occurs in high amounts in poultry manure and B&B, both of which should be used sparingly. If your courgette leaves are the size of dinner plates and your leaf beet is a metre tall, you have used too much.

Organic fertilisers As maintenance for the gross feeders of the cabbage family you may need to sprinkle organic fertiliser pellets once a month for 3–4 months. There are slow-release fertilisers also.

Potash Essential for plant growth and development. A small bag goes a long way and results are swift for ailing plants.

Urine Human urine is a sterile commodity and was once widely used in first aid to treat wounds when water was putrid. It is still used for the fulling of cloth and dying of wool in cottage industries. Urine contains the growth hormone auxin and comes free. A lidded bucket in the bathroom allows those household members who are purpose-built to aim well into it. Take the bucket to the garden tap and fill up with water. Spread liquid across yet-to-be-planted garden beds and around fruit trees, especially citrus. No smell lingers and since the stuff is sterile, no dangers to health occur. So cheap.

Wood ash Add sparingly to acid soil, or spread widely as it contains sodium that affects soil micro-organisms. Don't disperse it hot from the fireplace. Beetroot loves it. Pear and cherry sawfly hate it when applied to the leaves they are devouring. Keep a supply handy in the shed.

Grouping Plants According to Needs

Sometimes it may be possible to plant lime lovers together and lime haters somewhere else, or those that need much nitrogen here and those that prefer poorer soil over there. If you want to grow a variety of vegetables every year, plan your food garden in four plots, however small, and rotate crops seasonally so that root crops follow gross feeders and organic matter lovers take up the soil left by lime lovers, with additions of organic matter. A permanently no-lime corner may support a blueberry bush under-planted with potatoes, aubergine and the glorious red amaranth, an untried combination. It may not always work, but keep lime haters away from limed plots for two years. A planting notebook comes in handy here. Consult Part Four.

Truly gross feeders are the brassica family which need manure, compost and organic fertilisers.

Savoy — a gross feeder.

Moderately gross feeders While they establish themselves, feed aubergines, peppers, cucumbers, lettuce, potatoes, pumpkin, leaf beet, spinach, strawberries, sweetcorn, tomatoes, and courgettes as you would brassicas.

Extra nitrogen should be worked in well before planting and applied again in small amounts throughout the growing stages for amaranth, aubergine, garlic, leaf beet, and sweetcorn.

Low nitrogen Suits all root crops, beans, corn salad, and peas and can either be left-over nitrogen from last season's crop, or a sparse application.

No lime for amaranth, aubergine, blueberries, celery or potatoes.

Lime required and worked in three weeks before planting for beans, Florence fennel, garlic, onions, peas, and strawberries. Also use for parsnip, tomatoes and turnips in acid soil.

Organic matter comprises old compost, old manure, lawn clippings and leaf mulch and benefits beetroot, broccoli, cabbage, cauliflower, cucumber, Florence fennel, gherkin, and courgettes.

The Message of Mulch

With temperatures increasing due to global warming, and long dry summers with more frequent storms, our vegetables have come a long way since their ancestors grew in sheltered valleys in Asia and Europe where the best agricultural land was once found.

Even though our gardens may not have inherited pollution from agricultural practices, they are still subject to climate changes. Once soil repeatedly dries out, microbic life and earthworms disappear and water is not taken up when applied. Therefore we mulch.

However, for most of the year, in rainy and cooler conditions, there is no need for thick mulches. Wet straw can become a hotbed for slugs. So let summer mulch rot away, or fork it in and let the soil air a little, unless your region experiences continuous drought with erosive winds. If weeds come up, pull them for compost or liquid manure. Never let them set seed – keep track of weeds. Mulch again in late winter.

Mulches do not have to cost much. Newspaper, cardboard, old clothes and stones cost nothing. Stones trap moisture when placed around plants, be they lettuce, cabbage or tree seedling, but they also attract slugs and snails.

If your soil is rocky, acidic or unworkable, you may choose to start your square-metre garden from scratch like a no-dig garden, a method espoused by garden expert Charles Dowding.[16] Mark a square metre, or build a box with sleepers or planks. Lay down 12–20 layers of soaked newspaper, with cardboard and old T-shirts as underfelt to prevent persistent weeds breaking through. Make a doorstop sandwich by layering old animal manure, compost and straw.

After watering well, make holes in the straw, fill with soil or compost, and plant vegetables. The garden will gradually sink, so keep topping up with CM, hay or straw. In the first season plants may not grow fantastically, but the sandwich improves with time.

The most fertile mulches for vegetables are home produced compost and straw. If your climate is severely hot and dry, think in terms of 'putting the vegetables to bed'. As soon as plants are above ground, lay sheets of soaked newspaper between them, add wet bags, fabrics, top with CM, compost, hay or straw. After the first watering, watch how long the plants can go without. There is always one plant that is first to look distressed. Keep mulch slightly away from stems and trunks to prevent collar rot.

Laying out a no-dig garden on top of lawn. Despite carpet strips and wooden edging, grass roots did invade and sheet-metal strips had to be fitted later to a depth sufficient to keep them out.

Mulches

The following mulches are listed alphabetically, not for preference.

Black plastic is used for commercial strawberry growing and to suppress weedy lawns. But it cooks the soil and should not stay there long. Weed suppression is its main benefit and newspaper, cardboard and telephone books can do that and decay timely, so that you can mulch and plant on top.

Bracken fern I wish I still had our forest to pick bunches of bracken. Bracken contains nitrogen, phosphorus and potassium. Apart from spreading shredded bracken on beds to decay, use ferns as parasols for seedlings.

Cardboard is good for a path between new beds, or between straw-filled, no-dig garden plots. If used to suppress lawn or weeds, cover with chipped branches for good looks. Line slatted or wire compost bins with cardboard, pizza boxes or paper party plates, or use as underfelt in no-dig plots. Only use uncoated cardboard between vegetables.

Clothes can be slow to disintegrate. For that reason they are best used around the edges of plots for weed suppression or as underfelt for no-dig plots. Half-rotted clothes-mulch can still mulch fruit trees.

Fruit residue Apple, grape of coffee residue from orchards or cafes can be laid on your plots.

Gravel is a marvellous mulch if applied 3–5 cm thick. It is mainly used in ornamental gardens around succulents, cacti and sword-leaved plants, but should you have a supply, try it as a mulch on sturdy vegetables of the cabbage family. Most woody herbs prefer gravelly soil for drainage, just mix gravel with garden soil.

Hay Legendary tales are told about the effects on a garden of one bale of spoiled hay. Be wary of weed seeds in meadow hay. Great plant food, now sold in handy packs.

Herb stalks Should you have a flourishing herb plot, do as the Shakers did. They stripped herbs for tea, cooking and medicine, then spread the stalks as mulch under fruit trees, some acting as a pest repellent. Stalks are best over newly applied compost because they take time to break down as they shade the soil.

Lawn clippings are a quickly-decaying mulch, best mixed with coarser materials, such as leaves and broken twigs. Otherwise apply dried.

Leaves should never be burned as this causes air pollution and asthma and robs the soil of valuable mulch. First sweep a layer of leaves under the tree canopy as food, then compost the rest with other organic matter. To make leaf mould for mulch or potting soil, put leaves in a wire cylinder until broken down. Eucalyptus leaves make surprisingly good mulch for the ornamental garden, less so for vegetables. Leaves cleared from the gutter in spring are suitably decayed. Sprinkle lime to counteract acidity; B&B to encourage breakdown.

Mulch blocks are available commercially. Add water to a block to get a wheelbarrow of water-holding mulch to spread around plants.

Newspaper sheets make a weed-suppressing mulch in layers of 10–12, but cover this with leaves or straw or you get impervious papier-mâché. Don't use between small vegetables, which prefer an airier mulch, but use underneath and around the perimeter of plots and under fruit trees.

Oak-leaf mulch or bark repels slugs.

Olive-leaf residue In more Mediterranean climates, olive-leaf residue has been used as a mulch.

Pine needles are a great mulch around strawberries. Remember the pine tree needs at least a 10 cm layer itself.

Recycled household waste Where you are, you may be able to find or buy mulches from recycled household waste, either in bags or to gather yourself.

Rock Crushed or as rock dust, contains minerals.

Sawdust Must be from untreated wood, e.g. from your own workshop or your own trees. Use only on paths, in the ornamental garden and sparingly in the compost, balanced out with lime if the wood you use is acidic.

Stones If you are blessed with a million stones on your land, use them. By planting each plant in an earth saucer surrounded with stones and filling the saucer with CMC, you trap moisture and attract good beetles. To keep slugs and snails away, spread coffee grounds around the stones.

Straw Keep straw away from seedlings and young plants as there can be some harmful fumes during the breaking-down process.

Tea-tree mulch is another commercial by-product, from tea-tree oil production.

Tree prunings Prune a few branches. Mow or shred them to make a mulch, or separate leaves from twigs and spread as above.

Twigs If you are strapped for mulching materials, but have wattles or shrubs, prune twigs and spread cross-wise in layers between plants. This provides an airy mulch that in time breaks down into compost.

Weed mats Buy only the biodegradable type that lets through water and acts as a mild mulch. For a single square-metre vegetable plot, buy half a metre of the double width. Depending on the spaces needed between vegetables, cut weed mat into strips of 20, 30 or 40 cm. Place strips in a grid across the plot and plant vegetables in the interstices. Once young plants are well above ground, remove strips or cover with CM and water well. Re-use weed mats.

Woodchips Some electricity utilities and councils deliver free woodchips after pruning roadside trees. Use for paths in the food garden. Pine wood is beloved by strawberries.

At the end of summer when there is little food about for wildlife, your mulched plots may be dug up at night by unseen creatures – cats, foxes, rats, and early birds – because only there in the moist mulch can they find something to eat. Hence, when planting winter vegetables in autumn, wait with mulching until the days are getting cooler or protect plantings with racks and cages. Mulch again when plants are established and there is plenty of other food for the wildlife.

What to Do about Weeds?

It is useful to know that weeds have tremendous benefits as plants and are only weeds because we did not plant them where they are. I shudder at the sight of yellow dock carrying a seed head for a thousand potential deep-rooted dockies, yet know that deep dock roots bring nutriments to upper soil layers.

Our friends bought a property in a country area where everyone appeared to be members of a land care or tree-planting group, so they were expecting to join a community that took care of the environment. This was true only insofar as the neighbours were changing a farming district into a region looking prettier by the year with flowering natives marking boundaries and daffodils popping up in green grass during winter.

But spring was the neighbourhood's cue to spray weed killers. We saw large brown areas between the greener ones, poisoned and ready for weed-free planting. Our friends found that although the previous owners had maintained an annual poison program on the property, it still sprouted an abundant crop of multifarious weeds. They decided to abstain from the springtime ritual, save the money and get some exercise by controlling weeds by mowing. By not using poisons they prevented toxic residues running into their precious water courses.

Weeds are weeds because they are vigorous plants that survive without human interference. The first rhododendron, carefully collected in the wild, has become a weed in the UK! Each weed has unique properties. Some are toxic; others are beneficent herbs. Due to the war against weeds waged by humans for centuries, only the toughest survive. In nature, trees stand in fields of weedy herbs or herby weeds beneficial to their health. If you care to imitate nature, let some weeds and grasses grow in your orchard and just keep a circle one metre in diameter around young trees for manure, mulch and watering. You can still mow the orchard, or have it grazed and fertilised by geese and ducks – see **Easy-Care Fruit Trees**.

But what to do with weeds that overwhelm the garden in spring?

Start on sunny days in late winter and don't leave weeding till mid spring, by which time your chosen plants demand space. Pull one bucket of weeds every day as exercise. A feathered flock living in a run will thrive on these morsels. Chickens, ducks and geese each have their favourite weeds and some they all squabble over, turning them into eggs and manure. Poison those weeds and you get nothing, while streams and water courses collect toxic residues. Regard weeds as plant food to toss in the compost or liquid manure (see **Plant Food & Soil Food**) or spread on a vacant plot to dig in. To solve the problem in a few years, always pull weeds before they set seed.

For extensive areas, apply hot water or steam weed with appropriate equipment. Alternatively, cover temporarily with black plastic or weed mat, making slits to insert plants, and mulch with straw. Buy UV stabilised, permeable and biodegradable weed mat so the soil underneath doesn't dry out (consult advertisements in organic gardening magazines).

My friend Gay covered a weed-infested area with telephone books opened in the centre, placed in overlapping fashion. Collect them from friends and neighbours. Give the weeds 2–3 years to die down. Cover phone books with straw and potted plants to make it look pretty. For me this worked on suckering bamboo.

Different weeds pull up minerals from different soil levels: calcium, copper, iron, magnesium, manganese, nitrogen, phosphorus, potassium, silica, sulphur and more. Should you be so lucky to have nettles, you may be happy to know that your soil is rich. Nettles love growing near compost heaps and are an excellent fertiliser in a similar way to seaweed. Pick nettles before they set seed, steep in a bin of water and leave to rot. Scoop off some 'nettle tea', dilute and use on your vegetables. Dry young nettles to make a velvet herb tea for human consumption. Leave a few stalks going to seed.

Most of our weeds are alien species. Our orchard trees, crops, pets and livestock are not native either! Unless we believe we can feed our population from woodland and hedgerows, we have to grow imported fruit and vegetables for our imported appetites. So we may as well let imported weeds do the job they are good at, which is making soil nutriments accessible for other plants. Contrary to popular perception, a garden sporting a crop of healthy weeds spells good soil for cultivated plants, including vegetables.

That said, weeds going to seed spell trouble. Pull or mow weeds early and don't let them seed on waste ground. Don't let dandelions flower too long, because the 'clocks' are seed heads that will scatter their seeds over a very wide area.

Each area has its own notorious weeds. Some are edible. Talk to locals and find out how the worst weeds propagate themselves – by seed, bulb, root division or all three? Then eradicate each weed just before it sets seed or forms new bulbs. Most weeds can be composted, but never put couch grass or dock root in the compost! This sort of knowledge takes the panic out of spring and the weed issue. Suspect seed heads and roots should go into plastic bags, knotted at the top. Growing and managing weeds is part of healthy gardening and your compost heap makes short work of most of them.

All this good news about weeds should be enough to make you quite relaxed on the subject. In winter, spot what is coming up and saunter out for your daily bucket. Pull selectively, according to what needs to be stopped in its tracks rather than weeding a whole area, which is what you do just before the new planting season.

Enjoy your weeds, get to know them. Learn that the pointy leaf of English plantain is nicknamed 'gardener's band-aid' because it stems bleeding should you cut yourself. Simply rinse, crush a leaf and apply.

Crop Rotation & Green Crops

Crop rotation restores the nutritional balance in the soil and prevents plant diseases developing, but it cannot restore all nutriments taken from the soil by previous crops. Therefore soil needs additional nutriments through green crops, compost, manure and organic fertilisers.

The word has been out a while now that mono-cropping, the growing of one variety on the same soil year after year, leads to root diseases, fatal for root crops as well as those on big feet like the large brassicas. Mono-cropping is putting all your eggs in one basket and is frequently practised with vegetables that increase prolifically, delivering the greatest harvest for the least amount of cost and labour. Mono-cropping is performed by poor people who need to feed many mouths for next to nothing.

Such was the case in Ireland where potatoes were the staple food until, in

1845, the Great Potato Famine struck. Cold wet weather gave rise to a fungal disease and the potatoes rotted. One million people died of starvation and two million migrated, leaving five million to try to survive off the blighted land. In the hills where I live, the growers of an entire valley were prohibited from cultivating onions for five years because of a disease caused by continuous mono-cropping.

In Bali the hills have been terraced to grow rice for a thousand years. But with a recent surge in population to 3.5 million, in a climate where rice can grow all year, continuous mono-cropping was reducing soil fertility and causing problems requiring chemical spraying. Now Balinese farmers practise crop rotation with peanuts, corn, sweet potato, tapioca, and vegetables after two rice harvests. Their fields are small and those surrounded by shelter belts of mixed trees and weeds have the best-looking crops.

From a train window, travelling from Hong Kong to Guangzhou, I watched spellbound as we rolled past thousands of market gardens doomed to become concrete jungles during the 21st century. Chinese farmers in Guangdong Province practise the most intensive vegetable culture I've ever seen. They have many mouths to feed, but they can grow food all year in a subtropical climate with an annual rainfall of 76 inches. Every bit of arable ground between villages is taken up by straight beds, two arms-lengths wide and divided by narrow paths where people hunch to weed, hoe or harvest, filling huge reed baskets. Every second or third bed had bamboo lattice running through the centre with peas, beans, cucumbers, aubergines and squash vines shading rows of leafy vegetables underneath. Each bed grew at least half a dozen vegetables including onions, celery and broccoli.

Later I learned that apart from lots of manure and compost made from street sweepings, the only other fertiliser used was nitrogen in the form of ammonia or urea. This went on all the beds, whether they would grow brassicas or root crops, mainly to save time. About five combinations of vegetables inhabited the beds in turn, so crop rotation was assured. Only aquatic vegetables like kangkong, lotus, water bamboo and water spinach were grown as mono-crops in watery regions.[17]

Even rotating half a dozen crops is not always enough to keep blights, root disease and insect infestations at bay. A mixed farming approach is needed, taking into account mini-climate, indigenous pests and predators.

The home grower can use mixed farming on a small scale and succeed. Make each bed a mix of 3–4 vegetables with companion herbs and flowering plants. Read about rotating crops in Part One and Part Four. If you are not following the succession of plots in Part One, here are some other scenarios for

Else's attractive kitchen garden is situated on a slope between a bank and future orchard. It has four mulched plots for crop rotation and citrus trees in tubs.

you to try. Sometimes you will plant mixed vegetables, other times a mono-crop like onions and garlic. But a mono-crop on one square metre causes no problems if followed by mixed species.

Alternative Scenarios for Crop Rotation

Scenario 1 You might first plant your square in early autumn as a Curry Plot with carrots, cauliflower, daikon, swedes, red onions, kale and herbs.

Scenario 2 As you dig up carrots and swedes, sprinkle B&B and sow rocket toward a Salad Plot to fit in with onions that sit in the ground till mid summer. The kale keeps standing a long time. Cultivate around them, sowing red radishes, and when the weather warms up plant one prolific, staked tomato plant and a rambling cucumber. Rake mixed lettuce seeds in between and there's your Salad Plot.

Scenario 3 When the Salad Plot comes to an end and the onions are drying in the shed, add manure and compost. Plant cauliflowers, broccoli, tatsoy and bok choy around the edges and broadbeans in the centre. There's your Stir-Fry Plot.

Scenario 4 It's spring once more. Eat or freeze any green food left growing. Rake in CMC for pumpkins, squash, courgettes and melons, or peppers, aubergine and tomato.

Scenario 5 Add lime in autumn, three weeks before planting onions and garlic. Mulch between rows. Have an easy winter.

Scenario 6 Since it may be a while before the onions and garlic dry off enough to be pulled, now is the time to expand. Dig up another square metre of lawn and plant spring vegetables.

Scenario 7 The onions and garlic are harvested, it is mid summer and hot. Plant a quick green crop like mustard and dig it in before it sets seed.

Scenario 8 Time for a nitrogen fix – plant winter peas along the edges of the square with at least four Asian greens taking up the centre for a different Stir-Fry Plot.

Scenario 9 Give that square plenty of manure, compost and B&B for an Anti-Oxidants Plot.

The 1, 2, 3, 4 Method

Should you find that intricate pattern of mixed vegetables over four years too much to keep track of, consider laying out four strips, each of 50 x 100 cm, i.e. half the size of the square-metre plot. Mark them 1, 2, 3 and 4 with numbers on stakes and keep a notebook. Whether you start in spring/summer or autumn/winter, plant as follows:

Plot 1 – leafy vegetables (leaf beet, bok choy, cabbage).

Plot 2 – any root crop.

Plot 3 – any leguminous crop, beans in spring/summer, peas or broadbeans in autumn/winter.

Plot 4 – fruiting crops (cucumbers, pumpkins, melons, courgette, and in theory also aubergines, peppers and tomatoes*).

Next season shift these categories up one so that Plot 1 becomes a fruiting crop, Plot 2 a leafy crop, Plot 3 a root crop and Plot 4 a leguminous crop. Apply manure and other requirements for each crop – see Part Four.

* Some gardeners group the Solanaceae family separately as they have similar feeding requirements. This means you have a fifth plot for potatoes, tomatoes, peppers, aubergine, Cape gooseberry and relatives – cramming two of each on a 50 x 100 cm plot! This fifth plot rotates along with the other four. With six plots you can grow onions and garlic separately too.

The 1, 2, 3 Method

This simple method still assures reasonable crop rotation on the same plot if you are not trying to grow food for all your needs.

Season 1 In autumn plant any of the gross feeders, e.g. the cabbage family or leafy crops. In spring plant aubergine, peppers, cucurbits, pumpkins, sweetcorn, tomatoes.

Season 2 Plant root crops that can live off the residue of the heavy manuring applied for the above. Beetroot, carrots, onions, swedes and turnips are all good.

Season 3 Plant peas or beans, depending on the season, or a green crop to dig in.

As a rule of thumb, remember that rotation starts with gross feeders when you lay it on with CMC, CM, OF and/or B&B, plus a sprinkling of lime. For root crops (except potatoes) also add a sprinkling of lime and top dress with some CMC if soil is poor. Lime again for peas and beans, but hold back on OF and B&B. Then manure all other crops and lime where soil is acidic. Problem is, potatoes like manure but not lime.

In a notebook draw a plan of your plots on a double page, write the year and season in one corner and note where vegetables were planted. It's an easy record to help you plan following seasons. Rotation for a minimum of three or four seasons, and as many as six seasons, avoids troubles.

Now that your first plot is underway, plan to develop another square each year until you have four square-metre plots. This streamlines crop rotation. Simply shift the salad plot from Square 1 to Square 2 and so on, until it returns to Square 1 in the fifth season. The other three squares follow a different sequence, or carry a mono or green crop.

Let the peas and beans family only touch corners with the onion and garlic plot. In winter this four-square bed might be one square of cabbages – planted as a border or cross – a diagonal half square of leaf beet, a half square of carrots, another of leeks, and a whole square of mixed cauliflower and broccoli, all intermixed with swedes, parsley, rocket, marigolds and borage, and plastic butterflies hovering across the cabbages (see page 248).

Going into your second winter there will be a profusion you had not planned. Self-seeded rocket may have to be pruned. Kale seedlings are likely. Give some away, with the recipe for green soup!

While you eat out a plot as the season advances, start planting suitable vegetables in vacant spaces, so that by mid spring you still have some winter crops, interspersed with lettuces, peas and beetroots.

Of course such intensive growing depletes the soil and thus, whenever space becomes available, tip in a bucket of CM before replanting. This almost automatic crop rotation never grows the same crop in the same soil in consecutive years. Together with companion planting you can see how complex it threatens to become, but that is where green manures come in to give you a break.

158

By growing food in rotating beds, a section occasionally becomes vacant to plant a cover or green crop. In winter try barley, buckwheat, oats, peas or wheat. In summer try buckwheat, millet or sorghum. Dig in before they set seed. Buckwheat leaves are a fine vegetable, but some swear by wheatgrass.

Digging crops in is green manuring. It is the growing of a dense leafy crop for the sole purpose of fertilising the soil. Not only does the soil get a rest from producing crops that must grow to maturity as green crops are dug in before flowering, but plants returned to the earth at optimum vigour make the best green manure. Allowing a month to let the crop decay, this plot would have had a healthy rest for three months before returning to full production. Seeds of common green crops are obtainable in small to medium quantities.

Common Green Crops

Buckwheat Any season. Available from health shops or groceries.

Fenugreek Autumn and spring (see **List of Common Herbs**). Enjoy spicy leaves while young, then dig in.

Lupin Before flowering starts, cover plants entirely with a layer of newspaper and 5 cm soil or compost.

Millet Sow in a warm season. From groceries.

Mung beans Spring and summer. The same beans as used for sprouting. Need warmth to germinate.

Mustard Any season. Benefits soils harbouring nematodes. Available in large bags in Asian and Mediterranean groceries. Sow yellow or black mustard, a handful per square metre. Grow your own seed.

Oats Put a handful in a mix of green crops.

Red clover Widely used by farmers, very nutritious when dug in. Available at farm supply stores.

Soybean Spring and summer. The world's most nutritious bean. From health shops and farm supply stores.

Wheat If organic wheatgrass and wheat juice is so good for people, it must be good for the soil. Mix with other seeds, e.g. mustard and oats.

Nitrogen-fixing crops Peas and broadbeans in winter, other beans in summer. These are not dug in, but harvested. Cut plants at soil level, leaving nitrogen-fixing nodules in the ground. You can use comfrey, borage or courgette foliage and broadbean plants after harvest as a mulch between other crops. Cover the Broadbean Plot with its own stalks after cutting down the plants, until the leaves become one with the soil. Then carry the stalks to the compost heap.

Flowers between vegetables attract beneficial insects
that keep pests down and confuse predators looking for
a particular crop to settle on.

Pests & Predators

The **first line of thought** is: leave well alone. Most pests are temporary phenomena. The **second line of thought** is: every creature has a role in the great web of life. Pull one out and a connection is broken, pull out another and several connections break, until the web collapses. This is what the chemical revolution has partly achieved. Its other achievement is having made certain weeds and pest species resistant to simpler pest management.

Let your garden accommodate all insects, butterflies, bees, birds, frogs, rabbits and mice. You may be fonder of some than others and if there are rodents it is because no-one can stop them. Protect vegetables likely to be attacked by wildlife (see **Hardware in the Food Garden**). Usually there is but a brief time slot when certain crops become attractive to certain creatures, so why wipe out a whole species because they have your vegetable on the menu twice a year? My early artichokes were chewed by mice or rabbits. By placing cloches over the globes I harvested several months longer. The chewed plants grew more stems that produced late artichokes as well. Prolific bearers such as tomatoes and courgettes may get bugs, slugs or mildew, but you can still pick a fair crop.

The **third line of thought** is: since eradicating so-called pests has not been successful, and they are still with us despite the billions of tonnes of chemicals bombed on them (rather like humans do to humans, no?), shouldn't we perhaps accommodate them? Why not make them comfortable by planting their favourite habitat away from the vegetables or fruit we want to protect. The favourite dwellings of earwigs in hot seasons are roses and artichokes, i.e.

tightly folded, cool apartments where they spend the daylight hours. Planting these may keep them away from your cabbages. Before eating artichokes soak out earwigs; they never penetrate beyond the outer layers.

Identify the pests in your garden, then seek remedies that work with nature rather than against it. If you have a manifest problem with grubs and caterpillars, you may have to deep dig the vegetable plot where some lay their eggs and let blackbirds or chickens clean it out. Plant flowering native shrubs to attract small birds for future pest control. Read a book like Jackie French's *Natural Control of Garden Pests*, and allow your views to do a lateral arabesque. Let the creatures have some of what you grow. Learn to take tiny losses.

Snails are the logo of the Slow Food Movement. They love agapanthus clumps. It's too hot and rough a crawl from the agapanthus bank to the vegetable garden, so they leave the vegetables alone. What works in my garden and climate may not work in yours, but try not to overreact to a bit of damage. It is early days yet for the idea of accommodating other species instead of annihilating them, and the last word has not yet been spoken on the subject. Try out biological methods and observe what works in your garden. Apply coffee grounds, wood ash, sawdust or lime around plants susceptible to slug and snail attack.

The **fourth line of thought** is: pests attack the weakest plants, leaving others alone, at least in a multi-mix organic garden. This is nature's way of preventing weak plants from having progeny by setting seed. The other thing nature arranged is that even one old broccoli plant full of aphids will attract hordes of predators to take care of pest control. Isn't that wonderfully organised?

Unfortunately, humans mess up this well-laid, survival-of-the-fittest plan by spraying at the first, second and third sign of a pest, thus keeping weak plants alive at the expense of the wellbeing of the whole species and killing good bugs in the process.

My first impulse when spotting a seed-setting broccoli sporting a grey mess of aphids reminiscent of asbestos is to pull the whole plant out and throw it on the compost heap where birds and nature's processes do what they must do. I don't like unsightly plants in my food plot. But I have learned to look and see before I pull. Predators will invade the garden to clean up aphids, attracted by flowering vegetables going to seed, of which I leave several standing. If you pull the affected plant, aphids may attack the next weakest specimen. You must trust the organic process to have its way. Leave the aphids and its host. Should the whole garden become infested, you undoubtedly have an impoverished soil that can only produce poor plants. Read again the chapters on compost and soil and this time do it: add compost and manure, grow green crops, start all over again!

Add OF and LS for plant health. Use LS on weaker plants worth reviving – it's medicine! Rotate crops, plant companion plants and grow green crops. Strong plants cope better with the vagaries of pests, weather and climate change. These jobs are done in no time by intelligent gardeners on their tiny plots. Whereas a hundred years ago the cry was 'We must tame nature!', now it is 'We must repair and restore nature'. If we do that, nature will take care of its own. That includes us.

One way of assisting natural processes to attract beneficial insects is to plant herbs and flowers in the surrounding garden. Plant feverfew rather than using pyrethrum spray. See **List of Common Herbs**. You avoid killing beneficial creatures while keeping unwanted ones at bay. Practise companion planting.

According to research at Utah State University you can attract ladybirds by sprinkling some of your garden area with sugar water. Melt 150g sugar in warm water and top up to 1L with cold water. Apply with a watering can.

Do 2–3 L at once. Increases of 200–1300 per cent were noted in the ladybird population within a few days, which is a lot even if you only had one ladybird to start with. However, numbers could be smaller where you are. Ladybirds feed on aphids, mites, and cabbage moth eggs, among others. Sugar water also attracts lacewings and beetles.

Alternatively, buy some *Hippodamia variegata*. Not a variety of hippos, but a species of ladybird that come through the post as eggs on tape. See advertisements in organic gardening magazines.

What? No Sprays?

In our litigation-happy times it is not wise to give advice that encourages other people to use any substance whatsoever. What is an allowable chemical and what is not remains a contentious issue in government departments that seek to protect us all from harm. Not all substances used by gardeners have yet been classified. At the time of writing garlic and milk, used by organic gardeners as sprays, are unclassified in some states, although we use them freely in our cooking. You can see where this is going, can't you? I am not keen to advocate sprays or applications no matter how innocent the substances appear to be, lest you are allergic. I rarely use any myself, preferring to let nature do the healing.

When spraying, no matter whether a homemade brew or a commercial product, wear gloves, mask, goggles, long sleeves and trousers. If there is a label, read it and follow the directions for use.

An A–Z of Pests & Problems

Aphids If you decide to spray soapy water under the leaves, remember that soap kills frogs and probably toads as well. Study the list of herbs in Part Four that can be planted for long-term prevention. Feed the soil to return plants to health. Plant an artemisia in a large pot to shift between vegetables prone to aphids.

Birds Netting may seem drastic, but is necessary if you only have one or two square metres to protect. Don't use monofilament netting that snares and kills animals, but buy netting that does not endanger birds and wildlife, e.g. long-lasting, double-knitted netting with holes allowing bee access. Thrown over fruit trees it has to be clipped tightly underneath or the birds will come in off the ground floor. Netting saves most of the crop for you.

To discourage birds from pulling up seedlings, nipping beans in the bud, or shredding the lettuce for you, push in short stakes and crisscross sewing cotton above the plants. String aluminium yoghurt covers on wire, or peg on folded bread bags with the ends cut into fringes. Make pinwheels on sticks or push thin branches either side of seedlings and bend together. Evidently jars and bottles painted red and stuck on sticks do the job. It may look like a carnival, but if it works? Wire cages are my first protection – see **Hardware in the Food Garden**.

Cabbage white butterfly These pretty butterflies, celebrated by the poet Robert Graves, are a nuisance to the cabbage family. They feed on brassicas, nasturtiums and some ornamental flowers. You may find the urn-shaped eggs and greenish larvae and pupae, ornamented with one thin stripe, on the leaves of host plants. Plant brassicas in small squares with stakes on the corners. Cut simple butterfly shapes from white plastic lids and containers and tie these onto thin string at intervals of 15–20 cm. Or use Styrofoam packing fill that has a sort of butterfly shape. String butterfly garlands from stake to stake and diagonally across – they spell out 'occupied territory'. Or try a molasses spray, as below. Plant large pots with thyme and sage, or artemisia with chamomile and place between cabbages.

Codling moth If you see brown caterpillars on your apple, fig, pear or quince tree, pick them off because after feeding on your fruit they cocoon themselves to turn into larvae that pop up again as moths which lay eggs and give rise to the next caterpillar population. *Interception* is the name of this game, as once infected it may take years to free a tree of this pest.

In deep winter, buy some metres of thin unbleached cotton or similar material and sew a supply of small drawstring bags. In late winter fix corrugated cardboard around the trunk before the tree starts flowering. Caterpillars shack up in the corrugations. Clean it out twice a week after dawn and dispose of the contents.

When the petals start to fall make an exception and spray with a garlic spray – see Garlic Spray below. Next, cover fruit that has just set, but has not been bitten by a caterpillar – while the flower petals are still dropping – with cotton bags and tie the strings above the fruit. Through spring and summer inspect the fruit and pick off by hand whatever should not be there. Clean out old leaves in the crook of branches and periodically brush trunk and branches with a steel brush to rid it of loose bark where caterpillars full of apple pulp might want to spin a cocoon. Clear the ground underneath the tree of all fallen fruit, bits of wood, bark and leaves and dispose of them thoroughly. Don't put down mulch as it makes hiding places, but do empty pots of earwigs as these clean up coddling moths – see Earwigs below.

Unless you have chickens, under-plant apple, pear and quince trees with the sort of plants that attract hosts of small wasps, flies, beetles and spiders which dine on coddling moth, such as alyssum, buckwheat, carrot, daikon radish and parsnip in flower, dill, red clover, mustard, Queen Anne's lace and yarrow. *Mix the seed of a number of these to attract the greatest range of beneficial insects.*

Chickens will dispense with codling moth if allowed to scratch under mature fruit trees. Protect them from dogs and foxes by enclosing even a small orchard with a fox-proof fence, i.e. with an apron of wire netting buried outwards around the run and an outward curving overhang at the top of the wire to prevent a desperado vixen digging under or climbing up. Or invest in a 'chicken tractor', a tiny mobile run to wheel around where you want a couple of chickens to work for a day. Protect that too from dogs and foxes. It sounds like a lot of work, especially if you have three or more trees to treat. But you will get results and once you have these measures in place it becomes part of a seasonal routine. Write the dates in your notebook for next year.

Commercial products such as a horticultural glue fixed around the trunk to prevent caterpillars climbing up may help – or use Vaseline. Sticky traps and pads to render the male infertile are advertised in organic gardening magazines. Other baits that can be hung in jars from the tree are apple juice with a spoon of olive oil, or dissolved molasses with the same – but they could trap beneficial insects also. If you decide to use organic sprays, apply before fruit sets. Spray all hiding places in the trunk, branches, and the ground around the trunk and spread elderberry prunings. Pheromones issue a safe scent that disrupts the mating procedure, said to work on areas of a hectare and larger.

Leaf Curl The bane of stone-fruit growers. The old remedy was spraying with a cup of copper sulphate and a dessertspoon of agricultural lime dissolved in 15 L of water. This has to be done when buds are just appearing on the branches, or it will be too late.

Bordeaux spray, although organic, contains arsenic and is therefore not recommended. You could try a stinging-nettle infusion or LS before buds open and again a few weeks later. Spray under the tree as well. A more hands-on treatment involves picking off diseased leaves into a plastic bag – easier with espaliered trees than huge canopies. Burn the end points of each affected branch with a cigarette lighter – at last one good use for those! – as the disease starts in the tip leaves. Do this daily for a week. Give tree and surrounding soil a dousing with LS for the remaining leaves to take up. Hang a bag of diseased leaves inside another bag in the sun before disposal. Under-plant the tree with tansy, feverfew and yarrow to form a dense mat. Hanging mallow weeds in affected branches seems to work. Pigeon manure is said to help.

Earwigs If you can't plant a 'catch' crop like roses away from the food plot, put out pots on their sides, stuffed with moist newspaper. Empty the pots away from the vegetable garden; migrate the little darlings to under the apple, fig, pear and quince trees to take care of codling moths.

Fungi There are many, but when you see the first sign, spray with milk and water mixed 1:10 and repeat before going for heavier antifungal sprays. If the weather is about to change it may not be necessary.

Garlic spray A homemade spray for use with persistent pests or diseases. Make several days before needed. This recipe is from the renowned Henry Doubleday Research Association, reprinted in *The Organic Gardener's Companion*. Chop 70 g of garlic, mix in 2 tsp of liquid paraffin and soak for 48 hours. Add 600 ml of water and 7 g of an oil-based soap as a disperser. Only mix, filter and store in a plastic container. Dilute with water 100:1, or for persistent cases, 100:2.

Molasses spray Dissolve a tablespoon of molasses in a litre of warm water. This discourages flying and chewing insects, and maybe even grasshoppers. Being sweet, maybe it attracts ladybirds? There's still much to discover.

Eelworms These little things suck the fleshy roots of potatoes, cabbage and cauliflower, radishes and carrots, making them look pockmarked. Read up on marigold and mustard in the herb list in Part Four. It may take a few years to clean the soil, but damage gradually dwindles. Eelworms don't like fresh chicken manure, but neither do plants, so apply to soil several months before planting.

Sawfly Caterpillars suck the green out of pear, plum, and cherry leaves, leaving leaf skeletons. Douse with water, then dry sand or wood ash. For long-term prevention spread oak-leaf mulch.

Powdery mildew Vegetable families host specific powdery mildews that do not cross-infect other plant families. If leaves of pumpkin, cucumber and courgette are affected, that doesn't mean the grapes will get it too. Mildew thrives in damp conditions, where ventilation is restricted. Growing cucumbers and pumpkins on a trellis may prevent it. Sprays of milk and water mixed 1:10, or whey and bicarbonate of soda have been effective. Where fungal diseases and moulds persist, prune affected leaves and compost in a hot heap or bin them. Mildew weakens its host, so if productive plants have a bad case, it might kill the plant. Destroy leaves in autumn to reduce the infectious spores.

Rabbits Sprinkle B&B where they have been nibbling.

Rodents If you do not currently have rodents prowling your night garden, they may come when you start growing vegetables. They love germinating peas and beans, broadbeans, sweetcorn, melons and ornamental bulbs. Protect germinating seeds with cages, dish racks or similar obstructions, or use rings of PVC pipe with netting. Really keen rodents may still uproot these. Raise seedlings inside, because once seeds have sprouted a plant with 4–6 leaves, the attraction appears to vanish.

Snails and slugs They are beautiful creatures. Nice children look on in wonder when snails carry their elegant spiral houses slowly through the grass. They eat certain plants including weeds, so we don't want to eradicate them. Organic growers used to make their vegetables unpalatable to snails and other diners by making a spray from wormwood, garlic or white cedar. There is a withholding time of two weeks after spraying, so this method is not attractive if you want to pick greens daily.

The alternative is to collect snails or place a flowerpot with moist newspaper upside down on a stake overnight. Migrate the snails to another 'country' early mornings before they wake up. Oak-leaf mulch or coffee grounds repel slugs and snails and add nitrogen to the soil. After a wet spell with intervals of sunshine – great slug weather – I picked a lovely cabbage surrounded with coffee grounds. Only one slug lived in the outer leaves.

Strawberry protection Strawberries test the gardener's ingenuity. Everybody loves them. We've had all manner of insects and mammals coming to feast including birds, mice, slugs, snails and millipedes. Most objectionable are millipedes that tunnel into big strawberries and disperse their body odour through the entire fruit. The best protection I've used was horticultural fleece, as strawberries ripen as much with warmth as full sun. Spread fleece, propped up to raise it above the plants, then weigh down the edges with stones.

Weeds For infestations that can't be fixed with exclusion, hot water or mulches, an organic pine oil product is available.

Whitefly These sap-suckers attack beans and tomatoes, leaving plants yellow and stunted. Ladybirds, lacewings and other flying pest controllers clean up whitefly infestations. Try a sugar solution to attract these good insects to your garden (150 g of sugar per bowl of hot water; add enough cold water to cool it before sprinkling around plants) and provide a habitat for them of flowering herbs in pots and perennial flowers in borders. My friend Maureen sowed lots of marigolds along her tomatoes and whitefly disappeared!

For plant health, feed and mulch regularly, know what your water contains, do rain dances in dry seasons, and take responsibility for what you do in your garden. Even so, when making a garden pest-free with all the tricks you know, you and your garden are subject to forces greater than us all. Sometimes you can do nought but cut your losses. Learn to live with things you cannot fight. You can always sprout mung beans should the vegetable plot fail. But it will never fail entirely.

Study organic gardening magazines, as organic growers come up continually with novel ideas and harmless repellents. *To repel instead of destroying improves biodiversity.*

By practising the good gardening methods previously discussed, you find that the war-like terminology other gardeners use will disappear from your vocabulary. No more fighting plant diseases, combating, blitzing, bombing and zapping unwelcome insects. No more killing sprees. Instead, practise preventive health care in the garden. Protect and plant wisely so that nature can do its best practice. Then your garden will bring you peace, as well as the best food possible.

Companion Planting & Intercropping

Just as with humans, some plants retard each other's development while others flourish in each other's company. Companion planting and intercropping is a science born from millennia of observation by food growers. The oldest known example is from Mexico where some eight millennia ago the Aztecs grew corn, beans and pumpkin or squash together.

Two large beds of companion plants. In the foreground are borage, rocket, amaranth and tansy. Marigolds live on the paths surrounding a bed of onions with pansies, leaf beet, radish, shallots, pyrethrum, lavender, squashes, pumpkins and beans. The soil needs to be well fed.

Climbing peas under-planted with French and red chard, bordered by mignonette and oakleaf lettuces. Russian kale near the bee bath.

The main reasons for intercropping and companion planting are to group together those plants that chemically enhance each other's growth, stimulate fruit-set, protect each other from predators, prefer similar conditions and provide or seek shade. Plant shallow-rooted lettuce between deep-rooted carrots and beetroots that find nutriments further down and provide shade when planted south of lettuce. Tomatoes stay healthy with chemicals exuded by mustard plants.

Companion plants are listed in the **List of Common Vegetables**, but should you plan to expand your food gardening, buy a book on companion planting. Many of the companions listed I observed in my own food gardens. It was a surprise to see a tomato plant intertwine spontaneously with an onion plant to their mutual benefit, or lettuces gallop along with beans. Just observe your square to see what works and what doesn't. Get familiar with different vegetable groups in Part Four as their growth habits and requirements are often similar.

Intercropping is what the Aztec Plot achieves. It is a regulated type of companion planting, the beans enriching the soil for the corn in exchange for a climbing stake or perhaps chemical protection, while pumpkin leaves shade

Onions benefit by cohabiting with pansies.

the soil. Slow growers planted with quick ones save space, e.g. carrots with lettuce. Radishes sown with seeds of carrots, turnips, beetroot and swedes loosen the soil for germination and provide growing space for the others when pulled. Carrots, onions and lettuce are intercropped, growing roots at different depths. Radishes and spring onions are compatible while climbers like peas, beans and cucumbers benefit from having low growing lettuce or bok choy nearby to shade their roots. Sow small turnips, swedes and radishes between cabbages and cauliflowers, but don't forget them. Carrots with spinach, spinach with kohlrabi, lettuce and beetroot.

The seeds of any vegetables to be transplanted can be mixed and sown together. Any combination of plants that you see doing well can then be intercropped on a larger scale. Feed the soil beforehand and sow plants as close

A companionable border planting of courgettes, onions, beans, Russian kale going to
seed, savoy cabbage, red and french chard,
marigold, squash seedlings and leek.
The seed-setting plants need thinning out.

Pumpkin, garlic chives and pyrethrum
compose a poem.

together as their adult size allows – for radish and spring onions 2 cm, carrots 3 cm, onions 6–8 cm, beetroot 8–10 cm – on the understanding that you regularly pull the biggest plants to make space for others.

Some plants decidedly retard each other's wellbeing, or one grows at the expense of the other. Garden writers differ on what benefits and what impedes. Sometimes I wonder whether it was an onion that made my beans crumple or whether the soil was deficient.

When at a loss I put mustard seeds near a plant needing rescuing. Mustard comes up in a week and exudes a gas that keeps pests away. But when the mustard reaches a height of 1 m it robs nutrients from the plant it is protecting. Cut it down and spread the leaves and stalks between the vegetables. Such is mustard's fate. When space allows, let mustard grow to full height – the flowers attract a beneficial insect bonanza.

And if you find all this too confusing, just plant what you want, mix it up thoroughly and observe what happens. Do this for 10 years and then write the definitive book on British companion planting!

A happy confusion of half a dozen varieties is good company.

The Seasons

Think seasonally. Instead of assuming summer to be an ideal time for gardening because you like to be out in the sun, regard **summer** as a time to keep your plants going to produce their harvest – feeding, mulching, maintaining, watering and harvesting. Prune away dead matter and remove spent plants, keep sowing for the late autumn harvest and overwintering crops. Try not to replant as small plants may well not survive after their initial die-back. Cuttings can be taken in summer to grow in a greenhouse, roses and lavender in summer, daisies and geraniums any time – all make excellent hedges around the food garden. Apart from pottering to keep you connected, read garden books, start a garden notebook and make plans. Learn the habits of one or two vegetables and herbs in Part Four for next season.

The gardening year really starts in **autumn**. Plant shrubs and perennials to attract pest predators. Clear away spent plants, prune existing perennials and shrubs and mark out a composting area. Set up compost bins (see **Compost Compositions**). Autumn is a good time to start a worm farm. Study the autumn list of vegetables in Part Four and select what you want to eat in a few months time. If all the plants in your square are spent, spread CMC and replant immediately.

Establish a brassica plot, an Onion and Garlic Plot, or a Stir-Fry Plot. If an old plant is still forming seed, stake and work around it. Should you have more than one square, fork over plot after plot, apply CMC and then plant. Position racks or cages to protect seedlings and keep watering if no rain falls, even if there's dew. Within five or six weeks you will eat the first pickings.

Make a tiny greenhouse of fleece and stakes to raise next summer's seedlings. My greenhouse (240 x 140 cm, with salvaged racks) is also the plant hospital, where dead sticks return to life, slow seeds germinate, and sick plants recover.

Winter is still a busy time for the gardener. In between rain showers you are out in the fresh air preparing for spring, adding lime to acidic soil, planting shrubs, pruning fruit trees and berries. After cleaning up, the compost is made and the previous batch turned. In mild winters continue planting trees and shrubs so they can make use of good conditions.

Make an instant cold frame by bending a piece of reinforcing wire into a U-shape, folding plastic around it in such a way that you can open and close a front flap with a peg. Push the wire edges into the ground, place two bricks or pavers inside to capture the heat and place seed trays on top of these. Don't forget to ventilate and water! Or, find a crate to cover with removable glass, or plastic sheeting on a stick to roll up on sunny days. Place it on black plastic to hold the heat. Use a cold frame to raise spring seedlings of vegetables needing a long growing season. For a hot frame see **Seeds & Seedlings**.

Spring is the season of exuberance. Everything happens at once. That's why you did the preparatory work in autumn and winter. The weather goes from hot to cold and back again. Things want to grow but can't, or should but won't, yet trees and shrubs burst with buds and new leaves in 37 shades of green. Crab apples and flowering plums are clouds of pink and white blossoms and the orchard reveals daily miracles. Animals and insects wake from their winter sleep.

Bugs and slugs may have crept into the cold frame. Remove all the seed trays once a week on a mild day and clean the inside of debris. Replace trays and water with LS to strengthen growth. Open frame when the weather is warm, but always close up before dusk.

Press seeds of your favourite vegetables in trays of potting soil or seedling mix to keep the cold frame full. In its balmy atmosphere, many seeds can emerge within a week. Keep them growing with LS until they have 4–6 leaves. Don't plant out until danger of frost is over, but do plant potted plants you didn't get around to in winter. The rest of spring is taken up with weeding and mulching.

Start a Salad Plot now. Contemplate planting herbs. Take a look around the garden and see where you need to plug up a space or thicken a hedge. If you can't buy plants, this is another good time to take cuttings from perennials, while the sap is rising. Soak cuttings or 'heels' in water with honey or a willow branch, to help root formation, then stick deep into a pot of soil in shade. If you have a superb white daisy bush, stick 20–30 cuttings in a Styrofoam box, feed with LS, and do a mass planting next autumn. If you love buddleia, the butterfly bush, take shoots and tips for a small buddleia forest. Mass plant your garden with beautiful hedges at no cost.

For years I drove past a particular hillside vegetable garden. It always lay fallow in winter, was dug over in April and not planted until May. But this unknown gardener knew what she was doing, for by midsummer the vegetables in that garden stood as tall as mine. Gnash! They probably bought all those plants . . .

There's the choice. *By starting late you avoid hordes of spring-born insect pests.* Summer heat is advancing, nights are no longer cold. As long as you feed and water late seedlings they may catch up on those raised early, but some may not get a long enough season.

These choices of when to grow major crops depend on your own rhythms, working patterns and climate, or on whether you simply cannot wait after that first springy day struck you radiant in early March. If you have become an unstoppable food gardener, you plant in spring as well as autumn and do progressive plantings through summer on cool days, or plant in the evenings to allow new plants to brace themselves for dawn. This way you will have all the vegetables you need throughout the year. But it does require the patchwork method, planting in between maturing vegetables and seed producing plants. Somehow that takes care of crop rotation as well.

Summer comes around again, you have done those small jobs throughout the year and the garden looks vastly different compared with last year. Keep things growing with mulches, keep on top of the weeding and watering. Don't burn anything; there is enough air pollution and asthma already. Store wood for winter or pack a few bags for a relative. Dance on a heap of small twigs to make mulch, or compost them. Big pieces of wood shaped with an adze make natural borders for garden beds. Prune away dead wood on trees as high as you can reach, so that new growth has space and branches are safe. Now enjoy the results of your labour and sit near a tree with a garden book amidst growth, colours and bird song.

A list of summer, winter and all season vegetables and herbs precedes their detailed descriptions in Part Four.

Permaculture

Permaculture is a system devised by Bill Mollison and David Holmgren, and was first launched in Tasmania in 1980. Permaculture is aptly named as it strives to create agricultural and horticultural systems that become self-perpetuating. Human ingenuity blossoms in permaculture set-ups and no two are alike, although there are now many properties and gardens in worldwide being run on permaculture principles. Permaculture embraces not only the food garden, orchard and livestock, but birds, insects, surrounding gardens, land management, integrated functions of houses and outbuildings, and the use of people's time and energy.

There are permaculture books, courses, consultants and open days. Permaculture is being exported to countries that need more sustainable agricultural methods to encourage food gardeners to stay clear of artificial fertilisers that ruin their soils and GM seed companies that deprive them of control over their own seed production. Bill Mollison has been tirelessly spreading permaculture principles in Africa and Asia, while those who have learned from him and David Holmgren have fanned out through the Pacific and South-East Asia as far as Afghanistan.

Permaculture is about closed cycles in which each component aids the others. It means that if you grow something to provide mulch and food for animals, who then give manure to put around fruit trees and vegetables, and the cycle is sustainable, you have a closed cycle. For most home gardeners this means kitchen scraps going to chickens that lay eggs and produce manure for vegetables and fruit that produce more scraps. In dwellings it is about trapping heat in winter and excluding it in summer by using the orientation of windows, attached greenhouses and slate floors to retain warmth, the angles of roof over-hangs, solar and wind technology, and water management systems.

Another tiny closed cycle is created by excluding chemical sprays and instead running chickens in a fenced orchard to control pests where they scratch for insects, eat fallen fruit and lay bonus eggs. If you have more land than one garden, grow the little amount of wheat the flock needs and exchange it for manure mixed with soil and straw from their run. Use this on vegetable plots or in compost to grow fruit, herbs and vegetables of which the chickens get the peelings.

The closed cycle principle goes as far as the universe stretches, but you can attempt closed cycles in an ordinary backyard. Compost bins, worm farms, food production, pond life, energy, grey-water disposal, all these fit on a suburban block and further your self-reliance.

If you have acres, you might be interested in land contours, wind and weather and how to preserve and improve your piece of the planet and make the best use of it. Borrow a permaculture book from the library for a feast of ideas useful to your future. Put your thinking cap on as to how permaculture designs can apply to your patch of earth, your patio or balcony, and sketch your ideas on the back of an envelope.

Seeds & Seedlings

The giving garden has to be a sustainable garden, because above all it is the seed base for the future. The seeds nature drops, the ones the birds drop in, and the seeds we gather, dry and store, ensure that plant-friendly micro-climates continue as long as we are here to gather, maintain and sow and refrain from interfering too much.

Seeds

The inventors of the commercial seed packet were the American Shaker gardeners, adding value to their products. Growing vegetables from seed is extremely economical, especially with open-pollinated seed, as the resulting plants produce seed true to type to save and plant again. These well-tried heirloom and heritage varieties, kept going by farmers and gardeners since the beginning of time, produce seed reliably.

Why is this so desirable? Just as you appreciate the taste and quality of home-grown vegetables, so you will appreciate the taste and quality of heirloom vegetables. Some may not produce as prolifically as hybrids whereas others may outperform those. Grow a variety of vegetables, rather than overproducing a few.

An heirloom is something precious passed down through the generations. In my understanding an heirloom vegetable is from before the time of widespread commercial genetic engineering, like seed my grandfather grew because his grandfather told him it was dependable.

The word heritage could imply that something has inherited qualities or characteristics. That may apply to my great-great-grandfather's cabbage seeds, but with a bit of word wrenching it could also be claimed for a modern seed emerging from a GM laboratory, as ultimately its ancestor is also ancient seed. After all, everything has qualities and characteristics that come from somewhere, no matter what they have been turned into.

There was a time when large seed companies feared small seed companies offering open-pollinated, organically grown seed of common as well as unusual heirloom and heritage vegetables, herbs, flowers and trees. There are several such small seed companies now, as well as Garden Organic, that offer this type of seed. If you like buying from catalogues, take the time to ponder hundreds of varieties and write away for a few (look at organic gardening magazines and websites, carrying advertisements from sellers of seeds, roots and bulbs).

Commercial seeds in shops are increasingly based on fewer varieties, may be genetically modified and are often impregnated with toxic substances to ensure shelf life. Most are hybrids, bred by companies for improved size, production and pest resistance. Hybrids may grow fast but do not usually produce viable seed, or if they do it may not breed true to type (i.e. the hybrid type it grew from), or its offspring may deteriorate after a few seasons. Lack of quality control can occur under the biggest labels. A representative of a large seed company once tried to convince me that their packet of undersized and broken broadbean seeds would still grow good beans! Not for my money. Some commercial seeds don't germinate at all, which could be the fault of retail outlets. Never buy seed from a counter in the sun, for it will be cooked.'

Seed Saving Networks

Garden Organic, formerly Henry Doubleday Research Association, has developed an extensive seed library of traditional seed varieties. Dedicated to preserving our valuable organic heritage, they undertake targeted activities to protect diversity and encourage seed conservation. The Heritage Seed Library (HSL) aims to conserve and make available vegetable varieties, mainly of European origin, that are not widely available. They are not a gene-bank and all the collection, once there is enough seed, become available through an annual catalogue.

In Australia, the Seed Savers' Network is an amazing non-profit volunteer foundation that since 1986 has collected in a seed bank as many varieties of open-pollinated vegetable, herb and fruit seeds as they can find, including heirlooms from immigrant gardeners. Their newsletter offers seeds of unheard of vegetables. Each year, they print a swap market catalogue of seeds offered by members from which subscribers can buy varieties. Members grow these seeds on and some donate supplies back to the seed bank.

In America, the Seed Savers Exchange collected 18,000 vegetable varieties grown across the country. Such networks are of crucial importance in preserving global food resources. A tragic story of seed saving dedication comes from St Petersburg in Russia. During the Second World War German forces besieged the city, then Leningrad, and the population was starving. The Soviet Union's seed bank was located in the city, protecting a store of containers preserving the seed of many varieties of grains, oats, peas, beans and other food plants. These could have provided food for many people. But the seed bank personnel were so dedicated to their task that not a grain or bean was missing by the end of the war, even though some of the guardians died of starvation themselves. Director Nikola Ivanovich Vavilov, who founded that seed bank to eliminate hunger from the world, died of starvation in one of Stalin's prisons, suspected of espionage. He probably corresponded with seed savers abroad. The Vavilov Institute in St Petersburg still maintains a seed bank.

Asian Vegetable Seeds

Asian vegetable seeds can be found in most Asian supermarkets. Some packets have English text, but for others you'd better brush up your Mandarin and Japanese. Plant some seeds in spring and again in autumn to find out which season they prefer. Experiment using the pictures on the packets. Marrows, squash and beans are mostly summer vegetables, but many leafy greens like cooler seasons.

Asian vegetables still have good resistance against British pests and diseases, with the exception of the greenish-white Chinese cabbage, which gets attacked by snails, slugs, cabbage moth and aphids to the point where you don't want to deal with it in the kitchen. Most Asian vegetables presently available are the products of 40 centuries of companion-growing horticulture, mostly in China, and the Chinese were too hungry and too practical to waste time on vegetables that could not survive prevailing conditions.

Planting Good Seeds at the Right Depth & Time

The right depth is generally held to be the thickness of the seed, but sow beans two to three times their own thickness. Rake very fine seed through the top of the soil. A very loose straw cover provides protection. Use a fine nozzle or mist to water seeds.

There are systems to guide gardeners to plant seeds on beneficial days.

Planting by the moon is an ancient method based on the notion that when the moon is waxing it draws new seedlings toward its light, and when it's waning root growth takes place. Fruiting and leafy plants are sown in the last quarter, beans and peas three days before full moon, and root crops in the middle of the first quarter. That's a rough guide, but you can buy moon-planting charts and some magazines print monthly directions.

Alternate rows of lettuce and beetroot with carrots seeded under the straw.

Biodynamic planting calendar If you like order in your life, then the biodynamic planting calendar is for you. Biodynamics was Rudolf Steiner's answer to feng shui. This is where every possible function of plants and trees guided by the moon and stars is worked out annually by a very knowledgeable person, so the calendar tells you every morning just what you can and can't do in the garden. This presumes you are available for horticultural work at any time so it works best for full-time farmers.

If through necessity you are a weekend gardener you can probably manage to keep to the rough moon-planting scheme. If your gardening has to be done whenever life allows you a few moments, plant and harvest to your heart's content when you can. Nature always strives for the light, always prefers growth and ever renews itself, so you will have marvellous successes just the same, even if a little slower. You can blame the few fiascos on the weather. Even biodynamic and moon gardeners find excuses.

Soak hard-coated seeds such as beans in water with a few drops of LS before sowing. As seeds germinate, apply LS every few days. Seedlings can go into the ground when the first root tip comes out of the bottom of a toilet roll, or a seedling is about 6 cm high with at least four leaves.

Where to raise seeds Seeds raised outdoors, protected from the elements and raised up from the ground, will be hardy. But as a lot of summer crops need 5–6 months of warm weather to mature, an earlier start may necessitate starting seedlings indoors. This avoids rodent damage too. Seeds do not need much light to germinate, so you can start trays off in shed or cellar, moving them to windows when two leaves have appeared.

Bottom heat Seed trays set on a small electrically-warmed bottom-heat mat will have improved germination rates. For a one-square plot it may not be worth the outlay.

A cold frame warmed by the sun gives seedlings an early start (see **The Seasons**).

An old-fashioned hot bed is fun to make. Start late winter and find a glass window or door to place on top. In a sunny, sheltered place mark out a frame with four bales of straw, or make a frame with planks or bricks to fit under the glass cover. Dig out the floor area to a depth of 20–30 cm and fill with animal manure, straw and grass clippings. Water in well and spread the soil on top. Place the glass across the frame. Give it a week to hot up, keeping it moist. Then half submerge pots with seedlings or seeds into the soil. Read Jack First's excellent book 'Hot Beds'.

Weaning When seedlings have at least four leaves, wean them from the protected environment through 'hardening off'. Place seedlings outside on nice days, and back in the frame at night until they appear robust enough to go into the ground when the weather is fine.

Problems A number of things can upset your plans. 'Damping off', causing seedlings to rot, occurs in seed trays when the soil is too wet or air doesn't circulate. Resort to timing and hardware until it becomes routine. Once you master seed raising you will only buy shop veg trays as an exception. Water seedlings with weak LS solution twice a week.

Preventing transplant shock The roots of many seedlings get transplant shock when taken out of a seed tray and put in a hole in the ground. This may set them back weeks. No growth occurs; sometimes death follows. The way to avoid this is to grow seedlings in biodegradable toilet rolls – see below – so that most of the roots remain protected when the tube is planted in open ground. Transplant shock also occurs when directly sown seedlings are thinned out. Pulling them up by the roots exposes neighbouring seedlings and these may die. Better to let them grow to toddler size before pulling the bigger ones.

Tunnel cloches By covering a row of early seedlings while the soil is still cold, you help them get into gear in their cosy tunnel. Make your own covers by bending reinforcing or chicken wire in a V or U-shape and covering with transparent plastic punched with breathing holes, shading or horticultural fleece – see **Hardware in the Food Garden**.

Hardy vegetables can be raised in the open. You can't raise pumpkins in winter as they expire on cold nights, as do tomatoes, beans, squash and cucumbers. But the cabbage cousins are hardy customers. Cabbage, cauliflower, brassica juncea, broccoli, Brussels sprouts, bok choy, kale, tatsoy, Chinese cabbage and mustards can all be sown in open ground in autumn and mild winters, growing on into spring. If your winter is not mild, sow Asian greens in open ground in late winter and start broccoli, cabbages and cauliflower off in

190

the cold frame at the same time. A small Percy's portable plastic roof also helps germination – see **Hardware in the Food Garden**.

A seed-raising table is useful when temperatures rise and the cold frame starts toasting seedlings. I found a waist-high small workshop bench measuring 30 x 50 cm. Around the edges I placed water-filled plastic bottles in a metal filing system frame I just happened to have. Seed trays sit inside this instant mini-hothouse open to the air, but an old fridge grid with netting attached to it lies across the top to keep birds out. This table holds six seed trays containing 36 seedlings. By always keeping the space occupied, it provides plenty of well-formed seedlings grown to the stage where they can hold their own in the big world. These need no 'hardening off'.

Continuous sowings Raise single trays of six beans from April to July for a continuous supply. Also raise back-up pumpkin and squash seedlings, as in some years the weather destroys early ones in the ground. In late summer start raising autumn vegetables.

Toilet rolls Raise seedlings in toilet rolls to avoid root disturbance when planting out. This is not necessary for vegetables that are best sown directly into the ground, e.g. root vegetables and sprawling greens like leaf beet, spinach, Asian greens, mustard, rocket and the like. But toilet rolls can prevent mishaps with beans, broccoli, Brussels sprouts, cabbages, cauliflower, corn, cucumbers, melons, peas, pumpkins, and tomatoes. If wildlife digs up your directly planted sweetcorn seeds, re-seed in toilet rolls and place in seed-raising mini-hothouse as above.

Collect toilet rolls in a cloth bag hung in the toilet. Start saving today. Six rolls fit into a margarine container and many in a seed tray, so you need 40–60

Brassica and bean seedlings raised in toilet rolls in a sunroom.
The bowl contains six tubs with six rolls each, enough to fill one
magic square. The beans are ready to be planted out.

rolls to sow 10 varieties of 4–6 plants each. *Punch drainage holes in margarine containers.* Fill rolls with potting soil and tamp the tub a few times to compact soil, then fill rolls to the top. Push in one seed per roll, add a name tag and put in the cold frame, hot frame or on the seed-raising table, depending on the time of year.

The advantage of toilet rolls is that they double or triple the height of a seed tray, allowing strong root growth. Often the roots hang out of the roll when seedlings are big enough to go into the ground. At this stage the plants don't seem to suffer the brief exposure of root ends during transplanting. Dig a deep, narrow hole and half-fill it with water. Plant the toilet roll, push it down a little and tuck in firmly with soil. These plants grow much better than seedlings that have to be torn apart from a seed tray or have bunched roots from lack of space. The cardboard roll disintegrates to become part of the soil.

Saving Seed

Open-pollinated seed is seed that has been grown with the aid of bees and insects in the open and will breed true to type, unless several so-called promiscuous species of the same family grow close together and the bees cross pollinate one with the other. Familiarise yourself with the chapter on vegetable groups in Part Four and either grow one variety per season, or space members of the same family wide apart in the garden to avoid cross-pollination and reaping seed producing a 'cukin' or 'pumpcumber'! If your only square is full of brassicas, cut the flower heads off all but the one you want to grow seed from. Cook all brassica flower heads as broccoli or in stir-fries. Learn more about cross-pollination from *The Seed Savers' Handbook* (see **Useful Addresses**).

Saving your own seed is highly recommended because seeds grown in the conditions of your garden will do best when replanted there. Seed saving allows you to sow thickly – see Leaf beet and Brassica juncea in Part Four – and keeps open-pollinated varieties viable in your district as you share seeds with friends and neighbours. Sometimes seed saving leads to self-seeding so that new plants come up in their own good time in the plot or compost.

The general rule for saving seed is to let pods and seed heads dry on the stalks. This enables seeds to take up all the goodness of the dying plant. You then cut off the seed, place it in a paper bag and hang it in a dry, dark place for a few weeks. After this you can harvest the seed from the pods or casings and store it in airtight, screw-top jars or plastic containers kept in a dark, dry and cool place.

Reduce any humidity in seed containers with silica gel packets saved from vitamin bottles or photographic equipment. Humidity is a great spoiler of otherwise viable seed, either destroying or reducing the duration of its viability.

Don't keep seeds in the shed, you'll forget them. Total seed-saving buffs keep their seed in glass jars in the bottom of the fridge. Find a shelf in the coolest room of the house for your precious seed collection, the food of the future. Use a wardrobe shelf, for your seeds are more valuable than your clothes. Inside the wardrobe door pin a timetable of when to plant what. Also store here seed catalogues and a book on companion planting. Spread it all out on the bed for action.

When my **beans** start to bean, I tie a bit of red wool around the fattest, longest beans, so that I don't pick those for the pot. These seed beans dry off with the plant. Red wool also marks my best sweetcorn cob.

When **carrots** wave strong, green ferns, indicating that the roots are ready for pulling, save the strongest, pushing a tall stick alongside it. Tie it up when it grows a stalk and let that one produce seed. Carrots flower like Queen Anne's lace, attracting beneficial insects by the thousands. Let the large flower heads dry until they are full of tiny, disc-like seeds. Further dry the heads indoors, then shake out in a bowl and store.

All the **brassica family** (see Part Four) produce prolific tiny, round, black or brown seeds in pods 2–3 cm long. Hang the pods in paper bags to dry. Only radish seeds are bigger. To plant radishes break open the pods to release the seed. The others have to be winnowed, best done on a windless day. After a few weeks drying, transfer one type of seed stalks at a time to a pillowslip (e.g. kale). Slap the pillowslip from left to right on a table or hard surface to break the pods. Soon you will have seeds and chaff. Go to the vegetable garden and stand beside a plot where you don't mind a few self-seeded kales and take handfuls of empty pods from the bag, spreading them on the plot. The seeds will remain at the bottom of the pillowslip because they are heavier. Next, empty the pillowslip contents onto a tea tray with a rim and blow gently across the tray, holding it above the plot. The chaff will blow off while the seed remains. A few seeds may jump down to take their chances. Shake the tray gently from side to side to separate seed from chaff between blowings. This is one of my favourite harvesting operations. You end up with fairly clean seed to store; it will be viable for several years. Winnow all seed above the same plot for a carefree escapee's Stir-Fry Plot!

The **cucurbit family** of pumpkins, squash, melons and cucumbers have large seeds. Leave one fruit on the vine until the vine dries off. Open the fruit and scrape out the seed, wash and dry thoroughly before storing. Easiest are the pumpkins. Select your biggest, handsomest pumpkin and when it looks ripe enough to eat, the seed is mostly viable after drying. A spell in the fridge may improve it. The other cucurbits are messier.

Even seeds from the pyramids have been germinated in the 20th century, but generally there's no point keeping cucurbit seed for more than a couple of years. *Refresh your stock annually or whenever possible.* Once you have a well-stocked seed bank, and not before, use old seed to grow a dense green crop on a vacant plot and dig it in. Or let it grow and eat it. Or save new seed from it.

Saving Your Own Seed & the Law

Plant breeders' rights began in the 1920s. Originally, seed laws were introduced for a very good reason: to prevent unscrupulous seed merchants from selling poor-quality seed of unknown varieties. These laws have been added to over the years, so we now have Plant Breeders Rights (PBR) (which allows breeders to make money on the investment they put into developing new breeds) and more worryingly, the patenting of genetic material.

To protect customers and to standardise the seed business across borders, the EU intervened in the 1970s, making sure that seed varieties were properly tested. Unfortunately, testing is expensive and those varieties not tested were dropped. If a variety has been dropped from the approved common catalogue, then its seeds cannot be bought or sold. Hundreds of vegetable varieties have been lost from UK soils and may now be illegal to grow. There are already some fairly tough laws regarding seeds of the major food crops, both arable and vegetable. The 2012 the EU proposed broadening these to all vegetables, flowers and other plants, but also to include what they are calling plant reproductive material (or PRM), which will include baby plants, pot plant cuttings, fruit trees and so on. In the first draft of the law there were major cost and bureaucracy concessions for microbusinesses and seed and plant collections, like Garden Organic's Heritage Seed Library.

DEFRA currently have a very sensible risk-based approach with a simple and cheap registration for seeds destined for the amateur market. As a result there were nearly 700 seed companies registered in the UK in 2011.

There is a growing movement both in this country and across Europe opposing these new laws. Government, industry (seed companies, plant breeders and growers), NGOs and concerned citizens are united in their disbelief and dismay at these proposals. There is a lengthy process of negotiation between the EU commission and EU parliament. Together with DEFRA, the various NGOs and independent seed houses have been asking for a total exemption from the law for seed for home gardeners and small growers, and several of the UK MEPs supported this idea.

At the start of December 2013, the law was reviewed for the first time by the MEPs. Due to the huge amount of public objection, the MEPs realised that there was a problem and the law could not be passed as it stood. When the list of amendments for this law has was released incredibly there were 1144 detailed alterations, deletions and additions suggested from MEPs of every political affiliation.

Two committees have a say in this law, the Environment committee, and the Agriculture committee. On January 30th 2014, the Environment Committee voted unanimously (49:0) to reject the law entirely, and send it back to the Commission for redrafting from scratch. Then, in February, the Agriculture committee also voted (37:2) to reject the law and send it back.

Its not clear how this will go. The status quo (i.e. the already existing seed laws) have lots of problems, and potentially a new law that takes full account of the needs of the environment, organic growers and home gardeners could be an improvement. In some ways a 'worst case' scenario might be if the new law was abandoned entirely, and the EU pushes the UK Government to enforce the existing laws much more strictly. However, the thousands of suggested changes to the draft law were not all compatible with each other, and even spending just 10 minutes discussing each one would take forever. So we keep the campaign fresh.

Though it seemed the intention was that all commercial seed would have to be protected by Plant Breeder's Rights, few now seem to state this on their labels. By 2002 six of the largest agro-chemical companies sold 70 per cent of the globally used agricultural chemicals and by 2004 they also controlled 30 per cent of the global seed industry, selling seeds treated with pesticides. These seeds promise effortless growth, but the more pesticide-drenched seeds that are being sold the more soils, rivers and groundwater will be polluted.[19]

Some people questioned whether the seed companies claiming these Plant Variety Rights had paid royalties to the original owners of the seed they started with, i.e. those farmers who had grown that seed or plant for generations through the ages. It appears that is not how it is done. One apparently goes to a third world country and acquires plants and/or seeds cheaply and easily. One takes them home, alters them and then markets them under PVR, PBR or Plant Variety Protection (PVP) laws as new and improved seed burdened with intellectual property rights incurring fines when violated. The international seed industry is waging a global campaign to have all farm-saved seed declared illegal or subject to government royalties. Should they succeed, home gardeners may well be affected.[20]

The Food and Agriculture Organisation (FAO) didn't seem able to stop a new law in Iraq, as part of US reconstruction, that prohibits Iraqi farmers saving their own seeds, compelling them to buy seeds protected by PVP from a US-based corporation that operates under 'no competition' conditions. This could indicate that the genetic seed sources the FAO protects may not necessarily be preserved for the people who protected these resources for an untold number of generations. Ironically, the FAO had estimated in 2002 that 97 per cent of Iraqi farmers, whose ancestors were the first farmers ever to grow and improve wheat, saved their own seed. Now most of these wheat varieties may soon be lost forever.

In 2006 the United Nations Convention on Biological Diversity's meeting in Spain debated lifting the moratorium on terminator seed technology, urged by the governments of Australia, USA, New Zealand and others. Brazil and India on the other hand, have national prohibitions on terminator seed technology in place.[22] In March 2006 they upheld the moratorium on terminator seed technology. 'This is a momentous day for the 1.4 billion people worldwide who depend on farmer-saved seeds,' said Francisca Rodriguez of Via Campesina, a worldwide movement of peasant farmers. 'Terminator seeds are a weapon of mass destruction and an assault on our food sovereignty.'[23]

On the local front, you can buy seed from companies that carry open-pollinated, organically grown seeds that behave naturally. They have no inhibitors injected into them to prevent the resulting plant setting seed or reproducing true to type. Any improvements to the seed have been made by the gardeners who grew it on and selected best progeny. You can grow these seeds on, save the seed, share the seed and the seed increasingly produces plants that do well in your garden.

The 1990s saw the bizarre prosecution in Canada of farmer Percy Schmeiser, onto whose land had blown some genetically engineered canola seeds from a neighbouring farm which germinated. He saved his own seed and grew it on, whereupon Monsanto's seed police detected he was growing their particular brand of GE canola and was therefore guilty of patent infringement. Farmer Schmeiser claimed to know nothing of this seed but was convicted and the seed company won that day in court. The Canadian Supreme Court's decision in favour of Monsanto in 2004, was followed by some 90 US farmers being similarly sued. Percy Schmeiser now travels the world in the cause of farmers' rights. Injustice makes activists out of people who just wanted to farm in peace.

Opponents of plant variety and plant breeder's protection claimed that seeds were nature's gift to everyone, that nobody could own them, that all humanity had a right to use them to grow plants, especially food and medicinal plants, those that big companies want to monopolise. Patenting seeds is like patenting the air we must breathe, or taxing the rain that falls on our garden.

During a summit for indigenous peoples held in Rio de Janeiro, the right of indigenous farmers over their crop genes was formalised, recognising farmers' sovereignty over biological resources. More action is constantly required to make it work globally, but some countries have installed their own laws to protect indigenous seed.[24]

Indigenous seed may be easier to acknowledge than indigenous people when it comes to growing crops. Less then four per cent of the world population is indigenous in the sense anthropologists understand it, and most of them have lost their lands, so they are no longer growing food. Then there are millions of people who were dispersed centuries ago, resettled elsewhere and are living off the land. Obviously they have developed local crop varieties. Even I, a rank immigrant from a tribe of migrants covering the five continents, developed a new variety of radish in my forest garden. Food growers who put the better parts of their lives into working the soil they happen to live on, are in my book 'indigenous' for the purpose of claiming rights over their biological resources.

All seed saving networks makes available open-pollinated, organically grown seeds, grown on by members who sometimes inherited them from generations of ancestors. Therefore, while these debates rage on about who has rights to seeds and who has not, be on the safe side, obtain heirloom variety seeds, grow them and set up your own little seed bank. Learning from those who have gone before can in this case save our seed and food resources from being modified away by corporations who take out contestable patents, have in-house lawyers, and don't mind spending a few millions for a conviction to keep small growers cowed. Few of the corporate managers have any innate knowledge or understanding of growing food and preserving seeds. They are managers and may have started in the manufacturing of cars, or cheese, or football boots. Those markets became saturated so they looked for other products to develop, and hey, people will always need food grown from seeds. So they hired scientists and financial wizards who between them came up with a plan to corner one or another crop in the world market. It's happened to coffee, it's happened to tea, it's happened to soybeans. They now have their eyes on broccoli.

Hardware In the Food Garden

Those lovely pictures of vegetable gardens featuring colourful rows in beds of heaped black soil may be reality somewhere, but not in my climate and not always in gardens run on clean and green principles. Such ordered beauty is sometimes preceded by spraying the life out of soil and surroundings to keep weeds and pests at bay. In reality the opposite, an imitation of nature's chaos, spells plant health.

If you live in an agricultural district where spraying takes place you may not have many insect problems and you can garden organically by default. Yet, if spraying has been taking place over many years, you may have more problems as insects become immune to the chemicals applied. Find out what happens in your environment.

A late-winter garden with hardware.

For a clean and green gardener, protection of vegetables and exclusion of pests, without spraying, is the aim so that the micro-environment can find its own balance. Temporary protection of crops takes many forms, all highly visible and spoilers of poster versions of self-sufficiency.

Much recyclable hardware aids the gardener's work. Start by collecting cast-offs and recyclables, and visiting junkyards.

Baling twine Plait together 3–4 strands of differently coloured twine from straw bales for a strong rope to stop sweetcorn and broadbeans breaking in the wind.

Bamboo Makes tepees, trellises and temporary fences.

Bath tub Can be converted to become a worm farm.

Blinking night-light We heard that a local sheep farmer had placed a number of amber blinking lights, formerly used to mark a hole in the road, around his sheep paddock. Since then, none of his sheep were attacked by foxes.

As we were having trouble with foxes running across our roof at night and causing havoc in the food garden, we thought we would try it. The light runs on a large battery, comes on at dusk, and stops at dawn. We placed it on a plank in the food garden. No more foxes.

Since the light blinks on both sides, place it so that it does not blink into your neighbour's bedroom window or the chicken coop as that may deprive the flock of sleep and affect egg production. Our chickens seem to cope well with the winks being 10 metres away.

Bricks Can be used for propping up top-heavy plants, holding down a line of twine pulling a heavy plant upright again, placing under pumpkins to prevent rot, under a hot frame, or under mint pots to prevent 'rooting down'.

Cages You attract a lot of birds if you plant densely, plant shrubs suitable for nesting, or plant native trees and nectar-producing flowers. Birds pay rent by keeping your garden fairly pest free. Our lush valley garden was full of nests in fantastic places. Birds don't eat vegetables, but can pull up seedlings as they scratch soil for worms and insects. You can't have an organic garden without birds, but you can't always have vegetables with them!

The simple answer is cages. Not for the birds, but for the vegetables! Anything from an upside down dish rack to a carpentry job of wooden frame covered with chicken wire can be a cage. My cages are 40 x 90 x 40 cm of painted wood or steel rod with chicken wire attached. Each covers almost half a square and two cages fit on a square metre with 20 cm space between them where I can plant something without much chance birds will go there. When planting seed or seedlings, arrange them inside an imprint of the cage edges. When the first plant pokes through the top of the cage you can remove it as they can stand on their own at this point.

Carpet is the best cover for a compost heap. Clean with strong detergent, hot water and a broom to remove residual chemicals. Ask a carpet dealer for old pieces. Underfelt – without plastic coating – makes good mulch and is easy to cut. Lay along plots or around fruit trees to suppress weeds, or use to line wire cylinders (see below).

Chairs This is a tip from Chris who taught in the Strathalbyn square-metre vegetable-growing course. An old cane chair placed upside down makes a great frame for a sprawling cucumber or cherry tomato. So do old kitchen chairs. As for a cane sofa – wow!

Cloches Are as old as farming itself and they look better than cages. A cloche protects an individual plant from cats, cold or birds. There are pretty ones made of bamboo. Use cheap baskets with enough gaps for bees to get through, but not mice. Bottomless baskets past their use-by date can be given a cheese-cloth bottom to start an upside-down life as a cloche. As long as air circulates and bees can go in and out, most wicker ware can be used to make a cloche.

Fashion cloches for early seedlings from plastic food containers, bottoms cut out and replaced by clear plastic with breathing holes, fastened with rubber bands. Push into soil over bean seedlings for warmth and protection. In spring, when insect populations explode, you can't have enough tiny cheap protectors like these.

Colanders A plastic colander is great for spreading lime, B&B or gypsum if you are preparing more than one square. Or use a flowerpot with just the right array of bottom holes.

Egg cartons An egg carton provides 12 biodegradable seed-growing pods for tiny plants of lettuce, chillies, corn salad and tender herbs. Pierce draining holes in each pod. Sit the carton on a tray of compost and fill with soil. Plant seedlings in their paper pod, after cutting each off the carton. There is no root disturbance and the pod disintegrates.

Flowerpots During hot weather earwigs like damp, crumpled newspaper in upside down flowerpots on sticks. Place pots under apple trees so earwigs can help control coddling moth.

Kneeling pad Wrap a firm foam rubber pillow in plastic, then an old sack. Or stuff leaky hot-water bottles with sand – they hang nicely in the shed on their ringed lips.

Milk cartons The waterproof insides have obvious gardening possibilities, especially for the balcony gardener. Wash empty milk cartons in soapy water and cut two bottom corners for drainage. Stack a box full of milk cartons, fill them with potting soil enriched with a sprinkling of B&B, and put 1–2 seeds in each carton. Grow lettuces, beans, carrots, chives, garlic, radishes or anything small. Being stacked together avoids drying out too quickly and the extra height of the milk carton allows roots to go deep. Raise native shrubs and trees in milk cartons too.

Another use for milk cartons is to make plant tags. Cut each side through the middle and again diagonally. This yields four tags, 16 in total. Write on them with a ballpoint pen and they should last a season.

Netting and nets Push into PVC rings to protect germinating beans from rodents. See also Pot scrubbers page 209. Wildlife-safe fruit tree netting is also useful on vegetables if you have lots of munchers. Our little black dog likes to crawl under the net protecting the apple tree to eat one apple a day. From inside the net she stares at her bigger mate, who isn't so smart. But she can't always get out when she wants to and sometimes has to be rescued!

Net bags from bought oranges and nuts are useful to pop over three sticks to protect a small plant, or to wrap around ripening fruit. You can also make netting hoods with elastic to pop over large pots and seed boxes.

Pantyhose Onions, garlic and butternuts can be stored by hanging them in pantyhose in a dark shed. Alternatively, use orange bags.

Percy's portable roof See the picture of him opposite. Hills gardener Percy McElwaine built the roof to protect young plants in spring when the nights were still cold. He found that wherever he placed the roof young plants grew faster compared with those left unprotected. Pumpkins and spring vegetables benefited especially. He transfers the roof on his back by stooping under it, but two people can shift it with ease. Made of corrugated plastic sheeting on a metal cross frame, it is something gardeners in cooler districts may find useful. Make a few in smaller sizes.

Plastic bottles Fill plastic bottles with water and dig them in as edging around vegetable plots. Scratching birds don't like reflective obstructions, although mice will still go in. In winter the water absorbs the warmth of the sun and at night the bottles give off this warmth, keeping plot temperatures more even. In a region prone to night frosts this can help plants survive. (See **Seeds & Seedlings** for a seed-raising table turned into a mini-hothouse with plastic bottles.)

A dozen water-filled bottles placed around a plant in strife or danger will save it. In autumn my lemongrass gets a bottle fence to 'overwinter' it. Bottles placed on their sides make a safe area for small plants. You will find other uses.

Percy McElwaine extends summer or brings spring forward with his homemade portable plastic roof.

Plastic juice bottles filled with water regulate temperatures on winter days and summer nights and function as edgings.

When a bottle after some years of service starts to deteriorate, dispose of it immediately. You don't want plastic breaking down in your soil. It is said that plastic does break down invisibly, giving off gases we could do without. If you feel strongly about this, collect glass flagons and keep all plastic out of your garden.

Plastic lids Ice-cream bin lids are useful to put under growing pumpkins and squashes to prevent rotting where they touch the ground. Use margarine lids under baby squash, cucumbers or low-hanging tomatoes. Courgettes grow too fast to rot.

Plastic tubs Cut the bottom out of yoghurt tubs. Push into soil over a just-planted pea or bean in its toilet roll, to protect it from birds' beaks or cold nights. Seeds sown directly inside tubs have less chance of being scratched up. Have a dozen on hand in spring and autumn when things pop up.

Poles The traditional bean-pole structure is two rows of poles or long stakes leaning toward each other and crossing over a 1 m width of soil. Place one pole in the crossover at the top and fasten with string.

Poly pipe One of the best inventions by do-it-yourself gardeners is the poly-pipe arch. Choose poly pipe of a diameter that fits over a dropper or non-rotting stake – ask your hardware store. Set stakes a metre apart across your square plot. Or buy enough poly pipe and four stakes to make two diagonally crossing arches, tied in the centre. You can cover it with netting, fleece or plastic. Peas, beans, cucumbers, squashes and tomatilloes can be trained up the stakes. Or connect stakes with wire netting for vines to climb up themselves. Make poly-pipe arches to create height in your food garden. Place three in a row or in an L-shape.

Polystyrene boxes Useful for the balcony or box gardener, and in small gardens. Use boxes to grow chives, shallots, onions, lettuce, parsley, sorrel and varieties of garlic. Their portability is an advantage. Two form a nice backdrop for your magic square without new ground having to be dug up. Six will enclose the square on three sides.

Poly tunnels If you don't have a greenhouse, set up a few makeshift green tunnels of bent poly pipe, plastic-coated wire, or trellis held down with bricks or stones. Short pieces of corrugated PVC sheeting bent into tunnel shapes and held in place by stakes take little time to set up. As you have to crouch down to stick your hands in, keep these tunnels short. You can close them at night with plastic or bags and open up in the morning for ventilation, but even tunnels open on either end will help plants grow. They function as temporary cold frames for seedlings or late summer plants when cold weather arrives.

Pot scrubbers Push into PVC rings to protect germinating beans.

PVC rings Large vegetables like cabbages and cauliflowers need more space than a cage provides. Plant them in individual rings of PVC water pipe with a diameter of 10 cm, cut about 8 cm high. Or make collars from plastic bottles cut into rounds, or simply staple cardboard into rings. Push the rings into the soil around seedlings; they won't be bothered by any but the most brazen bird. See also Netting and Pot scrubbers.

Racks from old fridges or ovens are useful protectors. Place them across a few bricks, to give head room to seedlings, or over a Styrofoam box. No birds will crawl under such contraptions, although rodents may.

Stakes Stakes are needed for climbing tomatoes, beans and peas, although peas are happy to wind tendrils up a bunch of twigs stuck in the ground. Golden Rod twigs can support peas. Basic stakes are straight tree branches. Collect these, as wood products are expensive. If you know of a stand of bamboo you are in clover. Thin out carefully and trim to size. Bamboo is the hardiest and cheapest wood in the world and grows sustainably. Your garden may grow ready-made stakes: sunflower stalks and buddleia branches.

Ties Carry soft ties, such as pantyhose or cotton underwear cut into strips, in your pockets when gardening. You always see something in the food garden that flops when it shouldn't. Beans and peas need initial ties to the stake before they get the idea. If you grow heavier plants on stake or trellis (e.g. cucumbers, butternuts or tomatoes) tie them progressively as they grow. Wire and plastic ties will cut into stems as they thicken.

Tepee Much the same as bean poles, but placed in a circle and tied at the top. Useful for beans, cucumbers, small melons or peas.

Tools So what's wrong with a digging stick? Seriously, a square-metre plot can be dug over with a borrowed garden fork and thereafter with a hand trowel and fork. Should you extend, a small hoe is useful occasionally. An old table knife stuck in a brick with a hole is handy to whip out weeds or seedlings. So is a hammer to pound in stakes. Your best tools in a small food plot are your fingers, which don't hurt the worms.

Trellis Make one from wood, wire or branches, held by upright posts or attached to a fence or shed. Or use posts with strings attached for climbing vegetables. Use strong wire when espaliering fruit trees.

Umbrellas Tie them to stakes or saw off the curved handles and stick them in the soil to protect vegetables. Put up the garden umbrella to warm up the soil and then to protect young plans in a cold spell.

Wire baskets Use as cages over a seed patch or young seedlings.

Wire cylinder You need at least 2 m of chicken wire or green plastic wire. Make cylinders about a metre high for composting (see **Compost Compositions**, Part Three) and 50 cm for growing carrots, mooli radish or potatoes (see Part Four). Stake cylinders with three stakes or tent pegs. Line with wads of wet newspaper or underfelt, up to the height you want to fill up to. Layer the bottom with wet newspaper, followed by pea straw, CMC and straw mulch. Cylinders dry out quicker than ground soil, so don't forget watering.

Wire tower Form a 2 m high tower by bending a metre of open square mesh into a cylinder. The green plastic-coated type is best. Some wire has graded spaces, from narrow to wide. Wide spaces at the bottom of the cylinder allow hands in to cultivate. Secure the

In a mixed border kale, cabbage and broadbean seedlings take off in protective rings, surrounded by mature plants and seed-setting coriander in the foreground. Leaf beet seed is ripening. Mint grows in a pot at centre left.

211

wire tower with one stake.

In spring, plant one squash inside the circle to ramble sideways, and six climbing beans around it. Or try cos lettuce inside to shade two cucumber plants. Or pumpkin vines. After harvest sow nasturtiums. In late winter put in tall snow peas. Some garden centres sell wire towers for tomatoes.

Pruning, Pinching & Thinning

I'm having you on, am I? Too right I'm not! Pruning growing vegetables of excess foliage and stems promotes better growth of those parts you want to harvest. Pinching out tips does the same.

Pruning

Beans run out of steam mid season. Prune off dying sections.

Broccoli produces shoots for months after the head has been harvested. Prune as you pick shoots for the pot, but also prune woody sections and lower leaves to keep this hard-working plant in condition. In our household broccoli and cabbage leaves are eaten together with kale leaves as a 'green slurry' stir-fry with ginger, onion and garlic. The taste far surpasses the name. If you don't eat the leaves, strip the ribs for juicing and feed the leaves to chickens, worms or the compost.

Cabbage and cauliflower Where I am, the growers regularly pull lower leaves off by hand, laying them on the soil as mulch.

Courgettes plants produce a jungle of giant leaves to protect their fruit. But enough is enough. Regularly prune lower leaves, making sure the fruit remains protected.

Fruit tree pruning is discussed in the next chapter, **Easy-Care Fruit Trees**. For specific trees, see Part Four.

Leaf beet and spinach go to seed as they please. If a strong plant has the bolting stem cut out, you can harvest the leaves longer. Or cut off all but the main stem if you want to save seed. Even when slightly bitter, the leaves taste good in a mixed stir-fry.

Pumpkins have non-flowering vines that use food and water. Cut them.

Pinching

This is done more frequently than pruning.

Pumpkin vines need their tips pinched out or they will go on forever, producing longer runners with more infant pumpkins that won't have enough oomph or time to even get half grown before cold nights finish them off. Depending on macro and microclimate combined, calculate when new pumpkins will no longer mature and cut off the tip above the last viable pumpkin. Do this on all runners. These tender tips of leaves, including tiny pumpkins, can be steamed lightly and served in coconut cream, a favourite meal in Papua New Guinea. I pinch mine on Midsummer's Day, unless spring is cold and summer is late.

Tomatoes bearing heavily can also have their tips pinched, as can **aubergines** bearing more than half a dozen fruit. Some do it to **cucumbers**, but I let them ramble, not minding that the fruit gets smaller as the season advances. Pinch wherever you want strong growth.

Thinning

Whereas I apologise to plants about to be pruned – 'This will stop you feeling so exhausted, sweetie' – and it hurts me to pinch out young tips, I draw the line at the thinning of seedlings. My respect for the life force in every seed that has managed to break the surface of the earth is such that, if seedlings must be thinned out, I will transplant them immediately somewhere else. It is a gross waste of seed to sow pumpkins, cucumbers and corn in threes, then thin out two, only keeping the strongest one. That may be commercially preferable, but the home grower raising vegetables in toilet rolls plants each germinated seedling. We don't need giant sizes, preferring flavour and quality.

Carrots, onions and beetroot have to be sown thinly, but excess little ones can also have their time in the sun. In Part Four read under Carrots and other vegetables how to harvest thickly sown vegetables, or vigorously germinating ones. Respect for the life that goes on in your food plot could well be registered by the plants and discussed at night! 'Food should be produced kindly,' writes food scientist Colin Tudge.[25] Although he is referring to animals raised for meat, the same goes for fruit and vegetables. Love is not wasted on them.

Easy-Care Fruit Trees

Fruit trees are as sensitive to climate as vegetables, but have to cope with more wind, rain and sun, while providing shelter for lower plants. They may dry out at the wrong time when fruit is developing, have all their fruit blown off when half ripe, or attract unwelcome visitors, bugs and diseases. So for the beginning food gardener, fruit trees should be of the hardy, easy-care type.

If you think that by nature you are truly a fruit eater, buy, beg or borrow Ben Pike's book *The Fruit Tree Handbook* and fill your garden with every conceivable fruit tree and bush in the open, on walls and on fences. With dedication even kiwis, figs, passion fruit and peaches can be made to grow in the southern UK. I grew them in a greenhouse at 500 m elevation. I also raised a mountain papaya in open ground, but it was a male and no matter how much seed I germinated, none were female.

Easy-care fruit that leaves you time to be an intensive food gardener is a boon. Rhubarb cannot be faulted, for it raises it's head in early spring and can be 'forced' by covering with a bin to give it a crop 6 weeks earlier than in open ground. It continues to crop for a long time.

After rhubarb come strawberries, then early cane fruit and early stone fruits: apricots, nectarines, peaches, plums. Mulberries and bush berries follow. Near summer's end pears and apples ripen. The home fruit harvest ends with grapes and quinces in autumn. Because quinces keep so well, their fragrance perfumes the kitchen until January. My small espaliered orchard together with some old inherited fruit trees provided fruit three-quarters of the year, some of which was preserved. Lemon trees are only viable in a warm greenhouse or a conservatory.

Do keep in mind that even if a fruit tree is bred for optimum production, some revert to the natural system of carrying only a few fruit the year after a bumper crop. Don't expect big crops every year from each tree. Plant a mix of early and late fruit, feed them all spring and autumn and you will be richly rewarded. Stone-fruit trees often bear from their second year, others may take a little longer. Quinces and plums are quick to bear and berry bushes fruit in their first year.

The American Shakers, renowned for their food growing success, planted fruit trees in very large holes filled with rubble for drainage, old broken-down manure and compost. They tamped down the earth and put fences around the trees. They had magnificent fruit harvests.

Espalier is a system of training young fruit trees on wires. Run wires north-south if possible, to gain light and fruit on both sides. You can espalier on walls and fences, provided the fruit is well ventilated. Alternatively, set up poles at either end, with strainers, and run 4–5 horizontal wires at 30 cm intervals. Don't place wires higher than you can comfortably reach. Plant trees 2–3 m apart in a 10–14 m row. If you have less space, erect four posts with wires in a rectangle of 2 x 4 m and plant six fruit trees around it. Plant the rectangle full of companion herbs (see Part Four) to help the fruit trees. This arrangement is easy to net.

As each tree grows up, let the leader (the main stem) grow, bending branches to left and right on the first and second wires, attach with pruning tape or pantyhose strips which expand with growth (wire ties and string will cut into branches as they thicken). Prune off superfluous branches. In the next growing season let two branches reach the third wire and so forth until all wires are occupied and the leader has also been espaliered. In summer the tree looks like a curtain of leaves and fruit. Prune summer and winter to retain this shape. Espaliered trees fruit more heavily because they are restricted from putting effort into lots of branches.

Netting fruit trees is necessary if you want to eat the fruit yourself. Use appropriate wildlife-safe netting. The birds may get some fruit before you have netted and peck fruit pressing against the netting. Espaliered trees are easy to protect from birds. Throw a long length of netting over the wires, pull down and away on either side and pin to the ground with bricks to prevent birds

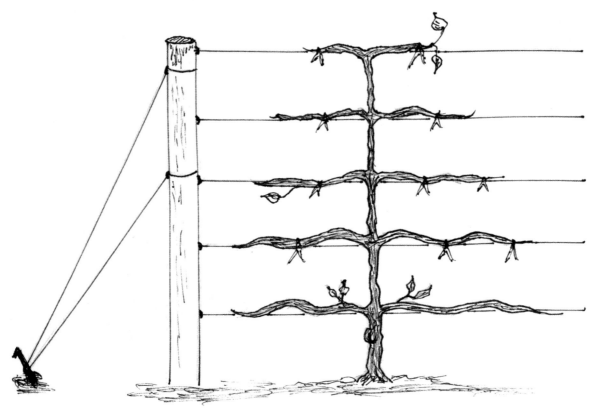

crawling underneath.

For freestanding trees you need one big square net per tree. Tie the net underneath the tree, for birds will try anything to get in. Knitted nets can be used for years with a little repair. Nets do double duty by protecting first the early-fruiting trees, then the late-ripening ones. Once you get serious about netting you will work out your own system. The price of posts, wires, trees and netting may be what you pay for shop fruit, but your fruit is sweet, organic and fresh and in following years you will buy nothing but a bag of manure.

Never water fruit trees with overhead sprinklers, instead lay out drip irrigation with a timer. Mulch trees to reduce evaporation and protect roots. During dry summers, water once a week for a set time. Once it has rained once in the week for about an hour, the trees will do with that.

The spraying of fruit trees against pests and disease is generally unnecessary in a small mixed orchard situated in an organic mixed garden with vegetables, herbs, flowers, shrubberies and hedges. This environment helps maintain fruit trees in good health, attracting birds to control insects and disease-bearing grubs.

Old fruit trees, other than stone fruits, need a good pruning and thinning out in winter. Remove grass around the trunk for more than a metre circumference and under-plant with feverfew, tansy and yarrow. Spread a load of manure and mulch under the tree's drip line (the perimeter of the branches) and see what happens in spring.

Now turn to the **List of Easy-Care Fruit Trees & Berries** in Part Four for more detailed descriptions.

Livestock, Birds, Bees & Frogs

Livestock

Chickens lay eggs, produce manure and are sociable. In suburbia you can comfortably keep 2–3 chickens, roosters usually being prohibited by councils for their melodious but premature announcements of daybreak. Chickens foraging around fruit trees keep these disease free, but in the food plot they cause havoc.

Consider enclosing a fruit growing area of 6–10 trees with wildlife-safe netting on high poles, fencing it off and using it as a chicken run. The feathered flock fertilises trees, gobbles up ground-dwelling pests and provides eggs. Feed mixed grains at dusk as they will peck a confined area pretty bare. Kitchen scraps, fallen fruit and spent vegetables complement their diet. Twice a week add a bucket of succulent weeds and a bowl of bran mash. Some gardeners prefer ducks on their gentle flip-flops, foraging for slugs and snails between the greens. Ducks don't dig.

No matter what animals you choose to inhabit your garden, make sure their quarters are dry in the wet, shady in the heat, and dog- and fox-proof. If you let them range freely during the day, ascertain they can find shelter when predators fly over. As for terrestrial predators, secure your fences and shut your flock in before dusk.

Birds & Bees

Water makes a garden come to life. Bird baths and ponds create a more moist atmosphere and microclimate. Although birds scratch up the food garden, they do so in their capacity as pest controllers. Place birdbaths throughout your garden. Earthenware bowls on a tree trunk look good. Place bowls well above ground where birds in flight can see them and the neighbour's cat and your dog can't. Birdbaths entice helpful birds to become permanent residents.

In the food garden fill a bee bath on a barrel or stand. Place a rock in it so bees don't drown when drinking and keep a stick nearby to fish out hapless bees. Attracting bees ensures pollination. In hot weather the bee bath is their pit stop.

Frogs

At the back of the food garden, hidden among daisies, lavender, sage and wild fruit trees grown from pips, is my frog pond. Just a deep plastic bowl dug into the ground, it has a 20 cm rim above ground so scratching creatures don't fill it with mulch. It contains plants such as papyrus and water iris. In the centre a brick stack with, at water level, two pieces of broken brick covered by a flat stone, makes a hidey-hole for frogs when predator birds appear. A wire rack covers all. Frogs can't stay underwater for long when danger lurks and coming to the surface to breathe could spell death. To disguise a frog pond, cover it with coarse chicken mesh, or two bent poly pipes crossing over each other, stuck on four stakes, and covered with mesh. Alternatively, tie a tripod of stakes or bamboo surrounded with plastic mesh, supporting climbing peas or beans.

Why accommodate frogs? They eat mosquito larvae, snails and slugs, and are an endangered species, no matter which frog we talk about. They are the first to die when the spray unit comes past. Could it be that in countries without frogs, or where people eat frogs, lethal malaria and dengue fever are rife? In Australia, where frogs are in decline due to spraying and loss of habitat, dengue fever is on the rise. Provide for frogs and learn to love their croaking concerts at courting time. When you hear a croak distinctly different from the usual ones, something may be going in the right direction.

Similarly, enticing a hedgehog into your garden will reap similar benefits. Leave a gap in your fence for them to enter and keep some leaves and debris for them to sleep over winter.

Warning It is necessary to erect a fence around or cover with mesh all bodies of water, however small, to protect the lives of children, even those that may wander onto your property without your knowledge.

A frog pond with lily pads and rocks soon becomes a home.

Ten Green Rules

Going organic makes gardening easier. There are a lot of things you don't have to do anymore and going back to basics allows nature a chance to show what it is capable of. Nothing is wasted; all is used or recycled. For organic farm certification the rules are very strict, but by using common sense the home gardener can achieve almost the same.

1) Think of a garden as a community where many different plants help each other and attract insects, which in turn attract birds to nest in thickets, contributing to a healthy balance without the need of toxic substances that harm birds, frogs, hedgehogs, wildlife and you.

2) Care for the soil. Don't leave it bare for long. Don't rotavate. Keep digging to a minimum. Use a garden fork when loosening is required. Build soil with compost, mulch, manures and green crops.

3) Compost manures or spread them under CM, keeping away from plant roots. Use LS, B&B, OF and natural pest-control methods.

4) Never burn garden waste. 'Cook' diseased waste in plastic bags in the sun. Don't bring healthy garden waste to the dump. Compost everything to make your own soil and mulch.

5) Set up a worm farm and frog pond *after* you have stopped using toxic sprays. Plan to enclose your orchard trees and put in a few hens to control codling moth and other pests.

6) Rotate crops in the food garden, plant fragrant and pungent herbs for pest control and practise companion planting.

7) Raise your own seedlings from open pollinated seeds, not genetically modified seed. Save seed from your best plants and swap with others. Leave some vegetables to go to flower to attract predator insects.

8) If you need to buy mulches, potting soil and other garden products, buy organic products or buy from unsprayed environments.

9) Never use toxic sprays, not even the one you are told breaks down quickly – yeah, sure – and disappears into groundwater until elements of it come up again to issue from someone's tap. Don't use snail pellets. They will kill frogs, hedgehogs, ladybirds, lacewings, worms, small birds and other assistant gardeners. *Contact your local council to dispose of your collection of toxic substances.* They have facilities to do this without the substances leaking into the environment, which would happen if you just put them in the bin. If you must spray, make garlic or soapy water spray and keep well away from pond and worm farm.

10) Utilise weeds for their nutrients in compost and green mulch. Control seed-setting weeds by cutting off flowers. Where weeds are rampant, mulch with wet newspaper, cardboard, telephone books and pea straw. Then plant ground covers and a tree, use that area as a pumpkin bed, or grow a crop of potatoes.

Think of your garden as your paradise
and paradise will emerge within a few years.
Celebrate your garden's birthday.

PART FOUR
Descriptions of Food Plants

- An A–Z of Vegetable Groups • Summer, Winter & All Season Vegetables • List of Common Vegetables • List of Common Herbs • List of Easy-Care Fruit Trees & Berries

L to R: artichoke, feverfew, lemon tree, verbascum, a young elderberry, gooseberry, borage and sage with strawberries in the foreground.

An A–Z of Vegetable Groups

Learning to recognise which plants are related makes it easier to recognise their seedlings and meet their needs. Individual species of plants belong to a genus, a group of plants having characteristics in common. A genus in turn belongs to a larger family of genera, but in practice the word family is often used for genus, e.g. the peas and beans family.

Aizoaceae/Ice-plants succulent stonecrops

Alliaceae/Allium/Lily group Chives, garlic, leek, onions, shallots and others. All produce one seed ball per stem. Around 500 species.

Amaranthaceae Amaranth species.

Apiaceae/Umbelliferae/Carrot group Flowers are from white and pinkish to yellow. Seeds form in 'umbels' looking like flat umbrellas, helipads for beneficial flying insects. Seed setting throughout spring and summer attracts predators to keep pests in check. Caraway, carrot, celery, chervil, coriander, cumin, dill, fennel, parsley and parsnip are the main food plants.

Asteraceae/Compositae/Sunflower group Artemisia species (the wormwoods), asparagus, chamomile, chicory, dandelion, endive, globe artichoke, Jerusalem artichoke, lettuce, salsify, scorzonera, shungiku, sunflower, tarragon and yarrow.

Chives, giant red mustard, yellow mustard, Siberian purple kale, marigold, leek, calendula and garlic chives keep each other healthy.

Brassicaceae/Cruciferae/Mustard group This group grows seeds in small pods like mini peas. Most have yellow flowers with four petals forming a cross. Includes bok choy, *Brassica juncea*, broccoli, Brussels sprouts, cabbage, cauliflower, Chinese cabbage (pe-tsai), collard, cress, horseradish, kale, kohlrabi, mustard, pak choy, radish (white and mauve flowers), rocket (arugula, cream flowers), swede, tatsoy, turnip, and watercress.

Chenopodiaceae/Goosefoot group Beetroot, Swiss chard, English spinach, perennial spinach, red orach, leaf beet.

Convolvulaceae/Morning Glory group Sweet potato.

Cucurbitaceae/Gourd group The genus *Cucurbita* comprises 25 species, the main ones being cucumber, gherkin, gourd, marrow, melon, pumpkin and squash. The terms marrow, squash and pumpkin are often used interchangeably, depending on local usage. One gardener's butternut pumpkin may be someone else's squash.

Fabaceae/Leguminosa/Pea group Beans, broadbeans, fenugreek and peas.

Grasses Comprise most grain crops and sweetcorn.

Malvaceae/Mallow group Okra.

Polygonaceae/Buckwheat group Buckwheat, rhubarb.

Solanaceae/Nightshade group These plants have five-petalled flowers, white, mauve or purple, with prominent yellow anthers. The family includes aubergine, Cape gooseberry, chilli, pepper, potato, tamarillo, tomato, the ornamental Chilean potato tree (*solanum crispum*), and inedibles like tobacco and belladonna. The toxicity of the latter indicates that toxic solanins exist in all *Solanum* plants to various degrees. They are believed to aggravate arthritis. A Solanaceae-free diet may make a difference to a sufferer. That said, tomatoes are claimed to be essential in the prevention of prostate cancer. But any potatoes showing green patches from exposure to light are toxic and must not be eaten by humans or animals.

Urticaceae/Nettle family Stinging nettle, essential plant food in compost, a delicious wild vegetable or herbal tea.

Summer, Winter & All Season Vegetables

Summer Vegetables & Herbs

Summer vegetables and herbs are mostly sown in spring, although repeat sowing of quick growing vegetables like radish, lettuce and beans are possible throughout the summer. For 'under glass' read also 'behind glass'.

Since local climates differ considerably, the starting dates of spring and autumn will vary accordingly. However, the following lists are useful when planning twice-yearly plantings.

Amaranth	From seed.
Asparagus	From seed.
Aubergine	Start (and best grown) under glass
Basil	Tropical, after frosts, late spring to early summer. Best grown indoors.
Beans	After frosts, repeat sowings until mid summer.
Beetroot	
Broccoli	Summer variety.
Brussels sprouts	Plant mid–late summer.
Cabbage	Summer varieties, plant early.
Carrots	All seasons variety.
Cauliflower	Early summer varieties.
Celery	Start early indoors.
Chillies	Start (and best grown) under glass.

Courgettes	Start under glass, plant out after frosts.
Cucumber	Start under glass, plant out after frosts.
Dill	In Spring, or wait for early autumn.
Globe artichokes	Sow seed in pots, transplant autumn.
Leaf beet	Sow thickly for young pickings.
Lettuce	Summer varieties, part shade.
Melons	Start early under glass, best grown in a greenhouse or on a hot bed outdoors.
Mustards	Tends to bolt in hot, dry weather.
Onions	Sow onion seeds in Autumn or plant sets in Spring or Autumn.
Peppers	Start (and best grown) under glass, plant after frosts.
Potatoes	After frosts.
Pumpkins	Start under glass, plant after frosts.
Radish	Small salad varieties.
Rocket	Early, outdoors.
Snow peas	Plant early, but can also be sown in autumn.
Squash	Summer varieties.
Sweetcorn	Sow direct when soil warms up, re-seed failures.
Sweet potatoes	Start early indoors, plant out after frosts.
Tomatoes	Start under glass, plant out after frosts.

Winter Vegetables & Herbs

Winter vegetables and herbs are sown in late summer and autumn while the soil is still warm. Establish perennials like artichoke, asparagus, rhubarb, sorrel and strawberries in early autumn.

Asian greens	Chinese and Japanese green-leaf vegetables.
Asparagus	From crowns.
Beetroot	
Broadbeans	
Broccoli	Winter varieties.
Cabbage	Most varieties.
Carrots	All seasons variety.
Cauliflower	Winter varieties.
Celery/wild celery	
Coriander	
Dill	
Endive	
Fenugreek	
Garlic	Plant while soil still warm.
Globe artichoke	Plant roots.
Kale	
Leaf beet	
Leek	Plant in a row while soil still warm, transplant when 10 cm.
Lettuce	Winter varieties, e.g. radicchio, corn salad, oakleaf.
Mustards	Including giant red.
Onions	Plant sets or seeds in a row and transplant when 10 cm.
Parsley	Seed or division, biennial. Sow every year.
Peas	Winter peas, or check seed packets.
Radish	Including daikon.
Rhubarb	Plant crowns.
Rocket	Annual, save seed – grows on till summer.

Snow peas	Check seed packet for climate directions.
Spinach	Perennial and others.
Strawberries	Late autumn to early spring.
Swedes	
Turnips	

All Season Vegetables & Herbs

All season vegetables and herbs are best sown in spring and autumn, as most seedlings won't take off in summer's heat or winter's dread. Some appear in previous lists as summer or winter vegetables, but can manage in all seasons. Others have special 'all season varieties'.

Asian greens	Most leaf vegetables.
Beetroot	
Broccoli	Depending on variety.
Broccoli, Chinese (raab)	Winter and mild summers.
Cabbage	Depending on variety.
Carrots	All seasons varieties.
Cauliflower	All seasons varieties.
Herbs	Most herbs can be planted any time, except tropical ones, although coriander, dill and rocket do best in cooler weather.
Jerusalem artichoke	
Leaf beet	
Lettuce	Cos, mignonette, radicchio and mesclun mix.
Mustards	
Swedes	
Turnips	

List of Common Vegetables:
How to Grow & Use Them

Unless otherwise stated, these vegetables are grown from seed. Some food plants are known as vegetable and fruit, e.g. melons. Some large herbs are also known as vegetables, e.g. sorrel. Brief cooking suggestions are included, especially for lesser-known food plants.

General Growing Notes

Colours Green vegetables contain chlorophyll. Carotenes are found in orange and yellow vegetables e.g. carrots, red pepper, melon, pumpkin, sweet potato and tomatoes. Anthocyanin colours red-purple vegetables and fruit; these are important in preventing cancers. They range from red and blue berries, cherries and plums, to purple Russian kale, red-brown lettuces and radicchios, red cabbage and beetroot. It has been claimed that anti-oxidants in reddish plant foods eradicate harmful free radicals 10 times faster than do green vegetables.

Plants carrying *officinalis* as their second botanical name were used as medicine before modern pharmaceuticals appeared. Some *officinalis* plants are once again being used in medicines after a period in exile.

Horse manure See caution regarding horse manure on Abbreviations page.

Lime Many soils in Britain are acidic rather than alkaline and may need a dusting of lime, particularly when growing peas, beans and onions. But amaranth, aubergine, blueberries, celery and potatoes don't like lime.

233

Nitrogen Found in commercial fertilisers and concentrated manures, e.g. poultry manure. Nitrogen generates abundant growth of foliage. Reduce applications for fruiting crops after plants are established, or they will grow more leaf than fruit. Fruiting crops are aubergine, beans, broccoli, Brussels sprouts, peppers, cauliflower, cucumber, pumpkin, squash, tomatoes and so forth.

For root crops, e.g. beetroot, carrot, onion, parsnip, swede and turnip, very little nitrogen goes a long way – too much and you eat leaves. Peas and beans fix nitrogen from the soil, leaving enough behind for root crops if pea and beanstalks are cut off at soil level rather than pulled up.

Planting note Sowing seasons are only a guide. Even throughout Britain there are vast differences in climate and elevation. Climatic conditions have become unpredictable and freak weather occurs everywhere. Watch seasonal cycles where you live and be prepared to sow again if first sowings fail due to bad weather. *Keep a garden notebook.*

Staple vegetables These are described here in greater detail than more experimental varieties. Consult seed catalogues for organic seed of more unusual varieties, or try aquatic vegetables in a pond or a water pot.

List of Common Vegetables

Amaranth (any variety of the *Amaranthus* genus) Sow in spring, after frosts have ceased. A prehistoric plant with a variety also known as love-lies-bleeding. Amaranth grown for its leaves is sometimes known as Greek spinach, although similar amaranths appear in South-East Asia, Africa and the Caribbean.

These tall, green-maroon plants have a counterpart (*A. caudatus*) grown in South America for its small grains that are ground into flour. There are more varieties, with maroon to yellowish feathery flowers, producing the best leaves or best grain and all are very nutritious. Pick young leaf tips for salads or mix mature leaves with milder spinaches. The plant doesn't like lime, fancies a little nitrogen, and accepts poor soil. Being drought tolerant, self-seeding and easily removed where not wanted, amaranth's glorious colours would grace a bare spot in an ornamental garden.

For a first crop, sow the fine seed indoors in a tray and transplant at 8–10 cm. Plant outside after frosts cease, keeping a few reserves in pots. Success in the garden means self-seeded plants next year, but do harvest some grains. This is a plant whose time is yet to come.

Asparagus (*Asparagus officinalis*) Plant in autumn or sow in spring. Companions: nasturtiums, parsley and tomatoes. A perennial indigenous to Central and Western Asia, Europe and North Africa. The Greeks have cultivated it from ancient times and a variant can be picked along our coasts.

Asparagus has male and female plants. The females are slim and pretty, too thin to cook, and produce tiny vermilion-seed berries. The familiar fat spears come from the male plants. Buy male crowns and be done, or buy seed and raise a mixture. The female spears are tasty enough raw, and the seeds will produce more plants. Spears are broken off underground at the point where they can still be snapped by hand.

Fork over a deep bed of extra good soil in autumn, as asparagus are perennials and remain permanently where planted. Score up the bed with planks or sleepers to hold layers of compost and straw mulch. Sprinkle lime three weeks before planting crowns deep enough to cover with compost and thick layers of animal manure and pea straw. Plant nasturtium seeds in pockets of soil in the straw to grow a ground cover when it rains. This bed is permanent, so the rest of your Pasta/Pizza Plot needs another square. I have seen an asparagus bed that had been producing spears for sixty years and gave no sign of quitting. It is something you pass on to the kids or the next owners of your property.

The test as to whether you are serious about your love for asparagus comes when the first spears appear in spring because *you must not pick any spears for the first two years*. Just let them grow and die down to build up the crowns, otherwise they will never be vigorous. Remember the origin of asparagus in the steppes, where plants need to gather courage to establish themselves. In the third spring you may pick a few spears here and there, mainly the female ones. Leave the rest till the fourth spring, then have a feast! But never pick the bed bare, as this exhausts the roots.

After the harvest is over, push nasturtiums to the edges and cover the plot again with compost, manure and straw. Nasturtiums usually drop enough seeds to recover the plot.

Chefs boil and steam asparagus spears in bundles, standing them up to their waists in narrow pots of boiling water. They garnish them with sauces and herbs, cheese or eggs, or include them in frittatas and fancy dishes. My asparagus seldom reaches the table. Like the nomad I am, I pick it fresh and nibble the juicy spears as I work in the garden. Try that before rushing to the cookbooks.

Aubergine (Eggplant) (*Solanum melongena*) Sow in spring. Companions: green beans. Also known as eggplant, the aubergine hails from India. By nature a tropical perennial, aubergine will still grow in temperate zones in warm spots. If the summer is short, or elevation causes cold nights, grow them in pots and bring indoors to mature. Aubergine does not like lime, but needs extra nitrogen. Choose round, egg-shaped, long-thin, or lavender varieties. Home gardeners can produce what they need to rival their crop of parsnips, turnips and swedes and are a popular choice for home-cooked dinners.

Start seed off under glass with LS. Prepare the bed with plenty of horse manure and compost. Plant outside or in the greenhouse border when warm enough and tie plants to short stakes when growing.

Writer Rana Kabbani wrote the following Syrian recipe for eggplant dip in Antonia Till's book, *Loaves and Wishes* (see **References**). Roast three eggplants over an open flame, sprinkle with salt and cool, before scooping out the flesh and blending it with a little olive oil, garlic and Greek yoghurt. It should taste smoky. Serve with hot bread.

Beans (*Phaseolus vulgaris*) Plant late spring after all danger of frost is over. Companions: feverfew and marigold. From South America as well as the Mediterranean and Middle East (*Vicia* spp.).

A few are perennial, dying down late summer and returning in spring. There are climbing and bush varieties and many different-coloured flowers, pods and beans. Old World beans have mostly black and white flowers, the best known being broadbeans. Broadbeans and the scarlet runner bean have separate entries below, as they thrive in different conditions from most other beans.

The history of beans and their travels between the Old and the New World is quite fascinating. Choose from borlotti, blue lake, broker bean, butterbean, noodle bean, redland pioneer, French bean, Spanish runner, stella bianca, snake bean, to name just half of those I've tested. Grow climbers on a tepee, trellis or wire cylinder. Green soy beans grown from dried soy beans are called *edamame*, a nutritious addition to rice, salads and vegetables. Beans are the peasant's great stand-by.

Garden Organic's seed savers offer many old-fashioned varieties never seen in shops, as do small seed companies. Plant a few dried beans from European and Asian groceries, e.g. borlotti beans. Buy packets of different beans, cook and taste them and if you like them plant some. See **References** for more on peas and beans.

Apply lime to the soil three weeks before planting, but don't overdo the B&B. Plant seeds in toilet rolls at the same time. In a wildlife-free zone you can plant beans directly in the soil, after frosts. Otherwise, beans sown directly are likely to attract night-feeding prowlers who dine on the sprouting beans. To foil freeloaders, germinate beans indoors, in a cold frame (aired during the day), or under a wire rack – see **Hardware in the Food Garden**. Prepare four margarine tubs with six toilet rolls each, filled with seed-raising mix or potting soil. Push in four different types of beans, bushing and climbing. I love the way beans pop up a week later. First the bent swan neck pushes up the earth, then two leaves unfold, remarkably big for having been folded up inside a small bean only days before. Start preparing their plot, away from onions and garlic. Soon the next set of leaves appears and when you lift out the rolls you will see root growth protruding already.

Do not plant out until they have four well-developed leaves and roots are hanging out. Dig a hole slightly deeper than the roll, pour in water, push the roll into the wet soil and pack earth around it. Surround with CMC. As they grow, provide initial B&B between plants and douse fortnightly with LS. It seems a long wait for flowers, but once they appear, beans are not far behind. Pick twice a week to encourage production. Fresh beans are delicious steamed on the plate, in salads, almost raw in a garlic-chilli-coconut dressing, and in stir-fries.

Plant new beans every month, as long as three months of warm weather can be expected. Climbing beans take longer to fruit than bush beans, hence sowing times are critical. Cut old plants at soil level to leave nitrogen in the ground.

238

Grow more beans then you need and dry them on the stalk. When bone dry, pod and store in jars for winter. Soak overnight and next day rinse then cook in fresh water for delicious bean dishes, soups, and salads. Vegetarians eat beans and lentils instead of meat, for excellent protein. Combined with rice their food value increases dramatically. Next time you want to give a friend a present, make a little box with 4–6 different bean varieties. Your friend may thank you years later!

Beetroot (*Beta vulgaris*) Plant spring, summer, or autumn. From Europe and Western Asia. Apply lime on acidic soil, but no nitrogen fertiliser – use LS. Sprinkle wood ashes around plants, but never coal ashes. Beetroot belongs to the same family as leaf beet and leaves can be eaten 2–3 times before harvesting the root. Beets come in colours of purple, bright red, gold, white, or red-and-white stripes. Golden beet has a delicate flavour, but white beet is soapy to some taste buds. Choose from round, long and flat beetroots. In common with other red-coloured fruits and vegetables, red beetroot contains betanin and rates high in anti-cancer diets, especially as a daily serve of fresh beetroot juice.

The seeds, like leaf beet seeds, produce 2–3 seedlings each. Plant seeds 10 cm apart to allow for 2–3 beets to grow sideways. They don't fancy being unravelled and transplanted. A hundred beetroot seeds fit on a square metre, but by planting 10 seeds to grow 20 plus beets and repeating two months later, you will get a continuous supply. Beetroot likes compost with animal manure, but using poultry manure will produce more leaf than root. Withhold nitrogen fertiliser to prevent forked roots. This goes for most root vegetables. Harvest beets as they grow, pulling the bigger ones. They can remain in the ground a long time before setting seed and getting woody.

To pickle, boil beets in the skin until a fork just goes in, but don't let them get soft. Cool, then rub off the skins. Cut into slices and pack into jars, alone or with onion rings and black peppercorns. Pour on a good vinegar, close the jar and leave for one month.

Beetroot served hot is delicious. Boil beets as above, cool and slip off their skins. Grate the beets coarsely and put aside. Finely cut an onion and some parsley and fry in olive oil. When the onion just browns at the edges, add grated beetroot and toss until thoroughly heated. Sprinkle salt, pepper, lemon juice and a little sugar and stir again. Serve with potatoes, as a hot salad on mignonette leaves.

Or pop mustard seeds in olive oil, sauté onion, garlic and ginger, and add ground cumin, grated raw beetroot and chopped beetroot leaves. Toss well before adding coconut milk to simmer until tender.

Try a dip made of boiled and pureed beetroot, mixed with yoghurt, salt, pepper and ground cumin, served with wedges of fried pitta bread.

Saving seed from beetroot can take two seasons. If you also have leaf beet setting seed, protect the beetroot flower head with a tied paper bag to prevent cross pollination.

Bok choy (*Brassica chinensis*) Plant autumn, winter, spring. From China. When bok choy first became available I gave some seedlings to a friend who soon exclaimed: 'I don't know how we lived without bok choy!' It can be grown in all seasons, but bolts to seed quickly in hot weather. This versatile Chinese vegetable has crisp dark green leaves shaped like a ping-pong bat with a strong white central rib. The entire rosette makes a great wok meal, but it is more economical if you pick outer leaves from several plants until they go to seed. Use also in pasta, soup and salads. A bok choy stir-fry with garlic, ginger, onion and a handful of other leaves such as amaranth, giant mustard or the like, makes a fine meal with rice noodles and crispy tofu.

Avoid early bolting by providing manure and water. Let one plant set seed, and next season sow thickly for a bok choy carpet.

Brassica juncea Plant in autumn. From Japan. Add manure and lime, feed LS. Sold under this botanical name in Japanese seed packets, as well as by local seed companies, brassica juncea stands for a group of mustardy Asian greens ranging from mild green to burgundy. All are favourites with me if grown quickly and picked young, excellent for steaming or adding to winter salads. Sow a half or quarter square by raking in seeds and patting down. Water regularly and when plants are 10 cm high begin pulling the biggest, making room for others to grow. Eat it twice a week – you will buzz with energy. Save the best plant for seed, tying red wool to it.

Brassica varieties from Asia These include bok choy, brassica juncea, Chinese flowering broccoli raab, kale and cabbage, giant red mustard, mibuna, mizuna, pak choy and tatsoy. Also see separate entries.

Alan D. Cook of Brooklyn Botanic Garden Record's publications[26], writes that no matter how proficient you become at raising Asian radishes, yard-long beans, cucumbers and water chestnuts, 'you can't be a good Asian-food gardener if you can't handle the *Brassica rapa* gang'. The problem lies with the quick-bolting habit of Asian brassicas when the weather changes to warm and/or humid. In Guangdong Province, China, where the climate is more often warmly humid than cool, I observed bunches of flowering broccoli, cabbage and kale on sale everywhere. In cool weather brassicas don't bolt. By not waiting, but cutting and eating before they do so, you get more value and the flowering tops are excellent.

Sow regularly. The best way to get on with the '*Brassica rapa* gang' is to sow varieties at different times and record the results in your garden notebook, remembering the best season for each variety. Easy. Not that I do this. I sow them all year round as fillers for spaces coming to hand, and use them as and when they please to come for salads, stir-fries, seed and chicken food. Adjust planting times given for Asian brassicas to your own microclimate. Experimentation is advisable.

Broadbeans (*Vicia faba*) Plant in autumn. Also known as fava beans. From the Middle East. Broadbeans help control wilt virus and can be planted after tomatoes. This native of Afghanistan and Western Asia became the main bean throughout the Mediterranean, Middle East and North Africa until Columbus

Red-flowering broadbeans in the foreground.

discovered the land of other beans. Known since Neolithic times, the cooks of the Levant ground broadbeans to create falafel, now a global fast food. The post-nouvelle cuisine movement rediscovered young broadbeans to garnish spring dishes. Flowers are white and black, or red.

The versatile broadbean, the only bean that grows in the cold season, can be eaten at four stages: first as young, finger-length pods, steamed with oregano; then as shelled beans when not too old. You can even tip prune the plants when they are in full flower and toss the tender leaves in a stir-fry. Later, shelled beans can be frozen.

Finally, dried shelled beans can be reconstituted or ground up to make falafel. Dry them in the pods on the plant. After soaking and cooking, mince beans with an onion, a raw potato, garlic, chilli and parsley. Add pepper, salt, cumin and coriander. Enjoy your own falafel made with home-grown ingredients!

Boil, steam or fry fresh broadbeans from 1–4 minutes, depending on their age. Serve with pasta, seasoning, olive oil, quince paste and sour cream. Team beans with sweet potato mash, or roasted carrots with lemon and Italian parsley. Or serve with crumbed goat's cheese. Some cooks peel the skins off beans after cooking, which is like eating only the heart of the artichoke. The skins are flavoursome and good roughage.

If last summer you grew the Aztec Plot, or just sweetcorn, plant broadbeans in autumn to put some nitrogen back in the soil.

Broccoli (*Brassica oleracea*) Plant summer, autumn, or spring, depending on the variety. Companions: coriander, dill, young nasturtium. From Europe, especially Italy. By preference a cool weather plant. Varieties include heading, sprouting, green, purple, Italian, or Chinese broccoli raab (with long edible stems). Commercially grown broccoli normally needs a flavoured sauce or a generous helping of grated cheese, but home-grown broccoli has a taste all its own.

A gross feeder (see **Plant Food & Soil Food**) broccoli needs plenty of organic matter. Lime the soil if acidic. I mention broccoli in the chapter on attitude, as it is half wasted when growers only cut the head. This cancer-fighting brassica can be eaten all year round with regular plantings and picking of the plentiful side shoots, if also fed and mulched well.

Plant in late summer to get it on its way by winter, developing rosettes of blue-green edible leaves and a gorgeous head. The art is to judge the state of swelling in hundreds of individual buds and pick the head before any lose their deep colouring, but not before it has reached maximum size. When the first yellow flower appears there's not a day to spare. At moments like this you will remember that growing a variety of food plants is one of the most intelligent things a human can do in life.

Yet I am duty-bound to report that broccoli side shoots with half the buds in flower are easy pickings, eminently edible, and good for you as well as tasty. But edible stems must be cut shorter as they go woody. Use shoots raw in salads. Sauté stems and florets in olive oil, adding lemon juice, salt and pepper. Should you care more for stems than heads, grow Chinese broccoli raab with edible leaves and flowers. As long as it is picked tender, broccoli is suitable for almost any mixed-vegetable dish. Try courgette, broccoli and grated carrot with a Vietnamese-style dressing, or soy sauce with Dijon mustard.

When the plant flowers profusely give it a severe pruning, saving the best flower head for seed, and you will still pick shoots for another month. Make sure no other brassica (see **An A–Z of Vegetable Groups**) is setting seed simultaneously, as they may cross pollinate. Cover one with a tied paper bag if necessary. Strange new varieties don't necessarily combine the best of both parents.

Brussels sprouts (*Brassica oleracea*) Sow late summer to early autumn for growing in the cool season. Originated in Belgium. Said to be the latest development of the cabbage, Brussels sprouts first appeared only a few hundred years ago in Belgium. They look like mini cabbages clinging to a tall stem with an open, cabbagy head. I have been spectacularly unsuccessful with this vegetable so far and plan to make it a special project next year. My sprouts opened up, perhaps due to too much nitrogen, but we still ate the heads!

Buckwheat (*Fagopyrum esculentum*) Sow in spring. From Central Asia. Buckwheat can be seen growing at very high altitudes in Asia, where it is sown in late spring and matures through the short alpine summer, which can still include snowfalls. Fast growing to 1.5m by 0.3m, it is frost tender and flowers from July to September, with the seeds ripening from August to October. It cannot grow in shade but thrives in all soils, even nutritionally poor ones.

This increasingly important plant is not a wheat at all; it is gluten-free. The small grains are ground up to make flour for pancakes, noodles and mixed baking flours. The reason I list it under vegetables is twofold. The triangular leaves can be eaten as a tasty spinach. Secondly, buckwheat is an excellent cover crop to grow on a bare plot. Harvest the seed or dig in the plants before seed sets. The plant has whitish to rose-pink flowers. Buy seeds from small seed companies or try buckwheat from health shops. Use cooked buckwheat in soups and as filling for a colourful winter vegetable salad, using a rudjak dressing (see pages 22–23).

Cabbage (*Brassica oleracea*) Plant autumn, winter, spring, or summer varieties. Companions: plant artemisia, mint, pennyroyal, tomato, sage, and wild celery to confuse predators with aromas of artemisia, chamomile, sage and thyme to repel cabbage moth. (Place the mint in pots between cabbages so that it doesn't get any ideas of taking over the plot.)

Native of Southern and Western Europe. Generally they like cool weather. Choose from green, white, red, savoy and mini cabbages.

Summer and winter varieties are planted respectively in late winter and spring, or late summer and autumn. Cabbages and Brussels sprouts top the popularity poll of home-grown vegetables, despite some of the problems they suffer.

A cabbage is a gross feeder (see **Plant Food & Soil Food**). It can also sit still and wait until the time is right. And that also goes for its cousins, cauliflower and broccoli. Cabbage seedlings can sit for two months without developing until the weather or other conditions change to their liking. Then they take off as if they'd been waiting for a starting signal – which of course they were. They still develop a head, even tardy specimens. Never abandon a cabbage and it will not abandon you.

Sometimes winter is too wet and cold or too dry and cold and you hope the cabbages will get by on dew. Then a few will suddenly bolt and produce seed heads out of a well-developed plant. Use them as broccoli, steaming the seed heads. The plant will produce shoots for a while. Pick leaves for chicken or worm food, saving the ribs for juicing with carrot and ginger. Thus a cabbage that missed its vocation is still a very edible plant.

Although modern cabbages grow all year round (check seed packets), water deep in summer or they won't produce. They are easier to grow over the winter. Grow plenty and pick outer leaves for stir-fries, saving the plant's energy for the cabbage head.

The main enemy are cabbage moths, pretty white butterflies with black spots. They lay eggs on the underside of the leaves and the grubs eat the cabbage head hollow. When you pick and cut the head, all you find is a grey mess in wrappings. Heartbreaking, I assure you. What to do? Some years ago a viewer sent in a clever idea to a TV gardening program. I tried it and it worked for me.

Hammer in four stakes around your cabbages. Cut butterflies from a white plastic container and fasten at hand-span intervals to thin cotton. Tie the cotton to each stake, crossing diagonally through the middle of the square in both directions. I have used Styrofoam twists from packaging as butterflies before, but have learned to avoid the edible kind made from corn as the birds make short shift of these.

Why would it work? The answer appears to be that the cabbage butterfly is territorial. Seeing the plastic butterflies it thinks the patch is already taken and flies on. I have used the method several years in succession after half my cabbages were eaten hollow, and although cabbage-white butterflies dance around my garden, they've left the cabbages for me. I have no idea where they now procreate, but not in my cabbages, thanks to an unknown gardener passing on a great idea.

Carrots (*Daucus carota*) Sow spring to autumn, or an all seasons variety. Companions: chives, coriander, lettuce, onions, radish, sage, shallots and violets. By mixing all these seeds together you can have your entire salad growing in one spot, as none of them need much nitrogen. Leeks

Plastic butterflies protect cabbages from the worst damage cabbage moths can do. They spell out 'territory already occupied'. Outer leaves have been attacked but the heads are firm and clean. Include a pot of mint as a companion plant.

and parsnips are carrot buddies too. Originally from Afghanistan, Pakistani carrot seed produces a deep-orange carrot with a purple top, close to the original. Great source of carotenes. Only feed a little OF. Choose from long or stumpy, pale or deep orange.

Gardening 'experts' will tell you growing carrots is dead easy, but many a gardener has troubles with this indispensable root vegetable. The main requirement is deep, light soil so carrots can penetrate downwards. If you have 'concrete' soil and no supply of sand to lighten it, go up instead of down. Dig over one quarter, then knock the bottom out of a waxed cardboard banana box, or use a large, deep pot. Fill with potting soil, preferably lightened with sand and a snuff of lime. Be careful with nitrogen, it produces forked carrots. Don't over-manure carrots, although they may need a top dressing with OF when reaching adolescence.

Sow half to one packet of carrot seed per box. Received carrot wisdom dictates they must be thinned out. Thinning out seems such a waste. Just when a healthy little plant has surfaced it gets pulled up by the roots and thrown on the compost because it hugs its neighbours. Instead mix carrot and radish seed, pulling the quickly maturing radishes to leave room for carrots to take up. Carrots seem able to postpone growing until room becomes available. Carrots tell you when they are well developed underground by developing a large tuft of greenery above ground. By carefully pulling those large tufts – pushing back smaller ones – you make room for others to grow. If the soil sinks from watering, top up with compost to prevent carrots turning green.

Germination is guaranteed by covering soil after sowing with a tea towel, T-shirt, or jute bag. Fit the carrot plot to the size of the cover. Water well and in 2–4 weeks green sprigs will push up. Remove the cloth when sprigs are a centimetre tall. Now cover with wire, to keep off the birdies. Sow one tea towel of carrots per month to always have 3–4 plots on the go from which to pull. Collect deep boxes with strong corners, tea towels, T-shirts and old racks and you shall eat baby carrots, sweet and juicy.

When the carrots go woody, give the biggest one its head and reap the seed. The flowers are as pretty as Queen Anne's lace. Carrot tops will be greedily eaten by geese. In former days farming families seem to have eaten them too. You can replant carrot heads, after cutting short the tuft, to grow several small carrots.

If you were born during the last half-century you may never have savoured real carrot taste. Carrots used to be yellow and purple in 16th-century, northwest Europe, and the Dutch developed orange carrots. But modern carrots must grow faster and taller, rendering them rather tasteless. Restaurants use them mainly for colour and fill, scarcely for their unique taste.

Pakistani carrot seeds I bought from a small seed company hardly came up or they started dying off. Those sprigs found themselves in the wrong place and climate, and were, perhaps, only a few generations removed from their source. I raked the ground and grew something else. The following winter a strong carrot plant rose between the broccolis. The Pakistani. Did I pamper that carrot! As it grew huge, I staked it. As it burst into flower, I fed it. I talked to it daily in plant lingo. When the weather warmed considerably, the seed heads formed and dried off. As they ripened unevenly I harvested heads for weeks, drying the seed indoors by daily stirring.

That home-grown seed produced seedlings that decided to grow in my garden. The resulting carrots were a deeper orange with purple tops, tasting like pre-war carrots. There are Japanese and Nepalese carrots also promising better flavour. Do not grow them simultaneously if you want to save seed.

Cauliflower (*Brassica oleracea*) Companions: coriander, cumin, dill, lemon balm. Originally from Italy. From the Mediterranean, but widely grown in India where hot climate varieties have developed. In the Indian Himalayas I came to appreciate curried cauliflower. Winter, summer and all seasons varieties are available, as well as purple and mini cauliflowers. They are gross feeders, needing plenty of organic matter like CMC and lime. See **Plant Food & Soil Food**.

Cauliflowers are real teasers. They grow large grey-green leaves, then fold them inwards so you can't see what's happening inside. After months of tending you begin to think they're having you on. Nothing seems to be happening. Then one day you see a snow-white or creamy bit of cauliflower peeping between the leaves. If you then go away for a fortnight's holiday you may return to find that the whole lot has collectively matured or bolted. Therefore, plant half a dozen periodically throughout the year and keep an eye on these most secretive of all brassicas!

Cauliflowers can be petulant about when they form a head, usually for lack of choice food. Once I left an unproductive one in a bed where it wasn't in my way, just to see how long it would take to make up its caulie mind and head up. The year came and went and she still stood there in full leaf, barren. It became a contest. She had time? Well, so had I. Then, in a very cold winter she started to bulge and after an 18-month pregnancy produced a respectable medium size cauliflower. It was difficult to cut her down after such a long contest of wills. Perhaps I should have let her go to seed for a breed of long-life caulies. Instead we enjoyed her valiant effort one chilly winter's day and she tasted very good. One cauliflower to remember.

When a caulie ripens in warm weather, snap the great outer leaves and fold over the flower head to protect the colour. You can do the same to protect in winter. Keep up manure and water. In autumn and winter they grow slower, but happier. Raise one seed per toilet roll and plant out when the roots come out the bottom. Never sprinkle seed in a seed tray, because you disturb the roots when transplanting and they may go dormant.

Depending on your microclimate, sow seed from late summer until late spring. Should three caulies bolt in one week, make thick cauliflower soup with cumin and freeze. Dilute as needed. Peel and slice the thick stem for stir-fries – tender and tasty.

Celery (*Apium graveolens* var. *dulce*) Sow in spring. Companions: bush beans, tomatoes. From Europe and Asia. See also Wild Celery in the **List of Common Herbs**. The celery we know best is stalk celery, obtained by blanching wild celery by heaping soil around the plants to grow longer stalks. But growing celery in a trench and filling in as she rises is easier and holds the water better. Dig a 30 cm deep ditch, fork in CMC, plant seedlings or seed in more compost at the bottom, and gradually refill the ditch as plants grow. The stalks are eaten and the leaves are excellent for stock, soup or stir-fry.

Celeriac (*Apium graveolens* var. *rapaceum*) Sow in spring. This relation of stalk celery produces ball-shaped roots with a delicious celery flavour for soups and stews. Grow like any root vegetable, in light soil with CM and LS.

Chicory (*Cichorium intybus*) From the Mediterranean and Western Asia where it grows wild – as it does on roadsides in Australia where the brilliant blue flowers contrast nicely with the usual yellow of roadside herbage. Linnaeus, who catalogued all plants in a comprehensive system, found that the chicory flower opened and closed with the regularity of clockwork.

Italian cooks, used to many varieties of chicory, sauté the young leaves with garlic in olive oil. For the salad bowl pick leaves before the plant sets seed and always from an unsprayed location. The Italian chicory rossa adds purple stripes or blushing greens to a salad – see Radicchio. Blanched chicory is particularly popular in Italy and France, known as witloof or chicons. Belgian Endive produces one of the finest and most delicious of winter salad crops. Excellent for forcing and easy to grow, the seed is sown in spring in a shallow drill and the plans thinned out to 9" apart. The Carrot-like roots are harvested in November and stored in a cool place. Three or four weeks before required, bring them into a dark, warm place when the delicious, succulent shoots, "Chicons" have formed. Ground chicory root makes a pleasant coffee substitute. Chicory is not choosy about soil; an underrated vegetable.

Chillies (*Capsicum annuum* and *Capsicum frutescens*) From South and Central America where they grew wild thousands of years ago. There are hundreds of varieties, hot or mild, red, yellow or purplish black. Long ones are milder. The tiny *Capsicum frutescens* is hot-hot-hot, grown in the tropics and turned into Tabasco sauce and cayenne.

Start seed off under glass in spring. The seedlings are very small and may get lost in a garden bed still full of cabbage giants and garlic. Tease them out and plant two to a small pot and fertilise. After a few days in the greenhouse they come out in the sun and once they show four leaves they can be replanted into a plot in full sun or grow in the greenhouse. After harvesting, use chillies fresh, removing seeds and white lining, or string them up to dry in the shade. Pickle chillies in vinegar and oil, or store in the freezer. Plants can be overwintered indoors.

Chinese cabbage (*Brassica pekinensis*) Sow all seasons. Also known as pe tsai, wong bak, Shantung, Tsientin, Nappa or Manchurian. There is a short variety, but the 30 cm long, light-green, crisp, tightly folded cabbage is the most versatile Chinese vegetable of all, used in all manner of dishes. Its delicacy results from quick growing in rich soil with plenty of water. Hence it is a matter of experimenting to find what the optimum seasons are in hot, cold, dry and wet climates. Build up soil around plants to blanch the leaf base. Experiment.

For a sweet and sour dish, fry red peppers, onion and shredded Chinese cabbage. Sprinkle with dressing of soy sauce, rice vinegar and sugar.

Chives (*Allium schoenoprasum*) Sow autumn to spring. Companions: cabbage and lettuce. Also garlic chives (*Allium tuberosum*, mauve starry flowers) with flat stems and mild garlic flavour, Chinese chives (*Allium odorum*, white starry flowers), and Chinese garlic chives (*Allium tuberosum*). Native of the Northern Hemisphere. Chives repel aphids and are easy to grow. Cultivate like onions. European chives have purple spiky flower heads. Plant seeds, or buy a pot of chives, split the clump and grow more. Find yourself adding chives to almost everything from salads, soups and roasted vegetables to dainties like curried eggs.

Collards (*Brassica oleracea acephala*) Sow late summer. Native to Europe. A cousin of kale with a strong cabbage flavour. Cabbages and kales have finer flavour, but collards grow so readily that if you have trouble growing anything, try them. Water and feed well, picking leaves from the bottom up. Use young leaves for salads or sauté with onion greens, ground cumin and quartered cumquats.

Corn salad (*Valerianella locusta*) Sow late summer and late winter in soil that is not too rich, e.g. after brassicas. It tolerates medium frost. Also known as lamb's lettuce, or mache. This small, almost wild European salad plant should be better known. Corn salad adds another flavour to salads or a garnish to pasta, polenta or couscous. Easily raised from seed.

Courgettes (or zucchinis) (*Cucurbita* spp.) Companions: young nasturtiums, but courgettes will be retarded if growing near leaf beet, which could be a good thing. From Central America. Courgettes should be picked when young as they will turn into marrows overnight. They belong to the squash family of the genus *Cucurbita*. They are green, white or black, smooth or ribbed. They like rich soil with some lime. Plant in a depression to hold water. It is said that growing courgettes is easy: all you have to do is turn your back. This, for once, is true. One summer it rained a few days. When I looked again, there was a marrow half a metre long of commensurate width. I juiced it for a week at one glass per day. If you make juice, you will cope with more than one plant. Delicious with apple, carrot and ginger.

Most families need just 1–2 plants. A seed tray of seedlings better be shared around. Or plant two seeds in toilet rolls. Pick courgettes young and regularly.

Courgettes, like pumpkins, produce male and female flowers, on thin and swollen stems, to be pollinated by bees. If your garden has no bees, plant bee-attracting herbs and pollinate by hand the first year by picking a just-opened male flower and pushing it into an open female flower, rubbing carefully. You feel you're invading their privacy. Place the used male flower in a tiny vase in the kitchen.

When courgette plants have produced their first spectacular burst of fruits they start looking like giant green centipedes lying with their feet in the air. Suddenly there are but few flowers and hardly any fruit. Rejuvenate them by pruning. Cut off all leaves from the beginning of the main stem up to where the fruit is forming, leaving enough leaves to shade new fruit. This enables plants to put all nutriments into a second production run, not as boisterous as the first, but satisfyingly regular. In late summer and early autumn let fruit grow to full capacity. The skin hardens and it becomes a marrow to keep for a while and save seed from.

There are more recipes for courgette than anything else. If all you have ever tried is fried courgette, battered male courgette flowers (only in the courgette and pumpkin world is it the males who get battered) and courgette soup, become adventurous. Try sliced male courgette flowers in an omelette, bake courgette cake and bread with marigold petals, or grate courgette into lettuce with herbs, oil, lemon and soy sauce. You can grill courgette with tomato, garlic, cheese and basil, serve courgette sandwiches with chutney or grilled cheese and mustard, and make velvet courgette soup with rocket, coriander, cumin and lemongrass. Or stir-fry courgette with green beans and broccoli or tomato chutney, and make up your own courgette relish, jams, and pickles. My favourite salad is grated courgette and carrot with chopped celery or grated apple and a dressing of Dijon mustard, curry powder, olive oil and balsamic vinegar. Pure health.

Cucumber (*Cucumis sativus*) Companions: bush beans, radish, lettuce, savoy cabbage, sweetcorn, sunflowers, stinging nettle and horse manure compost.

Possibly originated in the Himalayan foothills and was already growing in ancient India, Egypt and Greece more than 3000 years ago.

Lovers of hot weather, cucumbers like protection from the wind and need lots of water. This prolific producer diversified as it spread across the globe over centuries. Choose from green, yellow, white, crooked, straight, long, short, round, striped, horned, and baby-skin smooth. Or go by country: African, Armenian, Chinese, Dutch, German, Italian, Japanese, Lebanese, Russian, Syrian. Or by flavour: apple, lemon, or . . . cucumber!

Grow only one variety per season if you save seed, as varieties cross-pollinate. Cucumbers grow well on a trellis or draped over a cane chair, saving space and preventing mildew – thanks for that, Chris!

Sow seed in toilet rolls behind glass, apply LS. Prepare bed with CMC in a warm spot with dappled shade, or in a poly tunnel or under a plastic 'roof'. Plant out when the danger of frost is over and plants have several leaves on a strong stem. Avoid root damage. Keep up LS, mulch and water as fruit forms, to make the difference between a sweet cucumber and a bitter one. You'll be amazed how many cucumbers one little vine produces. If vines are long and many, pinch out the tips. Pick cucumbers twice a week or they'll stop producing. Some gardeners claim that two vines are more than enough. Plant herbs and flowers to attract bees for pollinating. To save seed, let one cucumber ripen fully on the vine. Wash seeds before drying.

If your red onions ripen in cucumber time, make a salad of the two with a dressing of rice wine vinegar, sesame oil and tamari or soy sauce. German immigrants brought cucumber pickle recipes to America. After sprinkling sliced cucumbers and hard onions with salt and leaving overnight, they went into jars with oil, vinegar, black pepper and mustard seeds. If you like sweet pickles try oil, vinegar, sugar and spices, mustard, celery seed, ground cloves and turmeric.

Endive (*Chicorium endivia*) Sow in autumn. Known in ancient Egypt and Greece and related to chicory (same blue flowers). Several varieties – all easy and hardy.

Apply CS plus a dusting of lime. As a kid in Holland I had a love-hate relationship with endive, which in that damp climate grew into large bunches, like non-heading lettuce. Mum used to wash, cut and cook it with just the last rinsing water hanging on, and serve it with a white sauce sprinkled with nutmeg. I gradually grew to like it, but its bitter tang is not for young children.

Appreciate endive as a salad vegetable, picking outer leaves while young so that half a dozen plants are plenty. Later in the season, pick the yellow hearts. Endive is easier to grow than related witlof, which has to be blanched (see Chicory). To get new plants, rub a handful of dry seed heads between your hands and rake in. This will ensure endive coming up in its own good time.

Florence fennel (*Foeniculum vulgare* var. *dulce*) Companions: appears to be a loner and may inhibit other plants. Probably from the Azores. Grows less than 50 cm high (for tall field fennel grown for seeds and foliage, see Fennel in **List of Common Herbs**).

Florence fennel needs rich soil with added lime to form the half-submerged fleshy leaf base, the most edible part. The flavour has a hint of aniseed, favoured in Mediterranean cooking. Eat steamed with pasta or as a salad with orange slices and chives. Try raw with cherry tomatoes and a cool dipping sauce. Cinquaterra cakes from Genoa are flavoured with fennel. When Florence fennel forms seed heads, cut off all but the central stalk to produce seed.

The ferny foliage is used as bedding for colourful foods. Place freshly picked leaves on a blue platter, arranging cubed cheese, tomatoes, olives and red onions on top. Serve alfresco with crisp bread and good wine.

Garlic (*Allium sativum*) Plant in autumn. Originally from Central Asia and cultivated in ancient Egypt and Mesopotamia, now worldwide.

Garlic is a natural antibiotic protecting you from colds and infections and is indispensable in most vegetable dishes. The price is high enough to consider growing this delicious condiment yourself. One square metre can deliver 100 big garlic bulbs – work out what that would cost in the shop. You will be able to use the greens, use garlic young and fragrant, serve whole baked garlic, and store a few plaits at the end of summer! Grow enough garlic for cooking, drying, pickling, and replanting. Grow different varieties in boxes filled with compost, placed on underfelt.

Do not buy imported garlic to plant out, in case of disease. Search farmers' markets for organically grown garlic, even if they carry names of waves of immigrants. Elephant garlic is the biggest and mildest. Red Italian has a fine taste. Try local Isle of Wight garlic and Rocambole and wild garlic, growing free and wild in England. Save the best of each for replanting.

In autumn fork over a plot one spade deep, adding B&B. Break up bulbs and push cloves half a finger into the soil, spaced 10 cm apart in both directions. Dust soil with lime. Cover with CMC and a thick layer of teased-out straw. Water in well. Green spikes will appear soon. As most garlics don't fully mature until the tops die off, the ground may be occupied for the best part of the year, but start using bulbs from spring onwards.

Sometimes I grow so much garlic that full-grown bulbs left in the ground start shooting as many spikes as they have cloves. These I use as a whole bunch in stir-fries for a delicious young garlic flavour. Garlic just bulbed and not yet fully cloved tastes mellow. Simmer three sliced bulbs in oil, green tops included, before adding other vegetables. Use green tops for soups and salads. Use fresh or pickled garlic to make traditional Mexican salsa. In a mortar mash 4–5 garlic cloves with half a teaspoon of sea salt, add finely chopped onions and tomatoes, fresh chopped coriander, lemon juice and black pepper. For a really hot one use minced red pepper.

Store garlic in net bags hung in a cool, dark place or between newspaper in a box in a dark cupboard. When some start to sprout it is time to pickle the rest. No need to peel. Just rub off loose skins and place whole blanched bulbs

258

in hot sterilised jars and top with boiling vinegar. The taste remains great and the vinegar is fine for salads. Garlic plaits of 3–5 bulbs are a welcome present for friends who like cooking, so you can never grow too much.

Gherkins (*Cucumis anguria*) Gherkins are from Africa and possibly travelled to the New World with the slave trade. They are cultivated in the West Indies and Eastern Europe, which exports gherkins. Seed can be bought specifically for varieties suitable for pickling due to prolific cropping and texture.

To pickle, sprinkle gherkins with salt and leave overnight. Dry off. Pack in jars, as above, with bay leaf, chilli, peppercorns, dried ginger, fennel and dill, as you like. Evidently one grape leaf per jar gives a gourmet touch. Pour on white vinegar and a layer of olive oil, closing the lid tightly. Save jars with plastic lids for pickling as these don't corrode.

Giant red mustard (*Brassica juncea*) Sow autumn to late winter. From China. This stunning plant prefers cool seasons, yet will grow any time although it bolts to seed quickly in summer. The leaves are the most superb burgundy-maroon and green with fine nerve undulations like a map of rural Guangdong Province.

The taste is pleasantly hot. One leaf cut in strips makes a personal salad or a piquant addition to mixed salads. Use shredded in pastas. One plant produces so many leaves that you can afford to cook it as spinach or in stir-fries where it loses its bite but still adds flavour. A head of yellow flowers attracts good insects. Cut off side shoots to let the central stem produce seed.

Globe artichoke (*Cynara scolymus*) Plant roots in autumn or sow seed in spring. This high-fibre perennial grew in North Africa where Roman conquerors learned to enjoy them in the first century. The Italians have been cultivating artichokes for at least six centuries. The French eat them cold for lunch, with vinaigrette, or hot with garlic butter. They made their way to Norfolk Island in the Pacific with British settlers in 1788.

Globe artichokes are thistles and if not picked will produce a brilliant blue flower followed by seed. The globe is the flower bud.

Seed is available from small seed companies and germinates easily in late spring to summer. When seedlings have two good leaves, pick them out, plant in individual pots (in part shade) and start feeding LS. If your soil is acidic, work in lime three weeks before planting out in autumn in a composted bed and when the plants have six leaves. They grow to be tall, handsome plants of decorative value, looking great along a picket fence, and will produce globes the next spring.

France and Italy produce artichokes for much of the British demand. In Britain, you can pick them from the first day of spring to mid-summer. Once a week, pull off decaying leaves and lay these as mulch around the plants. If night prowlers gnaw stems underneath the globes, pull an orange net bag over the top and tie it down.

When all globes are harvested, cut down the stalks for the compost heap. Cut off leaves and arrange between the plants. Place fertiliser underneath and top with straw. Soon new plants will sprout from the old stumps and the whole process will start again.

The following year, carefully slice off new plants with a spade, including a piece of root, and replant elsewhere to ensure continuous supply of this old-world delicacy. When cutting down old stalks, some may separate with new white shoots under the earth. Carefully saw the stalk into as many pieces as there are shoots and plant each in a pot with compost. They will soon form new plants to be set out where there is space to grow. Thus you continually renew your stock and create designer hedges of these toothed, grey plants of classical elegance.

I drive past a farm where one year they had a marvellous 10 x 2 m stand of globe artichokes. At the end of the picking season the whole hedge disappeared. I wondered why they would dig up this superb stand. But next winter it was back in the same spot. I concluded that in typical farm-management style the farmer mowed the stand down after harvest! However, setting out a new hedge every few years is a safeguard in case old roots with deep fissures rot in wet winters.

To prepare artichokes, boil the globes in plenty of water. I like eating the inside of the bitter stems as well and cook these separately in the same pot. Rich people only ever eat the hearts of artichokes, which is what you buy in tins. But apart from the stems, the outer leaves have much to offer.

Boil globes for 30 minutes, then with two forks pull off a leaf and scrape the inside with your teeth. If you can't scrape yet, boil till tender. Each leaf has a tasty fleshy base. Peel off each leaf, dip in vinaigrette or garlic butter, and scrape with your teeth. Green and purple globes taste the same. This is real peasant food, slow food to be enjoyed. As you come to the innermost parts of the globe the whole leaf can be eaten, but it is the heart – after removing the pluck of hair that covers it – that is your reward for approaching it so slowly! To eat the classical way, cut in halves and remove the heart and soft leaves to eat with lemon juice, olive oil and sea salt.

Japanese vegetables Japanese greens available as seed tend to belong to the hardy and easy to grow Cruciferae/Brassicaceae group of vegetables. Gourds, pumpkins and root crops are also available and more will no doubt appear. As the text on seed packets is usually in Japanese, use garden sense and experiment with planting times and LS. See also Brassica varieties from Asia.

Jerusalem artichoke (*Helianthus tuberosus*) From North America. This root vegetable gives some people unfortunate bowel symptoms. But if you have tried them without ill effect, do obtain a root, cut it in pieces, and plant. Soon you will have lots of edible roots. Any piece left in the soil will grow again, like horseradish, which is so hard to get rid of it can take over entire plots. If your garden thrives on neglect and sweet chaos, think twice before planting Jerusalem artichokes. Boil and eat like potatoes.

Kale (*Brassica oleracea*) Sow in autumn. Native to Europe. Named varieties of this non-hearting cabbage plant exist, including ornamental ones. One of my childhood delights was *boerekool met worst*, a Dutch one-pot winter meal of potatoes mashed with finely cut curly green kale and a smoked sausage on top. My love of the invigorating taste of kale remains and I grow green curly and Siberian purple kale. Kale needs to have a touch of frost to taste really good. By planting in late summer or autumn, they just catch a night frost when they are ready to eat.

True Russian kale is not curly but scalloped. It can stand low temperatures, but strangely enough is also quite happy in summer, even surviving heatwaves. It is tenderer than the somewhat tough curly kale. The leaves lend a wonderfully engaging taste to horta, salads, soups or stir-fries. The young seed heads can be eaten as broccoli shoots. Whereas curly kale grows to broccoli height, Russian kale can reach 2 m, setting thousands of seeds in order to survive Siberia's winter. The seed keeps well. Use it to grow a green crop for digging in or chicken food.

Pick leaves young – wonderful stir-fried in olive oil with ginger, garlic and onion. For Russian kale soup (not purple but green) that even my grandsons used to eat with relish: cook leaves with an onion, cool, put through the blender and season with soy sauce. This soup stands alone in terms of nutrition as well as having a convincing taste impossible to describe. When served to guests accustomed to pale soups with dollops of cream, some are likely to break into praise songs. As Russian kale is not available in shops, you have to grow your own to experience this amazing vegetable.

To grow kale, allow a quarter of your square. This big, beautiful, decorative plant may need staking. No one need go hungry as long as we grow on the seeds of Russian kale.

Kohlrabi (*Brassica oleracea*) Sow in all seasons. From Europe, but also grown in China (*Gai lan tau*) and Vietnam. Prepare soil with CMC and lime. Kohlrabi can develop rather quickly and goes woody if left to linger, so pick them young. A greenish-white or purple swollen stem base is the part normally eaten, but young leaves can be used in stir-fries. A taste all its own. Use in soups, as a cooked vegetable, or eat raw.

Leaf beet (*Beta vulgaris*) Plant any season. Companion: parsley. Also known as chard. From Europe and Western Asia. The homesteader's perennial standby, these tall, green plants have hung around many a backdoor for a quick grab of green to add to a stew, soup or casserole and these days a quiche. Leaf beet is tough and survives neglect. Trouble is that when it does, the leaves become as edible as old slippers. Yet the plant possesses the means to overcome this and be a true gourmet vegetable. Read on.

Leaf beet comes with stems in plain cream, deep red, golden yellow, orange, and purple. Those with thick stems and broader leaves tend to be known as chard, either French or Swiss. Chards have a fine taste and the stems can be steamed or baked as a separate vegetable and served with a piquant sauce.

Steam green leaves with a bouquet garni, touch of lemon and black pepper.

Leaf beet going to seed is a sight. A heady aroma of honey issues from a plant that may be 2 m tall. The stem becomes a trunk with hundreds of branches bearing rows of seeds. You don't need that much. Prune lower branches to feed the main seed head. Maturation takes time and you can't grow much under this leaf beet tree, as its roots spread far. When seeds start drying off, cut them quickly, as hanging in the sun for weeks won't improve them at this stage. Hang seeds in an old pillowslip or paper (never plastic) bag in a shady veranda for wind drying. After a few weeks, strip the seed off. You will fill a shoebox. Share some out and with the rest grow leaf beet in gourmet style.

Prepare half a square, or whatever the size your protective cage is (see **Hardware in the Food Garden**). Dig in plenty of manure or other organic matter and B&B. Take a handful of seed and rake thickly through the bed, patting it down with your hand. Push under any seeds still showing. Place the cage over the bed and water in. Soon you'll see a forest of young leaf beets standing shoulder to shoulder. Start picking a bunch of the larger leaves when 15–20 cm long. These have short stems and take but minutes to steam to superb tenderness. The manure will keep this bed going quite a while, providing tender greens in all weathers. To ensure continuous supply, plant a batch 3–4 times per year. Never eat old-slipper leaf beet again!

Since I started growing gourmet leaf beet I've noticed that one plot inter-growing with parsley was much less nibbled by tiny snails than one without. This may work where you are. Trim parsley regularly for soups, stews and tabouli and let only two stalks go to seed.

Use this gourmet leaf beet instead of spinach in recipes for quiche and spinach loaves. Dice and steam leaves and drain. While still hot, stir in a few eggs, herbs and spices, and firm up with bread crumbs until the mixture sits comfortably in a baking dish. Bake in a moderate oven. Add to a basic spinach loaf: onions, garlic, capers and beetroot, chopped nuts and citrus zest, courgette and carrot, grated white radish, or mashed potato. Replace bread crumbs with cooked rice and rice flower or chickpea flour – see **Cupboard Self-Sufficiency**. Get creative with leaf beet.

Leek (*Allium porrum*) Sow in spring, plant out by July, and don't count on using that plot for more than half a year. The Egyptians grew leeks in 2000 BCE. Leeks can be expensive as they occupy ground for so long. But they are easy to grow from seed, planted out like onions. Apply CMC and lime.

Don't wait for the tops to dry off as with onions. Harvest leeks when young and tender, when medium sized, and when tall and fat. If you see the flower bud – a papery sheath containing a ball of mauve sparklers – you're almost too late as they get woody, but you can still make a batch of concentrated leek soup

Leeks in seed are decorative.

to put in the freezer. Let the best leek go to seed. When black seeds begin to pop from the sparklers these are ready to be cut and dried. Old leeks pulled up may have little bulblets at the base. Plant them between cabbages and lettuces, as they take time to become 'leeklings'.

Make leek and potato soup or use sweet potato; dress it up with a dollop of yoghurt garnished with chopped chives stems and young flowers, onion greens, or rocket. Use leek with other greens in dhal and pies, or as a vegetable with hardboiled-egg sauce.

Lettuce (*Lactuca sativa*) Sow in all seasons. Companions: beetroot, cabbage, carrots, onions, radish and strawberries. From Asia Minor and the Middle East. Small seed companies may carry more than a dozen varieties: hearting and non-hearting. Some grow throughout mild winters (butter lettuce, cos, oakleaf), others only in summer, so you can eat lettuce all year round. Easily grown from seed with CMC and lime.

Lettuce remains one of the most popular home-grown vegetables in the British Isles. As commercial lettuce is grown with human-unfriendly chemicals, it's worth growing your own – see Lawrence in **References**.

The smaller, non-heading lettuces are picked from the outside while they keep growing; ideal for the single vegetable gardener. A packet of mesclun mix contains some of the following: green cos, green curly, coral leaf, coral curly and cos, butterhead, oakleaf, green and red mignonette, Lollo rosso, radicchio, rabbit's ear, lamb's ear and more. See also Chicory, Salad greens and Radicchio. To make the plot look pretty, sow lettuce in a small bed, then transplant, alternating red/brown varieties with green ones. This is basic kitchen gardening, where the eye wants to be pleased as much as the tastebuds.

Size is important when planting out lettuces. Cos is tall and erect. Once I saw cos 60 cm tall in an organic garden supplying restaurants. Start picking before they become so big. Other lettuces are ground hugging; good for borders until they send up seed stalks with tiny yellow flowers. Lamb's ear or corn salad is the smallest, sprawls, and is not a true lettuce. Radicchio, the tough, bitter and beautiful Italian stand-by, is a variety of chicory, sending up a tall stalk to produce seed. Before it does, enjoy masses of bright blue flowers.

Collect seed heads when dry, drying further indoors, rubbing between the hands to release seeds into a bowl. Dry another week before storing in screw-top jars. No need to separate different types of lettuces if they will grow in your microclimate through summer and winter. Sprinkle seed mix 3–4 times a year.

Melons (*Cucumis melo*) Companions: bush beans and horse manure compost. Melons probably originated in Africa, but found their home in Central Asia. Hami, near the Turpan Depression in Xinjiang, is known as melon heaven, thanks to ancient irrigation methods and plenty of sunshine. Afghanistan also once grew and exported beautiful melons.

Easily grown from seed in early spring, indoors. Plant out in a green-house border, preferably on a hot bed. Melons dislike cold nights, so choose a warm spot. Select canteloupe or green-fleshed honeydew, or heirloom varieties from the Amish, Ukraine, France or Israel. For a Hami melon you need a long summer, hence the need to germinate seed under glass. Yet the melon called 'Collective Farm Woman' ripened in Moscow. If you tried growing melons and failed, seek out seed to complement your climate. They need CMC, B&B and good drainage.

To create a warm plot, dig a pit, fill it half with compost, plant melon seedlings and cover with an old glass door or rigid plastic held down by bricks. Provide ventilation and open up on warm days. Or make a small plastic poly tunnel. Check drainage. Commercial growers use black plastic to warm up the earth and plant seedlings in punched holes. As the vines grow, apply B&B monthly or old chicken manure between plants. Sprinkle lime to deter snails and slugs.

Either grow vines on a wire trellis, supporting melons in net bags, or put planks under rambling melons to stop rot. When ripening, protect melons with cages or cloth bags against rats and other rodents. Harvest melons with a piece of stem. If you run out of warm weather, use immature melons for a honey and yoghurt desert with roasted sesame seeds.

Mibuna (*Brassica X rapa* Japonica group) Sow just a pinch of seeds late summer and late winter. This is a quick-growing hot salad green from Japan, widely used in restaurants. Pick leaves from the bottom up. Let one plant set seed.

Mizuna (*Brassica rapa* Japonica group) Sow autumn to spring. From Japan. In its small form a salad plant, but the larger mizuna, or Japanese endive, is a deeply indented green-leaved plant for cool weather. In summer it bolts easily. Rather than space out seeds, grow one densely seeded patch so plants shade each other, don't dry out quickly and, provided you pick twice a week, continue to provide tender leaves instead of bolting to seed. Add young leaves to a tossed salad for their peppery flavour. Use mature leaves as a steamed vegetable to accompany baked pumpkin or carrots, or mix into a stir-fry.

Mustards (*Brassica juncea*) Sow all seasons, but cool weather preferred. Will grow in acid soil. Natives of Asia and Europe. Giant red (see page 259), Chinese, black, white (*Brassica alba* or *Sinapis alba* syn. *Brassica hirta*). For others, consult the Garden Organic website (see **Useful Addresses**). All have yellow flowers. Easy and hardy. Mixed with legumes they assist fruiting trees, vines and tomatoes. Grow yellow mustard as a quick green crop after vegetables, dig in before flowering. Mustard is grown as a vegetable in many countries, as well as for oil and condiments, being prolific seed producers. They can grow to 1.5 m with dinner-plate leaves. Collect enough for your kitchen and the Horta Plot. Don't be without these fast-growing, maintenance-free, tasty and healthy additions to meals.

Onions (*Allium* spp.) Sow autumn, early winter and spring, depending on whether they are early or late onions. Companions: carrots, nettle, parsley, tomatoes and violets. (Onions and garlic are not always compatible with peas and beans, but are pest repellents where aphids cause problems.) From Western Asia. The Egyptians grew them in 3000 BCE.

Enrich soil with compost. For acidic soil, sprinkle lime three weeks before planting out. Choose from brown, white or red salad onions, shallots and spring onions. See below for heirloom varieties to grow from bulbs. Since onions need a long growing and drying off time, consider growing them in boxes to maintain a faster rotation of vegetables in your square. Or dig an onion square. Or plant a row of shop onions to sprout along a path and pick green straps for half a year!

Sowing onions directly and then thinning them out is a waste, unless you replant the thinnings. Better to punch holes in a margarine container, fill with fine soil and sow enough seed to cover. They come up like a forest! From a whole packet you may obtain a 3 m onion row. Calculate how many seed trays to sow for half a year's supply. When seedlings are 10 cm high make trenches with a hand trowel, pushing the earth higher on one side. Place seedlings at intervals the size of an onion along the low side of the trench, then fold in the high wall of earth. They will straighten up in a week. Water well.

Since onions look like grass, weed carefully. Top dress with CMC plus straw. Sprinkle OF. As they grow, heap compost around bulbs poking above ground. Pick greens sparingly for salads and stir-fries. Begin harvesting as tops shrivel. Most onion varieties store for several months, braided on a rope and hung in a cool dark place. See Chives for more onion material when stored onions run out.

Onions have one mystery habit. Some grow nice greens before drying off prior to harvest. Others set seed, handsome balls of white or mauve sparklers. If the onion is a good size and you want to save seed, let it happen. Seed growing will completely waste the bulb. Harvest seed when the stem goes yellow. Alternatively, snap flowering stems to let bulbs develop. Why do some onions set seed and others not? Different varieties are sensitive to planting time, too early or too late, and behave accordingly. As your garden's mini-climate needs to be factored in, you do best to follow general rules and experiment from year to year until you know what your onions tend to do where you are. This is what 'knowing your onions' means.

I adore heirloom Welsh bunching onions (*Allium fistulosum*), from Germany, where *welsche* meant 'foreign', as they arrived there from Siberia. Also known as Japanese bunching onions. Each bulb planted grows a bunch of elongated small onions. They can be propagated from seed or root division. Potato onions also bunch and grow from divisions. Pick green straps sparingly. Find them in markets or at heritage seed outlets. Grow shallots from bulbs. The Egyptian onion, or tree onion, grows a bunch of minute onions, no bigger than your thumb nail, at the top of the stem. I've never quite known what to do with these. I have pickled them, but peeling so many puts me off. They can probably be roasted in the skin like garlic.

Orach (*Atriplex hortensis*) Sow in spring, summer, or autumn. Known as Mountain Spinach, it is native to Western Asia and Eastern Europe. Grows like amaranth. A decorative red or yellow vegetable that stands hot or cold weather, grows to 2 m, and provides plentiful spinachy leaves.

Pak choy (*Brassica chinensis* var. *parachinensis*) Sow in spring. From China. Chinese greens with pretty yellow flowers that are eaten with the juicy stems. Sow fairly thick as it is a quick grower and you will pull whole plants, although it sprouts again if you use parts only. Steam, stir-fry, or mix in salads.

Parsnip (*Pastinaca sativa*) Sow in early winter. Companions: carrots, radish. From Southern and Central Europe. Add some old chicken manure and lime to the soil a few weeks prior to sowing. Sow parsnips as carrots. Pull the biggest ones to make room for little ones to grow. The main problem with parsnips is that the seed does not remain viable very long. Buy seed in a foil packet and sow soon thereafter. Let one parsnip go to seed – the beautiful umbrella head of flowers attracts beneficial insects. Sow new seed straight away; wrap excess seed in foil after drying and store it in a jar in the bottom of the fridge. Use as soon as convenient.

Slice parsnips and carrots in a baking tray, cover with red onion slices, orange or lemon slices, ground coriander seed, sprinkle with sesame oil and olive oil and bake under foil in medium oven until *al dente*. Remove foil to brown. Serve with noodles or sweet or mashed potatoes and a green salad.

Peas (*Pisum sativum*) Plant October to January and again in early spring. Companions: turnips, potatoes, parsnips, carrots, radish and beans. Cultivated as long as 10,000 years ago in Western Asia. Today most peas are podded and frozen, but snow peas and sugar snaps are eaten fresh in the pod. The latter two need climbing support, but a bush variety of sugar snaps is available.

Dig in old horse manure and lime. Don't use a high nitrogen fertiliser. For climbing peas rig up poles, wire tower, tepee, or trellis (see **Hardware in the Food Garden**). Plant peas 2 cm deep and 5 cm apart in a shallow ditch and press earth down by hand. If you have rodents digging up germinating seeds, raise peas indoors in toilet rolls. Plant outside when roots hang out the bottom. Tuck in seedlings with compost and cover with leaf mulch, grass clippings, wood ashes, compost or a mix of all these. Add B&B if plants are slow to develop.

Podded peas are best for freezing and can be used in many decorative ways, in almost any dish you care to prepare, as well as be served as an instant green vegetable when you've run out of greens.

Pea shoots Similar to bean sprouts, but grown outside. Easily harvested from peas left in pea straw. Cut them when 10 cm tall and use in curries, stir-fries and salads. Pea straw peas are called fodder peas, but are common podding peas quite suitable for human consumption.

Peppers (*Capsicum annuum*) Solanaceae family. Also known as capsicum, sweet pepper or bell pepper, they originated in South and Central America. Paprika is a milder and thin-fleshed variety. Choose from Hungarian, Italian, Japanese, Russian, Portuguese, or American. There are yellow, orange, red, purple and black peppers, but they all start off green. Sow seed early under glass or indoors, and feed LS. Build up the outdoor plot with CMC. Plant out after frost ceases and days are truly warm. Keep up feeding with fortnightly LS or OF and always water well. You can grow them outdoors, but they do best under cover in the UK, if kept fed and watered in a greenhouse border or plot. Pick peppers for size rather than colour to keep the plant in production. They can be eaten raw, grilled, baked, or fried. Preserve peppers by pickling in oil and vinegar.

Potatoes (*Solanum tuberosum*) Plant when no frost is expected for 4–5 months. Companions: nasturtium, corn, or grow after a broadbean crop. Potatoes date back to 11,000 BCE. Their homeland is Peru, where some 3000 varieties are still being grown on family farms. That's biodiversity! That huge collection may be needed in the future, if today's artificial farming methods smite one after another potato with blight, causing a new-age potato famine.

As quite a few plants are inhibited by potatoes, even its cousin the tomato, there is a case for growing potatoes somewhat separate. For winter growing, see below. As potatoes are an important staple food – used baked, mashed, in snacks, soups, salads, and as wedges – it is vital to grow heirloom potatoes to keep strong old strains in the system. Source them from Garden Organic. Potatoes return your investment tenfold. Choose from yellow, white, red and purple varieties, each with its own flavour and properties for cooking, baking or salads. Select shop or market bought tubers you like, grow them, then test how well they keep. Try another variety the following year.

If you can eat potatoes you are lucky. People with arthritis may not want to eat the fruits of the Solanaceae family (see **An A–Z of Vegetable Groups**). *Do make sure growing potatoes stay underground, for any exposed to light develop green patches, a sign of the toxic alkaloid solanines. Do not eat potatoes with green patches, they are toxic, especially for little people.*

Growing potatoes in straw If you have it, grow potatoes in soil, as friable as possible. *Potatoes do not like lime.* But you can grow them by spreading a thick layer of wet newspaper and a very thick layer of pea straw over a rocky hump where nothing else will grow. Make gutters in the straw and fill with compost, then bury cut potatoes or peelings, covering again with straw and sprinkling B&B. When plants are big and healthy stick your hand under the straw, feel around and steal the biggest potatoes for dinner without the plant even noticing. Keep covering this arrangement with more compost and straw. It's a different potato game from the wholesale ripping out of plants on commercial farms, after all tops have been sprayed to die off simultaneously. Eventually your plants will flower and stop growing. Harvest all and replant baby spuds. *Do not plant potatoes in the same place year after year.* Always dig a fresh plot or fill a new barrel. Store potatoes in a cool place away from light after rubbing off any eyes.

Growing potatoes in a wine barrel or wire cylinders This method may also work in winter, as it elevates potatoes above the frost line. Make chicken-wire cylinders lined with thick layers of wet newspaper or line the sides of a wine barrel with wet newspapers. Or use bottomless buckets or the body of an old washing machine. Place in a warm spot on high ground or stack between biscuits of straw.

For the wine barrel, cut 3–4 potatoes with eyes into pieces, place on 20 cm of compost, cover with old manure and straw. When plants appear, surround and cover them with more soil and straw, or add soft weeds and non-invasive grass clippings. Repeat this a third and fourth time depending on barrel height. Then let the plants grow up and make potatoes in the barrel. In a cylinder do the same, making sure plants get no more light than in a barrel. In other containers fill up as soon as plants appear, because they will reach for the light faster.

If your soil gets waterlogged in winter, grow potatoes on higher ground or use the above methods. If you expect true wet seasons, harvest all before the onset. Never plant in low-lying pockets.

Convert lawn to a food plot by laying small potatoes on one square metre of lawn and cover with manure and thick straw mulch. As plants appear add more mulch. The grass becomes potato food and after harvest you can plant other vegetables. May not work with some grasses.

Pumpkin (*Cucurbita* spp. See also Squash). Sow in spring. Dates back to 7000 BCE in Mexico. The variety of pumpkins is stunning. In our shops you mainly buy yellow butternut squash (not a true pumpkin) and Jack o'Lantern because these have long keeping qualities. But generally blue and green ones are the keepers while yellow and orange ones are for eating soon. If you see an unusual pumpkin buy it, dry the seeds indoors for a month, then refrigerate overnight. Rub off the silvery membranes before storing in an airtight container. If you have mice, don't leave pumpkin seeds uncovered; they'll bring the clan to devour them. Growers' markets, small seed companies and Garden Organic are sources for varieties of pumpkin seed suitable for all climates. There are also mini pumpkins for singles and giant pumpkins weighing in at hundreds of kilos for the whole clan.

Start seed early under glass to allow for a long warm season. Dig holes one spade deep and fill with manure, soft weeds, grass clippings and compost, adding lime for acidic soils. When this sinks down, add more compost and mulch and plant seedlings in a depression when all danger of frost is over. Although pumpkins survive dry days, to get results a daily watering at the roots is needed.

After a year's gardening you may find pumpkin plants coming up in the compost. These are strong and viable. Leave them in place, or transplant them with a clod of earth attached. One of our keeper pumpkins had begun to rot and I didn't want to insult the chickens with it. Thrown on the compost heap in autumn it dissolved over the winter, but in spring there were scores of dark green seedlings ready to transplant.

Mini pumpkins and butternuts are for small gardens, but most pumpkins need to sprawl. If you hope to limit your food garden to one or two squares, plant them on the edge to sprawl over, or make a pumpkin station somewhere else. Dig a bag of manure into a backyard corner, as long as the hose can reach it, raise a compost mound on top and plant seedlings in a circle, protected by bottomless yoghurt tubs. When they grow over the edges, remove protectors.

Pumpkin aficionados will pinch out the tips of pumpkin vines to encourage production of less but bigger fruit. When pumpkins are half grown, pinch every vine and carry the tips, complete with two or three furry leaves, flowers and embryo fruit, to the kitchen. Steam lightly, toss in coconut cream and serve hot. From mid summer on discourage the formation of more fruit by picking flowers. As a side dish, quick-fry these in batter, with or without vine tips, and sprinkle with Parmesan.

Pumpkins carry male and female flowers on the same plant, and are pollinated by bees. Observation tells gardeners that according to weather and temperature, pumpkins will, in some seasons, produce all male flowers for a long time, whereas ideally female flowers bloom simultaneously. Yet when male and female flowers are in attendance but the weather is dark and cloudy, bees don't leave the hive. Then the gardener should consider hand-pollinating. Every morning pick freshly opened male flowers (slender stem), and rub their pollen onto the stamen of the female flowers (swollen stem base), until the sun and bees return. Also do this when bees become scarce.

Pumpkins benefit from pruning in late summer to help maturing fruit. Cut vines to the nearest maturing pumpkin. Do this carefully, as half-grown pumpkins hide under leaves and you really regret cutting off a one-kilo junior. Now all the nutriments that course through the vines benefit pumpkins that will make the end of the season. If in doubt whether a small pumpkin has time to ripen, consider that even an unripe pumpkin makes good soup if you spice it up with onion, garlic, coriander and cumin.

Maddeningly, when cool weather arrives, the vines go into production again! With autumn on the doorstep, new tips with tiny pumpkins appear everywhere! Have another meal of steamed tips in coconut cream, or toss tips into an end-of-season stir-fry with the last beans, broccoli shoots or whatever is about to be pulled up and some Thai curry paste. Serve with rice – so healthy!

By autumn the vines take up a lot of space, yet they need to dry off before you should cut away the fruit with a short stem. Sometimes, when short of space, I carefully separate vines to clear space between them without disturbing the pumpkins. After filling the space with new compost, I may grow a quick crop of lettuce or radish, even cauliflowers that stay after the pumpkins are harvested. Or I'll pick up the end of a vine and coil it like a rope around its root, being careful to lift each attached pumpkin by hand. There they can sit – on a stone or plank – until they're done.

When the vines are dry, or if rains threaten to rot pumpkin tops, cut fruit with 5 cm of stem and place in a dry place, preferably in full sun, to harden off. In North India and Nepal you see pumpkins drying on roofs, holding down the thatch. If your harvest season is damp, harden them off in a covered porch. Hardy varieties will keep from several months to one year, so that you could be eating the last one when the new crop is getting ready. Occasionally a rat or a mouse will attack a pumpkin with a soft top, but well-hardened pumpkins are usually left alone. Not all varieties harden off like Queensland blues and butternut, so store others in a cool room. Uchiku Kuri and Sweet Dumpling keep well too.

A friend saw one pumpkin vine climb her apple tree in autumn and flower.

'Silly old thing,' she thought and left it to its endeavours. Mid winter, while weeding, she found a perfect pumpkin on a dried-up vine, gently sinking down in the grass.

If you have grown a colourful variety of pumpkins, squashes and courgettes, pile them artistically on a garden table, take a photo and send copies to friends. If they are astonished at your productivity, send them seed! Make yourself a batch of pumpkin pakora. Mix gram (chickpea flour) with your favourite spices and popped mustard seed into a thin batter. Leave standing while cutting pumpkin into thin wedges. Dip into batter and deep-fry until golden. The gardener's reward.

Radicchio (*Cichorium intybus*) Sow in spring and autumn. Companions: beetroot, carrots and onions, which all provide root shade in summer. From Asia Minor. Also see Lettuce. Italian growers achieve amazing red to purple colouration of the leaves by leaving them out in the cold, then digging them up, balancing them above water and covering plants with black plastic. On cold nights all that may happen spontaneously, except for the long curling shoots. Heirloom chicories from Italy are radicchio for the salad bowl. What Italian cooks do not do with radicchio is not worth mentioning. The leaves can be shells for Waldorf salads with olives, or covered with steaming bean soup, served with antipasto, or grilled with olive oil.

Radish (*Raphanus sativus*) Sow in all seasons. Companions: nasturtium (one seed will do!). Probably from the Mediterranean, but had dispersed to Egypt by 2000 BCE, thence to China and Japan. Choose from small round red, long red, red and white, European black, giant daikon or Japanese white, or the bulbous Chinese red radish (I wondered what people did with those). *Sow small ones in spring and most of the year, big ones in autumn.* Salad radishes grow so easily

278

Mooli radishes in flower.

that kids can do it. Big ones need deep soil, or a deep box, tub or wire cylinder.

There may be as many types of radish as there are chillies and with luck, or carelessness, you may create a new variety. Years ago I grew my first daikons alongside round, red table radishes. Plants of both went to seed and the bees must have cross-fertilised the daikons. The next year, using saved daikon seed, I harvested monstrous round red radishes. They were good to eat, some hot, some mild, but there were buckets of them. I saved their seed, calling it 'Lolo radish'.

During a stay in Singapore we lunched at a hawker's stall with our hostess. 'Try carrot cake,' she advised, 'it's my favourite.' We thought of British carrot cake and decided we'd rather have spicy noodles. Days later when looking for tea and cake we saw a sign announcing carrot cake. This time I was in the mood for it. We ordered, sat down and waited. After a while the hawker brought tea and a large plate of steaming something. 'I ordered carrot cake,' I pointed out politely. The cook looked annoyed. 'This is carrot cake,' he said decisively, pointed at the dish and walked away. We took a spoonful each. It was yummy and we began to analyse it. Scrambled egg and spring onions were easy to identify, but it took a sly walk past the hawker's stall to see that the unidentified ingredient was grated daikon, the large white radish. Perhaps it was translated as 'white carrot'.

So I started to make Chinese carrot cake at home with my monstrous round reds. It is a great feed. Asian cookbooks have more recipes, but try rolling grated daikon into patties with gram (chickpea flour) and spices, then deep-frying. Grated daikon gives new flavour to old stir-fry combinations. Try it in soups and use it to thicken sauces. But dig your soil very deep or the daikon will push up and turn green up top. Cut off any green parts before using.

Daikon (Mooli) prefers cooler winter weather. Like all root vegetables it should not grow in manured soil. Deep good earth with compost, topped with straw, is just fine. Tie a red ribbon or wool on the best one and let it flower. The giant plant produces hundreds of white or pinkish-mauve flowers visited by beneficial insects. Flowers turn into fat green pods. You don't need all of these for seed. Pick smaller pods while fresh and green, parboil a few minutes, drain, pack in small jars and cover with vinegar and a spoonful of oil. Large pods take time to fill out before seed is dry. Prune the bush down to what you want to save. To sow seed next year, break open the pods to release the seeds – this may have to be done in a mortar and pestle. Grow mooli sprouts by sowing seeds thickly in a pot. Harvest white stems with two green cotyledons at 6 cm for soups and salads. Or sprout seed like mung beans.

Finally, try grated apple and white daikon salad with a dressing of sweet and sour or spicy plum sauce. Daikon is useful in many dishes, produces bountiful seed, and attracts good insects. Do grow a few.

Rhubarb (*Rheum raphinticum* syn. *Rheum rhabarbarum*) Plant rhyzomes in autumn in well-manured soil topped with compost. Water well when stalks form in spring and summer. From Manchuria and Siberia; traded along the Silk Road in early times. The deep-red or pale-green rhubarb leaves are toxic, but if you have a bug problem in the garden spread rhubarb leaves around affected plants. Only the stems are edible. Red rhubarb has the looks, but the green ones also taste fine.

For a yummy dessert cook rhubarb, sweeten, and beat in cream cheese. Top with mint leaves and a strawberry. Or bake a rhubarb bread and butter pudding.

Rocket (*Eruca sativa*) Sow in late summer. From the Mediterranean. Also arugula or Italian cress, roquette, rughetta. There is also a perennial, wilder rocket (*Diplotaxis tenuifolia*) with long serrated leaves, a self-sowing sprawler with a milder taste. Rocket has moderate water requirements, grows profusely and produces enough lobed leaves to be treated as a tasty stand-by vegetable. The only gardeners complaining about rocket's fecundity are those who restrict its use to decoration on salads or risotto. The plant is easily pulled up where not wanted, appears disease free and bug resistant and loses its bite when cooked, making it suitable for soups and stir-fries.

Rocket is still a wild plant, like sorrel. It grows in the cool season, going to seed when the heat arrives, self-seeding freely so that by autumn you can start picking lush, deep-green leaves. It starts small, barely higher than a lettuce, but can shoot up suddenly, which may have given rise to its English name. One plant produces hundreds of tiny, pale-cream flowers, and sets thousands of seeds in tiny pods. Although rocket can be relied upon to drop enough seed to re-seed itself, pick enough dry pods to store for a thickly sown rocket bed in spring or summer.

Rocket can withstand some warm weather and still provide handfuls of fresh leaves for salads and pastas. During overproduction, make amazing rocket soup served with a dollop of yoghurt. Chickens love a meal of rocket. We all need rocket. It is one of the anti-oxidant green plants that boost our immune system, keeping us young. Let it set seed in at least two places because the flowers attract good insects.

Salad greens Salads start with lettuces, but the young leaves of many other plants can add interest, flavour and more nutrition to the bowl. Some are found in mesclun mixes, but not often in the shop selection. Farmers' market mesclun may be more on the wild side, as they are in France where these salads originated.

Pick young leaves to 8 cm of amaranth, beetroot, bok choy, borage, broadbeans, buckwheat, chervil, chicory, Chinese cabbage, collards, coriander, cress, dandelion, endive, kale, mibuna, mizuna, mustard, nasturtium, peas, rocket, salad burnet, salsify, leaf beet, sorrel, spinach, swede, tatsoy and turnip. Check edible flowers under Flowers in the **List of Common Herbs**. For salad dressings, see page 22–23.

Salsify (*Tragopogon porrifolius*) Sow direct in spring, 10 cm apart. Also known as oyster plant (not the ornamental variety). From the Mediterranean. The tapered white salsify root has a delicate taste when boiled or baked and served with butter sauce. Leaves are edible and good in salads. As salsify grows deeper than carrots, cultivate soil two spades deep. Apply CMC between plants, which can grow to over a metre. See also Scorzonera.

Scarlet runner bean (*Phaseolus coccineus* syn. *P. multiflorus.*) Plant in spring. Strong climber, but appears not to like hot dry weather, although it originated in Mexico's mountains. Mine succeeded up a mountain with cool nights. Stringy green pods up to 30 cm contain pink-spotted black beans. String, then thinly slice beans prior to cooking. It has gorgeous scarlet flowers and is prolific under the right conditions.

Scorzonera (*Schorzonera hispanica*) Sow direct in spring, 10 cm apart. Also known as black salsify. From Southern Europe. The tapered root, of delicate taste, is similar to salsify, though dark brown. Cultivate like salsify. If the top of the root is cut off and replanted it grows a second harvest of smaller spears.

Sorrel (*Rumex acetosa*) Any season. A perennial from the European mountains from Italy to Germany. Also known as French sorrel. A wild plant, usually bought as a potted herb, but prolific enough to be classed a vegetable. Seed is available. Sorrel is related to dock, a giant cousin producing thousands of seeds per single stem, sinking roots to the centre of the earth. Sorrel doesn't do that.

Depending on the soil, sorrel forms a migrating, self-seeding clump or is content with one fifth of a square, which is all you need. Water like lettuce. Not fussy and needs no fertiliser. Come winter the plant goes mostly dormant. I grow mine in a box.

Pick sorrel for a fresh sour flavour in salads. Sorrel soup is a delicacy. Sauté sorrel leaves and blend with stock. Serve with black pepper and a teaspoon of cream. The French also put sorrel into leek and potato soup for *la difference*.

Spinach (*Spinacea oleracea*) Plant in part shade to make it last. Sow in autumn with B&B and compost. Originally from Iran, it is widely grown in the

UK and is something of a gourmet green, taking up much space because it gets so reduced in the (very brief) cooking. A perennial spinach (*Beta vulgaris*) related to leaf beet grows virtually all year round in a clump and tastes truly spinachy. Pick the large light-green leaves. When it goes to seed let the best stalk have its head. Keep picking. Cut the clump down after harvesting seed, spread CMC around it and water well to encourage new growth. Spinach likes nitrogen, so add B&B occasionally. Next season, cultivate new clumps from seedlings.

See also Amaranth in this list. Chinese spinach (*Amaranthus gangeticus*) can grow metres high. Other plants going by the common name of spinach in their places of origin are Ceylonese spinach (*Basella rubra*) on long creepers, New Zealand spinach, also known as the Australian native Warrigal greens. Egyptian spinach, or *malu khia* (*Corchorus olitorius*), is an upright variety for salad and wok and is self-seeding. An Indian spinach named *saag* is popular in Indian cooking. Pick these vegetables from the bottom up as needed.

Young spinach is a delicious accompaniment for young potatoes and baby carrots in butter, spicy tofu with noodles, or in a real spinach quiche. For the baking of spinach loaves, triangles, pies and similar weekend food, grow perennial spinach and gourmet leaf beet. They take little space and shrink less than spinach.

Squash (also see Pumpkin) Sow in spring. Companions: nasturtiums. Squashes come in colours, stripes and shapes from buttons to giants. For the square-metre principle that inspired this book, look at baby squash, also called button squash or patti pan. You see them in baskets at gourmet greengrocers – toy flying saucers with scalloped edges in bright yellow, white, green, or striped. Expensive to buy, yet they grow readily.

Start 2–3 seedlings in toilet rolls under glass. Plant on one quarter when danger of frost is over, definitely before midsummer. They may need support. They benefit by having their roots in a shallow trench or earth saucer to hold the daily watering. Smaller squashes climb on wire netting. Female flowers need to be fertilised through bees or human hand to set fruit. They crop quickly and produce into autumn. At the height of the season you'll pick several each day.

Pick patti pans when 10 cm across or smaller, then cover with water, simmer until a fork goes in, drain and slice in wedges. Serve with mustard, lime pickle or homemade apple and rosemary chutney to retain the delicate texture and taste. Dice leftovers in a garden salad. Particularly good is sliced patti pan grilled or baked and served with garlic, ginger and herb butter.

To pickle patti pan pick fruit small, about 5–6 cm. Parboil until a fork just goes in with resistance. Drain and keep covered in a tea towel. Boil half water, half vinegar with a rosemary twig and bay leaf, remove herbs, and when liquid has cooled, pack them in jars, pour liquid to 2 cm under the lid and close tightly. Leave for a month. Eat all once jar is opened.

For large appetites the Hubbard squash (*Cucurbita maximum*), which is really a pumpkin, comes highly recommended. It keeps several months if stored in a dry, airy place. This ungainly fruit, resembling a retired football, has fine orange flesh and large white seeds that can be roasted, after saving some for replanting. And if you have too many, do what the Shakers did. They peeled, thinly sliced and dried pumpkin flesh, then ground it into flour for pumpkin bread.

Swedes (*Brassica napus*) Frost tolerant, sow spring to autumn. Companions: spread branches of elderberry around swedes to discourage borers. Keep mulch away from roots. With a name like that, swedes just have to be from Europe, no? But there are Chinese, Japanese, English and American swedes. Thet are the least popular home-grown vegetable, possibly because of memories of school dinners, or rationing in the war years. Yet these firm bulbous roots are sweet and juicy when eaten raw and young, or grated in salads. They can taste a bit earthy when cooked, but are great in soups, absorbing other flavours. Like radishes, they grow easily and rapidly, and are well worth cultivating. Fork soil lightly, but don't fertilise if they follow a previous crop of gross feeders. Do not plant after brassicas. Some LS for the seedlings should be enough.

Sweetcorn (*Zea mays*) Companions: beans, potatoes, pumpkins, squashes (see the Aztec Plot). From South America. Many varieties, including popping corn, are available from small seed companies and Garden Organic. Grow only one variety per season if you save your own seed. Maize is more starchy than the juicy corn on the cob and is grown for the processed food industry and as stock feed.

This ancient plant loves warmth and sun. Frost kills it. *Plant late spring and be prepared to sow again if a cold spell hits.* Sweetcorn needs five months to mature. Plant as late as midsummer if your summers are long. Several weeks before planting, dig in manure and an organic nitrogen and phosphorous rich fertiliser. Add lime or wood ash to acidic soil. See the Starchy Staples Plot. Sweetcorn can grow with less water than dark green leafy plants, but the cobs are bigger and better if watered well. Deep mulch around the plants reduces water needs.

Plant sweetcorn in a square and hammer in strong, tall stakes at the corners. Place corn seeds in pairs inside a protector (PVC pipe ring or bottomless yoghurt tub) to prevent night prowlers digging them up. Push in a piece of netting for good measure and don't remove either until the seedling pushes against the net. By then the seed is no longer attractive to prowlers. Apply LS. As stalks grow, wind a rope around the stakes to keep plants upright in the wind. Plant a short variety if you live in a stormy place. Don't plant sweetcorn in a long row, they need close proximity for cross pollination. Once stalks are up and away, apply chicken manure, OF or B&B, mulch with straw and water well.

When the silken tassels on the tops turn brown, the cobs are ripening. Strip down one cob leaf to see whether kernels have filled out and ooze milky sap when pinched. Don't let them stand too long; they get tough and starchy. In America, where corn is a favoured food, it is received knowledge that each kernel is attached to one silken thread in the tassel, so that a thin tassel means part of the cob has not filled out.

To foil rats, make collars under the cobs from large waxed paper plates, cut to the centre to fit around the stems like umbrellas. Staple the cut, then wrap the stem with a cloth strip to hold the plate up.

Freeze ripe cobs. No need to blanch. Peel and pack into the freezer. Eat corn on the cob with butter, after boiling in plenty of water. Barbeque or roast cobs at picnics.

The usefulness of the sweetcorn plant does not end there. Tassels are used in basket weaving or decorative loom weaving, and dried leaves make bread and fruit baskets. Leaves and stalks are used as fodder for domestic livestock, and cobs can also be dried for kindling.

Sweet potato (*Ipomoea batatas*) Plant late spring after frost. Probably from Mexico and now a staple food in the Pacific islands, Africa, and Asia. Sweet potatoes are generally larger than ordinary spuds and not related. The white, yellow, orange or purple tubers are a staple food in Papua New Guinea's highlands

Sweet potato is not related to potatoes. In temperate regions start
it off indoors before planting when soil warms up.

where the soil is volcanic and every afternoon at 4 pm the rain pelts down for
an hour.

Sprout a sweet potato on top of the fridge. Cut off pieces and grow in pots indoors until warm weather allows planting outside. Mulch thickly and keep moist.
As they need five months to develop, you may have to bring them in again later.

Having sprouted a sweet potato, take side stems of no more than 20 cm with
a heel (the bit that attached them to the main stem) and root them in a glass of
water. This way you make more plants to grow outside when summer arrives.

In Papua New Guinea we boiled sweet potato in coconut milk, made by
squeezing grated coconut in warm water, or baked it with bananas in an earth
oven. Following local custom we ate the heart-shaped leaves on tender vines
as a tasty spinach, also steamed in coconut milk. Sweet potatoes are delicious
boiled, baked, roasted or fried. In Hong Kong they are prepared with sugar,

nuts, ginger, nutmeg and cinnamon, and served as a sweet.

Tatsoy (*Brassica rapa* Narinosa Group) Sow late summer or autumn. Companions: bush beans. Favourite Asian greens. A flat, dark green rosette with an endearing flavour. Loves cool weather. Pick outer leaves while it grows on. Lends a distinct flavour to salads and stir-fries. Plant a quarter, because it shrinks like spinach.

Tomato (*Lycopersicon esculentum*) Sow in spring. Plant out after frosts cease. Companions: asparagus, garlic chives, young mustard, parsley, stinging nettle. From Mexico. Tomato plants protect goose-

Tatsoy can be densely planted.

berry shrubs from insect attacks. Organic gardening author Peter Bennett grows a green crop of barley before planting tomatoes to provide phosphorus. When I planted four cherry tomatoes, the one with self-seeded onion, nettle and young cabbage as neighbours grew to more than double the size of the others. The onion also looked better than its mates.

Choose bush or climbing, big beefy fruit or cherry size, in colours from red, orange, pink, and yellow to black Russian. There is even a tiny wild, currant tomato (*Lycopersicon pimpinellifolium*). Look to seed companies or Garden

Organic for heirloom gourmet varieties. Prepare soil with organic matter low in nitrogen, no chicken manure, and a little lime for acidic soil. Tomatoes are one of the most popular crops grown by the British gardener. When the staked plants stand tall, drooping with bright orange globes, the heart swells. There are as many tomato experts as there are tomato growers. The tomato is the food gardener's pride.

Unless you want to make tomato sauce, you need just one good cropper on a stake, or two cherry tomatoes or bush tomatoes, or one of each. *Start seed in toilet rolls under glass in early spring.* Plant out when all risk of frost has gone. Douse with LS. A pot of garlic chives nearby prevents wilt.

Save your own seed from a ripe tomato, wash off the pulp in a sieve, then place seeds on paper towelling 5 cm apart each way. Let this tomato towel dry thoroughly indoors before storing in a paper bag. Next spring, cut off as many seeds on paper as you want plants, lay each one on soil in a toilet roll, sprinkle with 2 mm of fine soil, water daily and raise behind glass. The paper disintegrates.

Freeze cherry tomatoes for use in sauce, juice or stir-fries. Let them ripen to a good red, wash and drop the daily handful in a freezer container. For pasta sauce, sauté garlic and onion, oregano, basil or parsley in plenty of olive oil before adding defrosted or fresh diced tomatoes. Add pepper and salt, but little or no sugar. Use wine vinegar to the degree of acidity you want. Bottle hot. Once a bottle has been opened, keep it in the fridge. Alternatively, make a Balti sauce – see Fenugreek in the **List of Common Herbs**.

Turnip (*Brassica campestris* syn. *Brassica rapa*) Frost tolerant. Plant spring to autumn. If soil is acidic, fork in a little lime three weeks prior to sowing. Companions: spread branches of elderberry around plot to discourage borers.

Described in Alexander the Great's time and probably from the Middle East and Iran. Cultivate like swedes, with whom they shared bottom place in a popularity poll among avid gardeners. They deserve better.

Plant after a well-manured crop, but not brassicas. Apply LS regularly. Choose white, yellow, green or purple top. Roots and edible tops are best when grown quickly and eaten young. Make several sowings during spring and summer and see whether they will grow all year in your microclimate, for turnips are actually biennial. They provide a pithy taste to soups and stews and bulk up other dishes, sliced, cubed or grated raw. Stir-fry the leaves, serve with mustard and soy sauce. Tenzin Palmo, the Buddhist nun who lived 14 years in a Himalayan cave, grew turnips all summer as the roots kept well into winter. Middle Eastern pickled turnip makes a good condiment. Use one part vinegar to two parts water, a quarter part salt, and add sliced beetroot or garlic cloves.

Sow turnips twice a year, in spring and in autumn

Water vegetables There are a number of edible plants that grow in pots sunk into a pond, or in a big water pot – e.g. lotus and water chestnut. Consult catalogues of small seed companies or specialist nurseries.

List of Common Herbs:
How to Grow & Use Them

Herbs included have culinary values and/or properties to ward off pests or promote plant health. Many are listed as companions to vegetables in the **List of Common Vegetables**. Some suggestions for using herbs in the kitchen are included.

Plants carrying *officinalis* as their second botanical name have medicinal properties. To discuss these properties is beyond the scope of this book – see **References** for further information.

General Growing Notes

Wherever it is recommended to grow a herb in a pot, either because its roots are invasive, or to act as a mobile pest controller, make sure to water regularly as pots dry out. Place potted herbs with invasive roots on a tile to prevent roots anchoring the pot. Herbs that like full sun, gritty soil and being well drained are mullein, sage, and thyme. Mints, lemon balm and other soft-leaved herbs prefer part shade and moisture-holding soils, compost, LS or B&B. Woody herbs tolerate poorer, stony soil. Try grouping plants accordingly.

Herbal teas Those herbs indicated as suitable for making herbal tea can be picked fresh for pot or cup, dried and mixed, or dried separately.

Native herbs Many British plants are suited for culinary use. Check with local nurseries or a hedgerow book what will grow where you are, as they may be location-sensitive.

Pest-repelling herbs All aromatic herbs will repel one pest or another. For good health in and around the food garden start collecting artemisia, basil, chamomile, feverfew, various mints, pennyroyal, rue, rosemary, sage, tansy and thyme. Plant these in large pots to be moved among vegetables. Plant some as edgings and hedges.

List of Common Herbs

Artemisia (*Artemisia abrotanum*) Sow spring to autumn or plant cuttings any time. Also known as southernwood. Native to Europe. Repels cabbage moths. Southern wood and Roman wormwood (*A. pontica*) are my favourite *Artemisia* plants for their stimulating fragrance. Southern wood was once used to accompany marriage proposals, perhaps because of its sweet apple scent. It grows ferny upright branches up to a metre. Plant in a mobile pot and in hedges pruned annually with big shears. Not invasive. Use in wardrobes and drawers against moths.

Arugula see Rocket in **List of Common Vegetables**.

Basil (*Ocimum basilicum*) Sweet basil. Sow spring to summer when cold weather has fled. Companions: tomatoes and beans (although the marriage may benefit basil more than the beans). From India, this tropical herb is an annual in non-tropical areas. When basil grows lush in summer you can afford to make pesto for pasta. Pinch out tips to encourage leaf growth. Try sacred basil for Thai cooking, bush basil, purple basil and flavoured basils. Although I'd rather combine basil with lemon juice then use lemon-flavoured basil, I could be wrong. Freeze basil in airtight bags at summer's end before cold nights kill off the plant, or bring it indoors in a big pot.

Basil mint has a good enough basil flavour, combined with the hardiness of mint, although you can lose it in a hard winter.

Bay laurel (*Lauris nobilis*) A slow-growing small tree. In Roman times emperors, senators and victorious generals wore bay-laurel wreaths on their curly heads. Fresh leaves flavour soups and sauces, but must be removed before serving as they are not edible. Use in a bouquet garni with thyme and parsley. Leaves can be dried and stored for years. A little bay goes a long way, so if you're pressed for space, just buy a packet. But for elegance in a big pot, she's your babe.

Borage (*Borago officinalis*) Prefers cool weather, sow late summer to late winter. Companion to strawberries. A soil improver. Originally from Italy. This proud herb with medium size, light-green, hairy leaves faintly tasting of cucumber, bears masses of tiny, star-shaped, bright blue flowers. Young leaves and petals are nutritional additions to salads or steamed vegetables. Mix finely cut leaves with cream cheese or yoghurt. Sprinkle salads with borage flowers, minus the black seeds, or freeze flowers and tiny leaves in ice cubes for summer drinks.

Borage adds delicate beauty to the food garden, and becomes a sight for weary eyes when mixed with marigold or nasturtiums. Grow borage to attract bees to pollinate pumpkin, squash and courgette flowers. Geese love borage and what they eat is good for you too. Let old plants decay – they return more to the soil than they took out. A must-have companion plant.

Caraway (*Carum carvi*) Sow in autumn. Probably from Asia. White to pinkish flowers. The seeds are used in bread and cakes. Added to boiled or fried cabbage they prevent bloat. Use leaves in salads and soups. Caraway attracts beneficial insects. Save an umbel of seed for next year, or let plants self-seed. Grind seeds with coriander for a nuts-and-spices pilaf. A versatile spice.

Catmint (*Nepeta* spp.) From our very own hedgerows. Choose between the large, sprawling, white-flowering catmint, and the elegant grey rosettes with mauve flowers, known as Persian catmint, which makes a delicious tea. They seed themselves and grow rootlings. Good insects visit the flowers and their scent keeps troubles away. Water during dry spells.

Chamomile (*Anthemis nobilis*) Sow in spring and autumn. The wild plant has been widely known in Europe, North Africa and temperate Asia, and many varieties are bound to exist. Keeps surrounding plants healthy, attracts good insects and repels white cabbage moths. Make chamomile tea with the flowers. Recent research confirms that chamomile boosts the immune system and relaxes muscles.

Chervil (*Anthriscus cerefolium*) Sow late summer or early spring. Needs shade in summer. From Asia Minor and the Caucasus. Chervil takes up little space, but needs to be re-sown in most climates. A much underrated small herb for fine food and egg dishes. Make chervil butter for artichokes, carrots, pastas and cheese dishes.

Coleus (*Plectranthus ornatus*) Plant autumn to spring. A deep-green succulent needing little care, it makes a dense patch with purple flower spikes resembling Italian lavender. This is another pest-repellent plant to shift to trouble spots, not for eating. Some say it stinks, others love the pungent odour of crushed coleus leaf. Dogs and cats avoid it. I lost mine in a garden move and have yet to find another plant in a nursery, as seed appears unavailable. Old-fashioned gardens may be a source.

Coriander (*Coriandrum sativum*) Sow thickly in spring in one quarter. Probably from the Mediterranean. Can grow in a mild winter. Fallen seeds germinate any time of the year, so a good location makes it an all-rounder. Prepare soil with B&B and CM. This unmistakable herb with its peculiarly pungent taste is easy to grow. Put a dishwashing rack over the plot until plants are 5 cm, to prevent wild things raiding the seeds. Start picking leaves when stems are 15 cm. Flowers and roots are edible.

Let several plants produce seed from the exquisite white-greyish-pink flowers beloved by dragonflies and lacewings. Or let all the crop set seed, harvest seeds when dried on the stalk, then strip and store. The seeds are a fragrant spice, having lost the pungency of fresh coriander that some writers have called fetid but most people find an absolute nostril-pleaser.

Cress (*Lepidium sativum*) Also known as garden cress. See also Rocket (Italian cress) in **List of Common Vegetables**. Cress seed is sown thickly in shallow trays for mustard-and-cress sandwiches. As cress takes longer to germinate, sow mustard three days later in another tray and hope they synchronise. Although both prefer cooler seasons, by sowing them in trays in a sheltered spot or in the kitchen, you can grow them all year round. Watercress (*Nasturtium officinale*) needs clean running water, which means it is a gourmet food now, and land cress (*Barbarea verna*) also needs lots of water to become edible.

Cumin (*Cuminum cyminum*) *Sow in autumn.* From Egypt and the Mediterranean. White to pink tiny flowers. Seeds are more pungent than caraway. Used in Indonesian and Indian food, curries, pickles, and sauerkraut. Self-seeds and attracts good insects.

Dill (*Anethum graveolens*) Sow in early spring, or in dappled shade in summer. From Western Asia and Southern Europe. Let some go to seed for the yellow umbrellas are beloved by beneficial insects. Use foliage in cooking and baking; use seeds for pickling dill cucumbers, dill vinegar, dill butter and dill bread.

Fennel (green) (*Foeniculum vulgare*) Sow late winter. There is also a bronze fennel. For Florence fennel see **List of Common Vegetables**. From the Mediterranean. Green fennel can seed very easily and after having one in your garden, you may find plantlets of it coming up everywhere.

Grow your own in a garden or orchard, but control the spreading of seed.

Red valerian and bronze fennel in a border adjoining the vegetable plot.

Whether you grow common fennel or the elegant bronze variety – a mystical sight on a misty morn – you have to collect all seed heads as they ripen, or cut the plant down. If fennel seeds spread on the wind, the neighbourhood may be less than pleased with you. Fennel is not easy to dig out after growing to teenage size undetected, but the taste of fresh fennel greens and the seed make it a wonderful herb, and the golden flowers attract thousands of beneficial insects. Do not plant fennel among vegetables as it inhibits other plants. If you have a herb garden, plant fennel with invincible vegetation like mints or crab apple.

Fennel is an ingredient in fine liqueurs. Grind seeds for a new gourmet flavour in plain soups and stews. Fennel bread and hot fennel buns are easy achievements, the seed used whole. Toasted fennel seeds stave off hunger. In India, from luxury hotels to humble roadside eating shacks, toasted fennel seeds are served after meals, to clear the palate and prevent flatulence. Sometimes they are mixed with sugar – delicious, but bad for dental health. One plant provides a year's supply.

Fresh foliage, green or bronze, makes a fragrant bed for arrangements of cheeses, olives, tomatoes and slices of red onion and orange.

Fenugreek (*Trigonella foenum-graecum*) From Western Asia and the Mediterranean. Easy to grow, it stands clay and dry conditions and will germinate in any season, so experiment. Begin by sowing a teaspoon of seed in autumn. Seeds are sprouted for a spicy addition to soups and salads. Shop-bought seed may grow plants but not sprout well, whereas home-grown fenugreek does so readily. Sickle-shaped pods contain the ochre seeds, an ingredient in curry powder.

Back in the 1980s, research led to a widespread belief that fenugreek would be hailed as a promising new crop because of its birth-control potential, but also advocated it as a high-quality stock feed – presumably not on stud farms. It promised to become a forage crop like lucerne – a high-nitrogen, legumous-cover crop, oil producer, sprouting vegetable, and more. The seeds contain oil, high protein, gum and resin and the plant contains high levels of carotenes. Seeds can also be roasted for use as a coffee substitute.

Fenugreek leaves are indispensable in a popular one-pot meal called the Balti – from Baltistan. The Balti originated in Himalayan fields and contains what shepherds have on hand or carry in their bag, supplemented with wild garlic, herbs and vegetables from the fields. You can design your own Balti at home.

Gather up literally any food at hand: vegetables, mushrooms, legumes, or any other protein food. Fry onion, garlic, ginger, and chilli in oil or ghee until golden brown. In a separate pan gently heat spice seeds – coriander, cumin, fennel, mustard, and a few peppercorns – for less than a minute (enough to release aromas) before grinding them up and mixing in some powdered turmeric, cinnamon, cumin or paprika. Stir all into the onion mixture and fry for half a minute. Now add the diced vegetables and mushrooms, the legumes and anything else that harmonises. Diced tomatoes or tomato puree is added with a little water and the pot set to simmer. Meanwhile, cut up fresh fenugreek or coriander leaves to stir into the Balti when the food becomes tender. Sesame seed can be used ground or whole to add a nutty flavour. Serve with chapatties made with atta (whole wheat) flour, or rice.

Balti sauce – widely available in supermarkets – is easily made at home. Just fry in oil the onion and spice mixtures as above, adding a whole bay leaf and a cardamom pod. Add tomatoes or tomato puree with some water and simmer half an hour. Remove the bay leaf and cardamom pod. When cool, puree in a blender and bottle. This sauce keeps in the fridge for a week, or can be frozen. For quick meals use Balti sauce on chunky salads, on parboiled, roasted or barbecued vegetables, or with rice or bread in any form. Add fresh fenugreek leaves.

Grind fenugreek seeds for your own curry or spice blend for chutneys. Use leaves through winter and harvest pods in late spring. Spend an hour podding them in a deep bowl before drying the seeds for storage. They will jump open when bashed in a pillowslip or pounded, but I like podding them and seeing the ochre, squarish seeds lying inside. Having started with 2 tsp of supermarket seed, I now grow enough fenugreek for our needs. Restore a harvested vegetable plot by sowing fenugreek in spring for a fragrant summer harvest.

Feverfew (*Chrysanthemum parthenium*) This medium-size plant with pungent serrated leaves is a garden insecticide. It carries heads of small white daisies with yellow hearts. Growing one in every vegetable plot removes the need for other insecticides, or grow it in a mobile pot. Feverfew self-seeds moderately and is easily transplanted to where it is needed. Root division is recommended as plants may die after a few years.

Flowers So many flowers are edible that it is impossible to list them all. Violets, borage, nasturtium and calendula are used as garnish in restaurants. Elderberry, hibiscus, hollyhock, pumpkin, squash and courgette flowers are fried in batter. The shungiku yellow daisy is added to Chinese dishes. The yellow flowers of broccoli and Asian greens can be eaten with the vegetables. Many herb flowers can be added to salads or made into teas. Mauve garlic-chive flowers are garlic flavoured. Lavender flowers enhance jams and biscuits, as do scented geranium leaves and flowers.

To protect people with allergies, always remove style and stamen from flowers before using. There are books on cooking with flowers. *Avoid flowers of plants with toxic properties unless you know they have been tried and proven safe to eat.*

Geraniums (*Pelargonium* spp.) Plant cuttings any time. Scented geraniums repel pests. Plant a low but tough hedge on the sunny side of the food garden, mixing peppermint, rose, nutmeg, coconut, lemon and whatever other scented geraniums you find in friends' gardens and markets. Apply mulch and water for great results. The flowers are unappreciated miniature beauties. Flowers and young leaves grace gourmet salads. Geraniums will put up with brackish water.

Horseradish (*Armoracia rusticana*) Companion to none, horseradish tends to push out any other plant. An invasive plant that annually conquers neighbouring territory, it is not advisable to grow horseradish in a vegetable garden unless you pound sheet iron half a metre into the ground surrounding it.

An ancient root, probably from Western Asia and Southern Europe. The roots are dug up when the poisonous leaves dry off. All harvesting and cutting of tops has to be done on the plot itself, because any piece of the horseradish plant lost somewhere else will start the formation of a new squadron. The roots should be ground up in a meat mincer. Face mask and goggles are recommended when doing this as the fumes attack nostrils and eyes.

How do I know all this? Because we did grow our own, and after having pickled some in vinegar for a month it made a divine condiment. After we moved we chose to buy little jars from the supermarket, not half as good. Horseradish is the Genghis Khan of the vegetable world. We learned to keep our distance.

Hyssop (*Hyssopus officinalis*) Sow or plant early autumn. From Southern Europe. This was once a favourite culinary herb for plain cooking. It has a strong aroma, deep-purple flowers, and is fairly hardy but can disappear in a prolonged dry spell. Worth re-instating.

Lavender (*Lavendula* spp.) Sow in spring, plant cuttings any time. From Southern Europe. There are English, French, Italian, Canary Island and Australian lavenders all in various shades of purple, pink and white. The old-fashioned lavenders from France and Italy have strong perfume. Lavender is a powerful insect repellent.

Plant a lavender and rosemary hedge on the north side of the vegetable garden as they stand cold winds well. Lavender puts up with brackish water, but likes alkaline soil. Apply lime or place concrete rubble around plants. In a garden where two rows of lavender showed a marked difference in growth and health although planted at the same time, the vigorous row edged a concrete path. Use leaves sparingly in salads, sauces, and jellies. Try apple and lavender jam, or lavender tea with honey and lemon.

Lemon balm (*Melissa officinalis*) Sow in spring or plant root any time. Also known as bee balm. From the eastern Mediterranean. Fresh lemon balm leaves make an invigorating tea. Used sparingly in cooking for a hint of lemon. Beneficial in the food garden as it attracts bees, but place it in a large pot as it can be invasive.

Lemongrass (*Cymbopogon citratus*) Grow from seed in spring and summer, buy a root, or try sticking a bunch from the market in good soil, cutting down the tops to 15 cm. Grows best indoors.

Indispensable for South-East Asian dishes. A tropical plant tough enough to survive a chilly winter if taken indoors to a greenhouse or the kitchen, or protected by a mini hothouse of water-filled plastic bottles.

The base of the stem is used in cooking. The spiky leaves are cut and dried for lemongrass tea. A lemongrass marinade with olive oil, garlic, tamari or soy sauce, and lime or lemon juice will flavour many dishes.

Marigold (*Calendula officinalis*) Sow in spring. Companion plant for all vegetables. The ruffled French marigold is said to be as good a companion plant as calendula due to its strong smell. Calendula does not have a strong smell but works in subtler ways.

Presumably native to Europe, but naturalised in India where it is used to make garlands and votive offerings. Also called English marigold, calendula or pot marigold. Orange or yellow flat daisy-like flowers. Also available are Himalayan marigold (*Tagetes lunulata*) if it likes your climate, and Mexican marigold (*Tagetes minutae*) growing to 2 m with bronze-coloured tufts. Both control eelworms.

The Mexican's leaves look embarrassingly like marijuana and whenever a helicopter or small plane hovered low over my second garden where they grew tall, I expected the drug squad to drop in for a chat. I looked forward to having them smell a leaf as the plant is called 'Stinking Roger' where it was let loose. They never came.

Calendulas adorn every organic garden as they attract good insects, need no maintenance, self-seed, and are easily pulled up when in the way. They are also a welcome addition to the compost. *Calendula flowers (but not the others!) are edible* and endowed with magic health qualities. Pick an uneven number as magic never works with even numbers. Sprinkle petals on salads and gourmet platters and dry for baking cakes.

Marjoram (*Origanum marjorana*) Sow in spring. Also known as sweet marjoram. Native to Portugal. More delicate than oregano. Plant in a large pot and move around to help vegetables. There are several varieties, some sweeter, some more aromatic.

Mint (*Mentha* spp.) Plant in spring. Native to Europe and North Africa, but now a global citizen. I picked mint in the Himalayan Spiti Valley. Grow in pots placed on tiles or planks to prevent roots invading the garden. I saw a food garden periodically left alone, almost entirely overrun with mint. Although the roots go wide rather than deep, it is a big job to clean up the soil as every tiny bit left behind grows again.

Move pots between vegetables, especially the cabbage family. Mints prefer temperate climates. Great as a companion plant in pots to put among crops. There are many varieties. Peppermint repels mice and makes a favourite tea, spearmint spells chewing gum, bunches of eau-de-cologne mint act as room fresheners, Bowle's mint is good in cooking, and ordinary garden mint can probably do all of those. Basil mint grows so fast you can make basil mint pesto. Mint goes with peas, fruit salad, and yoghurt.

Mustard (*Brassica alba* and *Brassica nigra*, white/yellow and black mustard) Plant any season. Companion: tomatoes, protecting them from diseases they are prone to. See also Giant red mustard in the **List of Common Vegetables** and Cress in the **List of Common Herbs**. White mustard was a native of Europe, but mustards are widely cultivated everywhere for seed and oil. Start with a packet of mustard seed from a grocery spice rack. Sow a few mustard seeds between tomatoes, but when they grow taller, cut and leave the stalks lying around.

To recondition a bed of run-down soil where nothing grows well, sow mustard thickly and dig in when flowering. Grow mustard each year in a different plot to keep the garden healthy and free of eelworms.

Use green leaves for salads and stir-fries. Ambitions to make your own mustard? Thickly sow a square metre and let plants set seed. Cut dry pods into a pillowslip without holes. Let them dry a few weeks more, then slap the pillowslip from left to right on a table to separate the seed and chaff. To separate seed, read about winnowing in the chapter **Saving Seed**. As I haven't made mustard yet, you'll have to chase up a recipe.

Nasturtium (*Tropaeolum minus*) Sow in spring. Companion plant to just about anything as it attracts good insects. Also known as *Nasturtium majus* or Indian cress. From Peru. Nasturtiums keep aphids away. Restrain nasturtiums by folding old plants under straw. Pick fat seeds just after petals have fallen and pickle in vinegar for a peppery pseudo-caper. Use leaves and flowers in bean salads.

Oregano (*Origanum vulgare*) Sow or plant in spring. Found in Asia, Europe and North Africa. This is the wilder, more pungent sibling of marjoram. An essential herb in pizza, pasta and bouquet garni. Grow in mobile pots as a companion plant.

Parsley (*Petroselinum crispum*) Biennial. Sow in spring in part shade. Curly-leaved. Native to Europe. Italian parsley is flat-leaved and more frost resistant. Plant parsley in the flower border to aid roses. As parsley is not perennial, collect seed in the first year and dry in a paper bag. Cut stalks right down and mulch for a second year's growth, while sowing seed in autumn for next year when the old root dies.

Parsley aids digestion, which may have given rise to the restaurant custom of decorating meals with a sprig. Unfortunately most people push it aside. Parsley has also been pushed aside as a garnish by dill, cress, fennel, rocket, nasturtiums and other fashionable herbs. Yet parsley remains an important food which is said to lower cholesterol. Grow plenty of parsley for tabouli, the Middle Eastern dish of chopped parsley, onion and soaked bulgur wheat with lemon juice, olive oil and pepper. If you can't eat wheat, use crushed buckwheat or coarse polenta. Tabouli makes a great meal with hot beans, just as a bean dish improves with parsley. In some countries, flat-leaved parsley roots are eaten as a vegetable.

Rocket see **List of Common Vegetables**

Rosemary (*Rosmarinus officinalis*) Sow spring or plant cuttings any time. From the Mediterranean. These aromatic evergreen shrubs should grace every garden. They are water-wise, low maintenance, and provide the greatest amount of herb for the least effort. Bees love the blue flowers. Add rosemary to a bouquet garni for gourmet leaf beet. Pasta improves with finely chopped rosemary. Homemade drinks of lemon or other fruits benefit by a rosemary infusion. Apple and rosemary chutney goes with patti pan, rice and beans. Rosemary tea helps the memory – mix the rosemary with purple sage. A rosemary rinse makes your hair shine. The list of rosemary's benefits goes on and you simply should find space for *Rosmarinus officinalis* and then take cuttings. Cultivars have brighter flowers, but you want strongly fragrant foliage. Plant a rosemary hedge along the western boundary of the food plot.

Sage (*Salvia officinalis*) Sow spring or autumn. From the Mediterranean. Repels cabbage moths and carrot fly. Although there are many sages with flowers ranging from white and pink to night blue, *Salvia officinalis* is the culinary herb. Use sparingly in cheese and breads. Sage crispy fried in olive oil is good on pasta. Medicinally, sage makes a throat gargle and a tea to reduce fever. Pineapple sage (*Salvia rutilans*) is a great tea herb. Purple sage tea is said to aid the memory in old age.

Salad burnet (*Poterium sanguisorba*) Sow in spring. From Europe. Also known as lesser burnet. A pretty, upright rosette of fine stems, with serrated tender leaves tasting of cucumber. Adds beauty to the herb plot. Sprinkle leaves on salads, or in *raita*, the Indian cucumber and yoghurt dish.

Shungiku (*Chrysanthemum coronarium* var. *spatiosum*) Sow in autumn. From East Asia. The leaves and flat yellow flowers are used sparingly in Asian cooking to add a distinct aroma and taste. Collect seed heads to sow annually.

Stinging nettle (*Urtica urens*) Sow spring to autumn. Companion plant for many crops to improve soil, compost and you. Found in Asia, Europe, South Africa, South America and Australia. Stinging nettle in the garden is a blessing.

Eat young nettles as spinach – they taste good and the sting disappears when cooked. Make velvety nettle tea from fresh tops or dried leaves. Cook nettles like sorrel soup, blended and with a dollop of yoghurt. Before supermarkets and greengrocers, Europeans ate stinging nettle in many dishes, as it is a nourishing, wildly profuse vegetable.

Let only one nettle set seed. Although plants are easily pulled up where not wanted, neighbours may complain if seeds blow across. *To contain the seed, tie a paper bag over the top.* In compost and liquid manure, nettle is a prime ingredient.

Sunflower (*Helianthus annuus*) A native of Peru. Not so much a herb as a food plant for its seed and oil. Sunflowers make a great addition to food gardens as background and as windbreaks. Use them as live stakes for climbing beans. Handsome varieties come in golden yellow, brown and caramel. Harvest seed heads, dry indoors, then lay them out one by one for birds during the hungry season on a rat-proof board hung from a tree branch.

Tansy (*Tanacetum vulgare*) Sow spring to autumn, plant rootlings any time. Companion for fruit trees as an under-planting against various diseases. From Europe. Not recommended for cooking or baking nowadays, as the plant is somewhat toxic (though 19th-century cooks flavoured biscuits and cakes with tansy). Both flat-leaved and curly-leaved tansy carry clusters of golden buttons. The roots are invasive, but easily pulled up.

Tarragon (*Artemisia dracunculus*) Sow in spring. From the Mediterranean. French tarragon is lauded as the only one to use for cooking. There is also German tarragon. Mexican tarragon is a strong grower with a fresh aniseed taste – to be used by the branch rather than the single leaf. The Russian variety is called 'false tarragon', even though it is an *Artemisia* and has that artemian whiff about it. They're all good, just different.

Thyme (*Thymus vulgaris*) Sow spring or autumn. Companion to many vegetables. Repels cabbage moths. Known as 'mother of thyme' as all varieties sprung from this common thyme of Southern Europe and then conquered the globe. It clings to Himalayan mountain sides in a blaze of mauve flowers. Essential when cooking with tomatoes, and in a bouquet garni. Use lemon thyme in pasta and caraway thyme in Indian cooking. Serve garlic and thyme butter with courgette. Search markets and nurseries for flavoured thymes or settle for one in a mobile pot, guarding a vegetable plot.

Parsley, tansy, thyme and rosemary keep struggling young fruit trees healthy.

Wild celery (*Apium graveolens*) Sow in autumn. From Europe, but known in Asia as Chinese celery. Prefers cool seasons, setting seed in summer. Collect seed and prune stalks to the ground for new growth. May only last a few seasons, therefore sow again next autumn. It is a versatile clumping plant providing aromatic leaves for soups, stews, stir-fries, omelettes and sandwiches. The stalks are not tender enough to eat, but the leaves add celery flavour in cooking. Root divisions grow readily and make a nice present in a generous pot. If growing real celery seems too much trouble, grow wild celery.

Wormwood (*Artemisia absinthium*) Sow spring or autumn, plant cuttings when pruning after flowering. Native to the Northern Hemisphere. The sacred bitter herb of China used to ward off evil. A South-East Asian artemisia is important medicinally against malaria. *Artemisia annua* is the wormwood that ekes out a living along farm fences, washed only by rain, with never a decent haircut. Wormwood makes a powerful pest-repellent hedge for an organic garden, but plant it several metres away from vegetables as it tends to retard other plants. After flowering, cut it back by half for vigorous growth. The silver leaves are gorgeous in bouquets. Wormwood keeps chickens lice-free when planted near the coop.

Yarrow (*Achillea millefolium*) Sow spring to autumn, plant rootlings anytime. From Europe. White and cyclamen-pink yarrows are hardy. Cultivars come in pastels. Yarrow roots are invasive: a 1 x 1 m patch may result from one plant. This is a very good herb in the orchard, working as a pest repellent and growth promoter for other plants, especially apple trees. It is also an excellent compost starter. Yarrow tea, made with flowers and leaves, soothes the spirit when you are stressed or fatigued, or just had a hard day in the garden.

List of Easy-Care Fruit Trees & Berries:
How to Grow & Use Them

Read the chapter **Easy-Care Fruit Trees** in Part Three before making your selection from the list that follows on page 314. Trees marked with an asterisk (*) are super easy to grow.

General Growing Notes

Cultivation Fruit trees need care in their first three years while making deep roots. After that they continue to need manure and/or fertiliser with mulch in spring and lime and deep mulch in autumn. If you grow dense herbs under a fruit tree little mulch is needed, but it does need food to produce well. Many trees can survive without watering after the first summer, or just three deep waterings per summer, depending on your climate.

Disease prevention When planting new trees, consider heritage varieties, as many are more disease resistant and have better nutritional properties – see **Useful Addresses** and organic gardening magazines. By spraying fruit trees with liquid seaweed early in spring and the root area in autumn, you may prevent diseases. Grow companion herbs under fruit trees (see **List of Common Herbs**) to prevent infestations and attract predators. Mix borage, comfrey, fenugreek and feverfew with recommended companion plants for each fruit tree. Nettle is very beneficial. With chickens in the orchard, only deep-rooted herbs like yarrow, lemon balm and tansy survive and must be protected while establishing themselves.

Dwarf fruit trees Ask your nursery. Another space saver is a 'fruit salad tree' with a number of stone fruit, pear or apple varieties grafted onto the same trunk.

Eradicating weeds and grasses Always keep soil around young trunks weed-free. Chicken tractors are small A-frame cages, half timber, half wire netting, housing a few chickens to dig up grass and weeds. Move around the tree as needed. Chickens are perfectionists. Without chickens, consider a fence-to-fence herbal carpet after eradicating competing weeds and lawn grasses by other means. Alternatively, spread large flattened cardboard boxes in autumn – ask the electrical goods store. Or spread weedmat through three summer months.

Espaliered orchard Save space, increase production, and keep fruit within reach by espaliering fruit trees. Apart from the common fruit trees, I have espaliered mulberry, fig and quince. Citrus varieties will only thrive and bear fruit indoors.

Grafting With permission, cut buds from a neighbour's different fruit tree and graft onto yours, pome to pome and stone fruit to stone fruit, in mid autumn. If this interests you, borrow a library book on budding and grafting, as it is easy to learn.

Horse manure See caution regarding horse manure on Abbreviations page.

If you have little time Plant the fruit you love best in the first year, your second love in the second year, and so on. It is better to prepare an excellent hole for one tree, look after it, see it flourish and be proud, than to bang in six to see them flounder for lack of attention and feel sorry. Most trees take a few years to fruit, but berries produce in their first summer, black mulberry and plum in the second.

Planting note Fruit trees are best planted in early winter when dormant, unless otherwise indicated by the supplier. *Citrus trees should be kept indoors.*

Dig a hole much larger than the root ball. Fill hole with water two days before planting. If the water drains away it's a good spot. Put a spadeful of rubble, gravel or broken tiles and clay pots in the bottom to prevent wet roots. Spade in compost mixed with old manure. Cover well with more compost for the root ball to sit on. Place the tree so that the graft (the knobbly bit above the root ball) is well above ground level. Fill in with good soil. Mulch and top dress with B&B after planting and water well to settle roots. Do a foot-stomping dance around the trunk to compact the earth. If the level sinks and forms a saucer, level this out with mulch, keeping the graft above it.

Pruning note To prune espaliered trees see chapter on **Easy-Care Fruit Trees** in Part Three. For freestanding trees keep pruning simple:

1) Prune when trees are dormant. Shaping is your choice.
2) Prune away dead wood and crossing branches.
3) Prune trees to keep fruit within reach.
4) Prune away excess growth in summer.

Seedling trees Seedlings of apple, quince, plum and nectarine may bear good fruit, sometimes better suited to cooking or juicing. Such trees show strong growth and disease resistance. Worth trying with any seed if you have space. I've had excellent fruit from seedling nectarines, plums and apples.

Apple* (*Malus x domestica*) Companions: yarrow, chives, apple mint, self heal (*Prunella vulgaris*) and nasturtium. All apples originate from *Malus sieversii* in the Tien Shan, the Heavenly Mountains range in Central Asia, where they survive in the wild. They love cool nights.

Apple trees are amazing. They can grow without being watered or otherwise tended. Yet young nursery-raised trees may die in a bad year. We inherited three apple trees in acidic, non-wetting soil which blossomed and annually produced good fruit. We have newly inherited a cathedral of an old apple tree that has survived on rain. Its fruit is only fit for pies, yet its presence and shade are immense. I have had good fruit from a sucker, grown from an excellent old tree that produced good eating fruit. I've also nurtured self-seeded trees whose apples were good enough for chutney, apple stew and sauces for the freezer. Apple trees love growing in hedgerows where their roots are protected by herbs and shrubs.

Brown rot and codling moth are the apple tree's enemies. See **An A–Z of Pests & Problems** in Part Three.

Apples from a sucker off an old-fashioned nameless apple tree. They were good to eat and to cook.

Apricot* (*Prunus armeniaca* syn. *Armeniaca vulgaris*) Companions: feverfew and garlic – keep cutting garlic tops for best results. Also chives, comfrey, tansy and yarrow. From China, cultivated worldwide, and a main crop in Pakistan's Hunza Valley. Given their exotic image, they are not the tender treasures you may imagine. Apricot trees can be espaliered. Taste ripe home-grown apricots straight from the tree! Apricots can be dried, preserved, stewed, frozen or devoured instantly. Team with cream cheese, cinnamon or polenta, one at a time.

Berries* The brambles: raspberries (*Rubus idaeus*), blackberries (*Rubus ulmifolius*), boysenberries (*Rubus* spp.), loganberries (*Rubus loganobaccus*), and youngberries (*Rubus* spp.). Other brambles are tay berries and wineberries. See below for blueberries, gooseberries and currants. Companions: try borage mixed with noninvasive herbs without overpowering aromas, e.g. chamomile, dill and nasturtiums.

Northern Hemisphere natives. Take cuttings in autumn or spring. Should these fail, take cuttings in the optimum growing season in your area. Soak cuttings in water with honey for one hour, then plant immediately, providing water and shade until rooted. Cuttings must never dry out. Thornless blackberry and youngberry are available.

Having grown all of the above, the youngberry proved to produce not only large, delicious and firm fruit, but was the only one to survive a prolonged dry spell in full sun for several weeks. The canes sprouted back to see another summer. *All berries tolerate part-shade.* Imitate their natural environments with a mulch of old leaves, or twiggy compost with straw. Check the pH of the soil – they don't do well under 6 or over 7, and 6.5 is just right.

Blackberries are best grown on a wire trellis, preventing the formation of wild, rambling thickets and allowing access from two sides to pick fruit.

An espalier wire arrangement between droppers or posts will do. Position the trellis north-south to make the most of the sun. Plant cuttings or canes under the wire and, when they lengthen, gather them up (with gloves), and twist and wind them around droppers, posts and wires to tie up. Tying them in a fan shape gives the best crop. If you only plant 3–5 canes, place them around a wire tower (see **Hardware in the Food Garden**).

Improve soil with CMC to retain the moisture essential for all berries. In the wild they thrive in dark muddy glens. After harvesting, prune out the canes that bore fruit, as next season's fruit appears on new canes. Add young leaves of raspberry and blackberry to any tea for fragrance and health.

Blueberries* (*Vaccinium* spp.) From North America. A thornless bush. They like it cool and stand half shade, although full sun increases production. Wind protection is important. Grow blueberries if you have acid soil and can make it drain well by digging in loads of organic matter. Lime in the soil will inhibit blueberries. They must never dry out so mulch thickly with pine needles, sawdust, leaves or shredded branches. Ask your nursery to provide two different plants for better pollination. Be prepared to fuss over blueberry bushes like a brown bear would. Be prepared to wait for first fruit.

Cape gooseberry* (*Physalis*) As these are not hardy in the UK, many treat them as an annual, which is such a shame. Lift before the first frosts, potting into a large container and over wintering in a frost free greenhouse or similar; of course due to their tenderness they are a perfect subject for container growing.

Currants* Black (*Ribes nigrum*), red (*Ribes rubrum*), white (*Ribes sativum*). Companions: try tomato plants and the same herbaceous mix as for berries, although they can go it alone. Northern Hemisphere natives. Red and white currants are small shrubs; the black currant grows taller.

The red currant produces fruit on old wood, just to be different. Even in my Uncle Wim's garden in overcast Holland the currant bushes grew in the shade of a massive walnut tree, where light was dappled. They like it cool and need a winter and regular waterings. Uncle Wim applied plenty of old poultry manure.

Black currants grew wild on the sandy heights of the heather in full sun between his village and ours. They grow fruit on last year's wood, so take care in pruning. They can be espaliered. As children we filled small buckets while stuffing ourselves with this curiously winy-tasting fruit. Mostly, black currants were made into jam, liqueur and jenever. Add the young leaves from currant bushes to herbal or black tea for fragrance and health.

Elderberry* (*Sambucus nigra*) Sow spring or plant cuttings in autumn or any time. A tall shrub of the honeysuckle family from England, but there are North American (*S. caerulea*), Canadian (*S. canadiensis*) and Australian species (*S. australasica* and *S. gaudichaudiana*). I have only grown a self-pollinating elderberry.

The fruit should not be eaten raw (see recipes below). *Leaves, bark, roots and seeds are toxic, yet the elderberry provides food and drink, as well as pesticide.* The tall shrub grows fast if treated with CMC and watered when stressed. Plant 50 cm apart for a dense windbreak. Leave some gaps to prevent turbulence.

Elderberry exudes a pest-repellent substance due to its glycoside content. Cut branches for vegetable seedlings under attack. In autumn, prune hard after fruiting. In spring the shrub will be laden with umbels of creamy flowers which precede the black elderberries that can be used to make the famed elderberry wine, jam or pies (remove the seeds).

Before berries form, pick trays of elder flowers to dry and store. Fragrant elderflower tea acts as a decongestant. Finely chopped flowers can bulk up scones, cakes and biscuits. Make cordial by boiling flowers in water with sugar. Keep in the fridge and dilute for a refreshing drink. Adding 50 g citric acid per 1.5 L of water and a few sliced lemons makes it keep longer. You can also make an elderflower and gooseberry preserve, as well as elderflower fritters in a batter of flour and egg. Any berries I leave are eaten by birds who didn't read these notes. Despite the toxicity of the plant and some of its parts, elderberries have been used for centuries, cooked or processed. Elderberry varieties may play important pest-control functions in future food gardens.

Elderberry flowers make a distinctive cordial. Elder branches and leaves can be spread where there is a pest problem.

Fig* (*Ficus carica*) The edible fig we know is one of the oldest cultivated fruits from Iran, Turkey and Afghanistan. It starts as a multiple-branched shrub that grows into a medium-size tree that can be espaliered. Fresh figs are purple ecstasy. Even fig haters eat fig jam or fig tart. Give the tree a good start with manure and mulch, water when the fruit is forming, but apart from that do not fuss. I picked five figs from a tiny fig tree, then espaliered and manured it and the next year picked almost 100 figs. Restrict its roots.

Guava The favoured guavas for the UK are the Chilean guava (*Myrtus Ugni*) and the Pineapple guava (*Acca sellowiana*), both evergreen, outdoor plants that occasionally give small fruits; unlike the Central American guava (Psidium guajava) which is tender in the UK, but can be grown in a heated greenhouse

Figs bigger than a pea need to come off the plant in late autumn.

or conservatory.

Gooseberry* (*Ribes grossularia* syn. *Ribes uva-crispa*) Companions: tomato plants, chives. These low-growing, thorny shrubs originate in Europe. An infusion of chives is supposed to stop gooseberry mildew, so try growing chives as companions. Oak-leaf mulch also helps. My Uncle Wim grew them on the sunny side of his walnut tree and we only ever picked them fully ripe with a red blush, sweet and succulent. Fork in poultry manure and mulch heavily. If you want a row of gooseberry bushes, layer low branches. Scoop out soil, bend a branch into the trench, cover with soil and pin down with a bent wire. When it has grown roots, cut it from the mother plant and plant it independently. Make sure you have access on both sides.

Grape* (*Vitus vinifer*) Companions: floribunda bush roses. I have found grapes to be about the easiest fruit to grow, but that may be due our soil and climate conditions. An open position where the wind blows through, even a western wall, have produced grapes for me on mere cuttings from friends' grapevines and without mildew attacks. But in my third garden half a dozen bare-rooted vines from a nursery all died in acidic soil with brackish dam water.

Grape cuttings are inexpensive and if they take they bear in the second year. Cuttings should be 40 cm and have two buds. Dry dark grapes for raisins, light grapes for sultanas and if you can get it, the small seedless black grape is suitable for drying as currants.

They seem to tolerate drought, unpromising soil and harsh pruning, even neglect. To grow a vine on a pergola let the main stem grow up and spread branches across the structure. Prune bush vines back to two buds after harvest. In spring make dolmades, young vine leaves stuffed with rice.

Grapes on the vine in late autumn, ready for harvesting.

Loquat (*Eriobotrya japonica*) Drought tolerant. Bantam chickens love roosting between the broad leaves, fertilising the soil underneath. From the Himalayas, but will grow in subtropical and Mediterranean climates, tolerating moderate neglect. Often starts bearing in the second year. Prune after harvest to keep fruit at reaching height. Each year the crop will increase, ripening gradually over two months.

If space is a problem, prune loquats to stay small. Unpruned they become grand, shady trees. As urban gardens become smaller, loquat trees disappear. Yet we should not lose such a long-bearing tree. Plant it, prune it and rave about fresh loquats, the first fruit of spring, and the ideal fruit for an alfresco dessert. Hardy in the UK, evergreen, but may need winter protection to fruit well. Eat loquats skin and all or peel. Serve with sour cream or yoghurt dip with a drizzle of honey. Then pop a few big seeds in pots to grow loquat trees for friends. Loquats are seldom available in shops as they bruise readily. They contain betacarotene.

Mulberry* (*Morus nigra*) The black mulberry. From Iran (Persia) or Africa. Given its head, the mulberry tree forms a beautiful spreading canopy, loved by children. But with increasing urbanisation this big tree is also heading for extinction in our cities. Only the black mulberry is worth growing for fruit. It bears in its second year. The white mulberry produces insignificant fruit, while another variety is grown for its leaves to feed silkworms doomed to die for the luxury rag trade.

Although I have espaliered mulberry, I'd much prefer to grow the untamed tree. My first mulberry tree still sits on its stony hillside 20 years after planting, and although it has not received any attention and is not very big, the new owners say it bears fruit reliably.

Nectarine (*Prunus persica* var. *nectarina*) Companions: chives, garlic and tansy (keep garlic cut to release its odour). The name is derived from nectar, the food for the gods that the Romans didn't have. Nectarines are an exhilarating fruit. They are related to peaches, but are smooth-skinned and have a more decisive flavour. Small tree, easy to grow, and can be espaliered. A seedling grown from a nectarine stone can bear fruit true to type. Bury a few stones in compost in an area where you won't need to transplant them. When birds start pecking the still unripe fruit, it is excellent for jam making. Protect with netting to ripen fruit. The bane of nectarine growers is leaf curl affliction in early spring. If neglected it can reduce the crop considerably because the tree feels sick, unable to function through its leaves. See **An A–Z of Pests & Problems**.

Olive (*Olea europaea*) Companions: mixed herbs to imitate meadows. Olives grow on stony hillsides in Mediterranean countries. Drought tolerant. Another tree that has survived, despite neglect, for some 10,000 years. Their leathery leaves don't wither in the blazing sun. The fruit is tough and bitter and needs pickling, or processing into olive oil.

My olive tree literally fell from the back of a truck. It lay on the road in its black tube, the top broken. When planted, it grew. We moved house and it moved with us and grew. Then a lost cow broke it in half and it regrew!

Italian urban gardeners are known to prune their single olive tree to within an inch of its life each winter, for large crops to pickle. Olive trees in Britain have been know to grown small crops and may grow accustomed to our climate, but in general they are grown for their distinctive leaves, as an ornamental tree only. Ask your Mediterranean greengrocer to get you a case of black olives in autumn.

Papaya (*Carica papaya*) Sow late spring and protect into winter. Presumably from Mexico. Although a tropical fruit, I include this to encourage experimentation. If you don't live in Scotland or a frost pocket in a valley and have a south-facing sun trap or greenhouse, you can try growing tropical fruit. I grew a banana plant in a south-facing tank yard, heat bouncing off iron tanks and shed, keeping out winds and ameliorating night temperatures.

Papaya is the easiest tropical fruit to germinate. The *New Oxford Book of Food Plants* calls it a 'tree-like herb', which shakes up our perceptions about what a herb is. The seeds are chewed by travellers with dysentery, and the pulp prevents fresh wounds from becoming infected. This 'herb' shapes up to be a tree of 2–10 m, depending on circumstances. In Papua New Guinea's highlands, where nights can be cold, papaya trees grow simply from discarded pips.

There are male and female trees, but also self-pollinating ones. Hoping for the latter I bought a papaya at the market, scooped out the seed, and within weeks had 50 seedlings. I potted some to give away as pot plants with attractive foliage, but kept some in the greenhouse on a mountain side. One produced a reasonable-size fruit.

The mountain papaya (*Carica candamarcensis*) comes from the Andes. When sowing seed in the 1980s I found it was not prolific in germination and I ended up with just one viable tree: a non-fruiting male. But it was a beauty – surviving on a mountain site and backed by native forest bathing in sun all day. Though it germinates easily, the plant needs winter protection and may not be hardy out of doors in all of the UK.

Passionfruit (*Passiflora edulis*) This vine from Brazil is not long-lived. Many legends of success and failure exist about this plant. I grew my first passionfruit in a square foot of soil surrounded by concrete near an east-facing backdoor. It stormed up the wall, spread several metres along the gutter in a glory of bright green leaves, produced a bucket of sweet purple fruit and died. Rather like a Brazilian carnival. Next, I planted passionfruit facing south with organic material, nitrogen and a trellis. Three times. None survived.

If you love passionfruit, ask your local nursery for the hardiest variety and growing advice. Once established, the plant needs a couple of handfuls of B&B in spring and likes sulphate of potash, something I was ignorant of when I lost my passion for growing passionfruit.

Peach* (*Prunus persica* syn. *Persica vulgaris*) Companions: chives, garlic and tansy (cut garlic tops during fruiting to release odour). See **A–Z of Pests & Problems** for treatments of leaf curl. Originally from western Tibet, where we bought some small but sweet fruit from a valley farmer, and the Tien Shan mountains of Central Asia. Peaches reached Europe via Iran (Persia).

Peaches can be dried, preserved, stewed, frozen or eaten daily as they ripen. Trees are small and can be espaliered. A sun-warmed peach straight off the tree is a treat. If they like your place, they crop impressively. If not, they're still a thrill. White or yellow flesh, find your preference at the greengrocer.

Pear* (*Pyrus communus*) Companions: catmint, rosemary, sage and yarrow. From the Tien Shan mountains. Hardy and prolific. They like a cold winter, but seem to take heat better than apples. A full-grown pear tree spreads a shady canopy. If space is limited, prune your pear each winter to manageable size, or espalier. They start bearing within a few years if there is another pear tree in the neighbourhood for pollination. If not, buy the self-pollinating Williams pear for its big juicy fruit and prolific crop. For sawfly on the leaves see **A–Z of Pests & Problems**.

Harvest from a yet to be espaliered tree.

Plum* (*Prunus* spp.) Companions: chives and tansy. From Europe and Japan. Many varieties, hybrids and colours. Carefree trees, hardy, prolific, fast growing. Apply dolomite. One early and one late plum may overwhelm a family, so get one special plum instead.

325

Greengage is special but bears only every other year and needs another plum for pollination. Do you want a firm or juicy plum, to eat, dry or preserve? For drying choose *Prune D'Agen*.

Pomegranate (*Punica granatum*) From Iran. Often associated with much warmer climates, pomegranate 'Provence' is surprisingly hardy in the UK, tolerating temperatures down to –15°C (5°F) when grown in a sheltered position. In particularly cold areas, it can be grown in a large container and moved to a warmer position during the winter months. A tree-size shrub with deep-orange flowers and red fruit, although dwarf varieties do exist. Seeds are surrounded by juice, which has been rediscovered as a health drink. Children love pomegranates. Serve whole for dessert at a garden lunch.

Quince* (*Cydonia vulgaris*) Companion: yarrow. The shell-pink petals of quince flowers in velvet leafy rosettes herald spring. One of the earliest fruit trees to blossom, but the last fruit to ripen. Autumn's fragrant harvest suggests quince paste and jelly, preserves, salads, desserts and perfumed juice. They need cooking, but even the cooking water is divine! Leave one in the fruit bowl to scent the whole kitchen.

The hard pomes will keep in a cool place for several months while you eat your way through stewed quinces and quince crumbles. To peel a quince, lop off top and bottom, stand fruit upright on a board and with a sharp knife shave the skin off all around. Then chop pieces off the fruit until reaching the core. Much easier than trying to quarter them, as the core is stubborn.

Strawberries* (*Fragaria* spp.) Sow from seed in spring or plant runners in late autumn. Companions: borage, bush beans, lettuce and spinach. The cabbage family is not a favourite of strawberries and the Solanaceae family (pota-

Espaliered quince laden with ripe fruit in its fourth year.

toes, tomatoes etc.) should be kept at a distance. Wild ancestors such as alpine strawberries do best in cool to cold areas and wild strawberries are native to all Northern Hemisphere woodlands. Once I was smitten by the sight of North American alpine strawberries flowering in May along Mount Washington's icy mountain streams.

The appearance of cultivated strawberries is a story of wild reluctance, chance encounters and a persistent English horticulturist. This delicious little fruit can be found as far north as Finland and as far south as Australia, fruiting from spring to autumn. Buy certified virus-free roots and prepare your plot generously with CMC and B&B. Slightly raise rows or hillocks for essential drainage and mulch with clean straw mixed with pine, spruce or other needles.

Adjust soil to a pH of 6 – if acidic add lime. Apply LS regularly for disease resistance.

In autumn the plants throw out runners to take root in nearby soil. Prepare a new plot. Cut and transplant runners from autumn to spring, manuring and mulching as above. Clean up the old bed by removing any dead leaves. *To prevent disease build-up, don't keep any bed longer than three years.* Protect with netting or a cage and pick off slugs and snails. Water at the roots to avoid fungal problems. Strewth! Yet they are easy to grow.

Strawberries are loved by all wildlife. In my forest garden mice dropped by for dessert, as did some two-legged ones! We never had better-tasting strawberries than those reared near the forest's edge, mulched with rotting fallen apple pulp. Visitors would rave at tasting a long-lost memory. With strawberries it's the plant food that determines the taste.

White strawberries are also available. They taste good and reputedly don't attract birds, but millipedes are colour blind.

Tomatillo* (*Physalis ixocarpa*) *Solanum* genus. Sow in spring. Companions: same as for tomatoes (asparagus, garlic chives, young mustard, parsley, stinging nettle). Also known as jamberry. It is the cousin of Cape gooseberry. From Mexico. Tolerates dry site. Grown like tomatoes, they produce small yellow or purple fruit in papery lanterns. Used for salsa with garlic and onions, and in sauces and salads.

Enjoy your meals!

This productive tomatillo was allowed to sprawl, keeping the weeds down.

Notes

1. J. Chatto and W.L. Martin, *A kitchen in Corfu*, Weidenfeld and Nicholson, London, 1993, p. 29.
2. *Seed Savers' Network newsletter*, Seed Savers' Network, No. 37, Spring 2004.
3. Interview with Terry Lane, ABC Radio National, 23 July 2005.
4. Julian Cribb, 'Perspective', ABC Radio National, 5 March 2007.
5. Colin Tudge, *The time before history*, Scribner, New York, 1996, p. 278.
6. *Encyclopaedia of lands and people*, Kingfisher, London, 1999.
7. DEFRA, *The expert committee on Pesticide Residues in Food (PRiF) Annual Report,* 9 September 2013
8. *Permaculture International Journal*, No. 74, March–May 2000.
9. Jeanette Fitzsimons, 'The state of the planet' in *South Australia newsletter: The Greens*, Autumn 2005.
10. *Round-table 2004 report*, Environment Protection Authority, Adelaide, 2004.
11. *Organic gardener*, November–December 2007, Australian Broadcasting Corporation, Ultimo, New South Wales, pp. 11–12. Also *Age*, Melbourne, 5 December 2007.
12. Chris Alenson, 'The use of nitrogenous fertilisers and their effects on the health of plants, animals and humans' in Barraclough's Backyard, *Green Connections*, Issue 31, September–October 2000.
13. Organic Growers of Australia, http://www.organicgrowers.org.au.
14. *Organic gardener*, FPC Magazines, New South Wales, Summer 2000, p. 59.
15. Hogan Gleeson, *Organic Gardener*, FPC Magazines, New South Wales, Spring 2002, p. 47.
16. Charles Dowding, *Organic Gardening: The natural no-dig way*, Green Books, UK, 2013.
17. Ernest L. Bergman, 'Vegetable farming in China' in *Oriental herbs and vegetables: a handbook*, Plants and Gardens Series, Brooklyn Botanical Garden Record, Vol. 39, No. 2, Summer 1983, pp. 37–38.
18. 'Bush Telegraph', ABC Radio National, 22 November 2004.
19. Felicity Lawrence, *Not on the label*, Penguin Books, London, 2004, p. 61.
20. See websites http://www.grain.org and http://www.fao.org/ag/cgrfa/itpgr.htm.

21. Ibid.

22. See website http://www.geneethics.org.

23. See website http://www.banterminator.org.

24. *Seed Savers' Network newsletter*, No. 37, Seed Savers' Network, Spring 2004; *Seed Savers' Network newsletter*, No. 39, Seed Savers' Network, Spring 2005.

25. Colin Tudge, *So shall we reap: what's wrong with the world's food – and how to fix it*, Penguin Books, London, 2004, p. 46.

26. Alan D. Cook, 'Supermarket on a stalk' in *Oriental herbs and vegetables: a handbook*, Plants and Gardens Series, Brooklyn Botanic Garden Record, Vol. 39, No. 2, Summer 1983, pp. 42–43.

A few well-fed and densely-planted garden beds also attract birds, insects and other small wildlife.

References &
Further Reading

Bergman, Ernest L., 'Vegetable farming in china' in *Oriental herbs and vegetables: a handbook*, Plants & Gardens Series, Brooklyn Botanical Garden Record, Vol. 39, No. 2, Summer 1983, pp. 37–38

Bartholomew, Mel, *Square foot gardening*, Rodale Press, USA, 1981 (Still available from Green Harvest website, see Useful Addresses.)

Baxter, Lynette, *Balti: the complete cookbook*, Greenwich Editions, US, 1998

Bennett, Peter, *Organic gardening*, Australia & New Zealand Book Co., Sydney, 1979

Berger, Sue, *The Allotment Book*, Green Books, UK, 2005

Bittman, Mark, *Leafy greens: an A–Z guide to 30 types of greens plus more than 120 recipes*, Macmillan, New York, 1995

Buchanan, Rita, *The shaker herb and garden book*, Houghton Mifflin, Boston/New York, 1996

Collins, Judith, *Companion gardening in Australia: working with Mother Nature*, Lothian, Melbourne, 1997

Conacher, Jeanette, *Small-scale farming and horticulture*, Organic Growers' Association Western Australia, Western Australia, 1986

Crawford, Martin, *Creating a Forest Garden,* Green Books, UK, 2010

Crawford, Martin, *How to grow Perennial Vegetables,* Green Books, UK, 2012

Cundall, Peter, *The practical Australian gardener: using sensible organic methods*, McPhee Gribble/Penguin, Melbourne, 1989

Dahlen, Martha and Phillips, Karen, *A guide to Chinese market vegetables*, South China Morning Post Ltd, Hong Kong, 1981

Deans, Esther, *Esther Dean's gardening book: growing without digging*, Harper & Row, Sydney, 1977

Donaldson, Stephanie, *The Shaker Garden: beauty through utility*, David & Charles, Newton Abbot, UK, 2000

Dowding, Charles, *How to Grow Winter Vegetables*, Green Books, UK, 2011

Dowding, Charles, *Salad Leaves for all Seasons*, Green Books, UK, 2008

Fanton, Jude and Fanton, Michel, *The seed savers' handbook*, Seed Savers' Network, New South Wales, 1993 (See Useful Addresses for contact details.)

Flannery, Tim, *The future eaters: an ecological history of the Australasian lands and people*, Reed Books, Sydney, l994

Food for plants, Discovering Soils Series, No. 6, CSIRO Publishing, Melbourne, 1978 (Refers mostly to chemical fertilisers, with a note that we must return to organic, even human fertilisers, as fossil reserves run out.)

Foster, David and Foster, Gerda, *A year of slow food: four seasons of growing and enjoying food in the Australian countryside*, Duffy & Snellgrove, New South Wales, 2001

French, Jackie, *The earth gardener's companion*, Earth Garden Books, Victoria, 1990

French, Jackie, *Natural control of garden pests*, Aird Books, Melbourne, 2002

Fukuoka, Masanobu, *The one-straw revolution: an introduction to natural farming*, Rodale Press, USA, 1978 (A classic on true organic growing.)

Grieve, Margaret, *A modern herbal: the medicinal, culinary, cosmetic and economic properties, cultivation and folklore of herbs, grasses, fungi, shrubs, and trees with all their modern scientific uses*, Penguin Books, 1980 (First published 1931. Still the herb bible, although classifications may have changed for some plants.)

Gross, John, *Food preserving at home*, Choice Books/Australian Consumers' Association, Sydney, 1999

Heazlewood, Anne, *The organic gardener's companion*, Reed Books/The Organic Gardening and Farming Society of Tasmania Inc., Sydney, 1990 (First published 1982.)

James Jr, Theodore, *Cultivating the cook's garden*, Council Oak Books, Tulsa and San Francisco, 1998

Kingsolver, Barbara, *Animal, Vegetable, Mineral: A year of food life*, HarperCollins, 2007

Klaus, Carl H., *My vegetable love: a journal of a growing season*, Houghton Mifflin Co., New York, 1996 (About the pain and the ecstasy of growing food!)

Larkcom, Joy, *The salad garden*, Doubleday, Sydney, 1984

Larkcom, Joy, *Vegetables from small gardens: a guide to intensive cultivation*, Faber & Faber, London, 1986 (Both titles by author are informative and practical with novel ideas. Disregard lip service given to chemical pesticides. Written for Northern Hemisphere conditions, but turn seasons around and use common sense.)

Lawrence, Felicity, *Not on the label: what really goes into the food on your plate*, Penguin Books, London, 2004

Macdonald, Janet, *The ornamental kitchen garden*, David & Charles, England, 1994

Mobbs, Michael, *Sustainable house*, University of Otago Press, New Zealand, 1998

Mollison, Bill and Holmgren, David, *Permaculture one: a perennial agriculture for human settlements*, Transworld Publishers, Melbourne, 1978

Mollison, Bill, *Permaculture two: practical design for town and country in permanent agriculture*, Tagari Community, Tasmania, 1979

Mollison, Bill, *Permaculture: a designer's manual*, Tagari Publications, New South Wales, 1988

Mollison, Bill and Slay, Reny Mia, *Introduction to permaculture*, Tagari Publications, New South Wales, 1992

Murray, David R., *Growing peas and beans*, Kangaroo Press, Sydney, 1999

Murray, David R., *Successful organic gardening*, Kangaroo Press, Sydney, 2000

Nearing, Helen and Nearing, Scott, *Living the good life: how to live sanely and simply in a troubled world*, Schocken Books, New York, 1970

Nearing, Helen and Nearing, Scott, *Continuing the good life: half a century of home-steading*, Schocken Books, New York, 1979

Nicholson, B.E., Harrison, S.G., Masefield, G.B., and Wallis, M., *The Oxford book of food plants*, Oxford University Press, UK, 1969 (Superb pictures and text – there were many reprints until a wholly new edition appeared, see Vaughan & Geissler.)

Norberg-Hodge, Helen, 'Bringing the food economy home', viewed at http://www.isec.org.uk

Okera, Shamim, *Scented kitchens: recipes and remedies by Australian Muslims*, Muslim Women's Association of South Australia/Peacock Publications, South Australia, 1996

Philbrick, Helen and Gregg, Richard, *Companion plants and how to use them*, The Devin-Adair Company, Connecticut, 1982

Phillips, Karen and Dahlen, Martha, *A popular guide to Chinese vegetables*, MPH Bookstores Publication, Singapore, 1985

Pike, Ben, *The Fruit Tree Handbook*, Green Books, UK, 2013

Pollan, Michael, *In defence of food: the myth of nutrition and the pleasures of eating*, Allen Lane/Penguin Books, 2008

Pollan, Michael, *The omnivore's dilemma*, Bloomsbury, UK, 2006

Shearman, David and Sauer-Thompson, Gary, *Green or gone: health, ecology, plagues, greed and our future*, Wakefield Press, South Australia, 1997

Stewart, Amy, *The earth moved: on the remarkable achievements of earthworms*, Algonquin Books of Chapel Hill, Chapel Hill, North Carolina, 2004

Temby, Ian, *Wild neighbours: the humane approach to living with wildlife*, Citrus Press, New South Wales, 2005 (A useful book for urban householders.)

Till, Antonia (ed.), *Loaves and wishes: writers writing on food*, Virago Press, London, 1992

The good bug book, Integrated Pest Management Ltd, Hertfordshire, England, 1995

Tudge, Colin, *So shall we reap: what's wrong with the world's food and how to fix it*, Penguin Books, London, 2004

Vaughan, J.G. and Geissler, C.A., *The new Oxford book of food plants*, Oxford University Press, London, 1997

Wickham, Cynthia, *Common plants as natural remedies*, Frederick Muller Limited, London, 1981

Woodward, Penny, *An Australian herbal: a practical guide to growing and using herbs in temperate Australia and New Zealand*, Hyland House, Melbourne, 1986

Woodward, Penny, *Asian herbs and vegetables: how to identify, grow and use them in Australia*, Hyland House, Melbourne, 2000

Woodward, Penny, *Pest-repellent plants*, Hyland House, Melbourne, 1997

Vandana, Shiva, 'Terra Madre: a celebration of living', viewed at http://www.banterminator.org and http://www.geneethics.org

Warren, Piers, *How to store your Garden Produce*, Green Books, UK, 2008

Useful Addresses

Organic gardening magazines carry lists of organisations, publications, nurseries, seed companies, new products and service providers. If you are interested in growing native food and fruit, consult your nursery and library.

Companies supplying organic or open-pollinated seeds

Jekka's Herb Farm
Rose Cottage, Shellards Lane, Alveston, Bristol BS35 3SY
www.jekkasherbfarm.com

Franchi Seeds of Italy 1783
D2 Phoenix Business Centre, Rosslyn Crescent, Harrow HA1 2SP
www.seedsofitaly.co.uk

Garden Organic
Ryton Gardens, Wolston Lane, Coventry CV8 3LG
www.gardenorganic.org.uk

Laura's Organics
19 Westminster Street, Wigan, Lancashire WN5 9BH
www.laurasorganics.co.uk

Moles Seeds
Turkey Cock Lane, Stanway, Colchester CO3 8PD
www.molesseeds.co.uk

The Organic Gardening Catalogue
Riverdene Business Park, Molesey Road, Surrey KT12 4RG
www.organiccatalog.com

Poyntzfield Herb Nursery
Black Isle, By Dingwall IV7 8LX, Ross & Cromarty, Scotland
www.poyntzfieldherbs.co.uk

The Real Seed Catalogue
PO Box 18, Newport near Fishguard, Pembrokeshire SA65 0AA
www.realseeds.co.uk

Seed to Plate
Broadmeadow, Drewsteignton, Devon EX6 6QW
www.seedtoplate.co.uk

Stormy Hall Seeds
Stormy Hall, Danby Head, Whitby YO21 2NN
www.stormy-hall-seeds.co.uk

Heritage Apple & Quince Tree Varieties

'Grow' at Brogdale Farm
Brogdale Road, Faversham, Kent ME13 8XZ
www.brogdaleonline.co.uk

The Heritage Fruit Tree Company
27 Walton Ave, Twyford, Banbury OX17 3JY
www.heritagefruittrees.co.uk

Ken Muir Ltd
Honeypot Farm, Rectory Road, Weeley Heath, Clacton-on-Sea CO16 9BJ
www.kenmuir.co.uk

Orange Pippin Fruit Trees
33 Algarth Rise, Pocklington, York YO42 2HX
www.orangepippintrees.co.uk

Organisations

Friends of the Earth
The Printworks, 139 Clapham Road, London SW9 0HP
www.foe.co.uk

Garden Organic
The working name of the Henry Doubleday Research Association
www.gardenorganic.co.uk

The National Allotment Society
O'Dell House, Hunters Road, Corby, Northamptonshire NN17 5JE
www.nsalg.org.uk

The Permaculture Association
BCM Permaculture Association, London, WC1N 3XX
www.permaculture.org.uk

Royal Horticultural Society
80 Vincent Square, London SW1P 2PE
www.rhs.org.uk

Ryton Gardens
Wolston Lane, Ryton on Dunsmore, Coventry CV8 3LG
www.rytongardens.co.uk

Via Campesina
www.viacampesina.org

Events

Slow Food Movement, Italy, holds an annual Terra Madre (Mother Earth) exhibition and coming together of traditional food growers from all over the globe. A major aim is to prevent loss of food diversity.

Acknowledgments

Primary gratitude goes to my mother and grandmother; excellent plain cooks with the ingredients available to them. They put all their efforts into my survival during the famine in western Holland that became known as the Hunger Winter of 1944–1945. By a miracle they survived themselves to cook again. Uncle Wim shared out vegetables from his small farm until that severe winter closed down the earth. He was my gardening teacher from the moment I could toddle, introducing me to his beloved pole beans, currant bushes and happy chickens.

I thank all vegetable-growing friends for stories that found their way into this book. Special thanks go to Chris Watters and Daryn Howell who helped design and run an eight-week course in Strathalbyn about growing vegetables on one square metre. We charged a nominal fee of one dollar per session for potting soil and seeds to give participants hands-on experience in raising their own. Chris, passionate tomato aficionado, introduced us to mixed salad boxes. Daryn, who grew carrots in his driveway, was a mine of horticultural information. Both shared their food gardens with the participants, some of whom returned to do the repeat course. Thanks also to Jane Henderson who demonstrated vegetarian gourmet cooking, and Thelma and Mario Ielasi for sharing their skills in preserving home-grown produce. Percy McElwaine allowed me to photograph his food garden and bequeathed me his portable plastic roof. Else Jansen started a kitchen garden just when I needed more photos. My first herb, a yarrow, came from Mrs Moss whose pioneering herb nursery at Mount Barker spawned most subsequent herb nurseries, including my tiny Middle Hill Herb Nursery. Gratitude goes to three gardeners, Louise, Jeff, and Vivienne, who over the decades helped out with the ornamental gardens on a regular basis, allowing me more time to experiment with vegetables.

Two authors who profoundly influenced my thinking about food growing at home were Mel Bartholomew, author of *Square Foot Gardening*, and more recently Colin Tudge with *So Shall We Reap*.

My thanks is also due to an enthusiastic officer at the Commonwealth Bureau of Statistics, who complemented the 'Home Grown Vegetables' figures from Catalogue 7110.0 of 1994 with backyard statistics from Catalogue 2015.0 of the year 2001. Australia then had 5,327,309 separate houses, most if not all of which were expected to have backyards. There were 632,176 semi-detached, row, terrace and town houses, and 923,139 flats, units and apartments, most of which would also have had backyards, however small. And finally there were caravans, tents and other dwellings, whose inhabitants may well have had access to a square metre of soil nearby.

At Wakefield Press, Michael Bollen acted as the devil's advocate every non-fiction book needs and Bethany Clark edited the text with tender care and much enthusiasm. I accept that any errors or omissions may well be mine, but regret having let go of some elaborating little chapters. All the same, neither time nor effort was spared by all involved in producing this book to make it the most accessible grow-your-own text for food gardeners born and yet to be born.

Lastly, a very special thanks to my partner Burwell Dodd, computer and compost specialist, who turned a spade when I couldn't, put in posts for fences and espalier fixtures, and has eaten the results of my food-growing experiments without a murmur.

Lolo Houbein
2008

Index

For quick information and tips about growing particular vegetables, herbs, fruits and berries refer to the alphabetical lists in Part Four.

Also from Green Books

For our full list, see **www.greenbooks.co.uk**

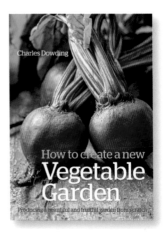

How to create a new Vegetable Garden
Producing a beautiful and fruitful garden from scratch

Charles Dowding **Published February 2015**

Any plot of land, whether it is currently lawn, overgrown with weeds, or even a building site, can be turned into a beautiful and productive vegetable garden.

Charles' no-nonsense, simple advice is the perfect starting point for any beginner or experienced gardener, taking you through everything you need to transform your land.

Organic Gardening

Charles Dowding

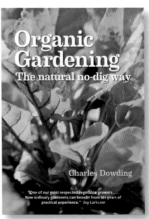

How to store your garden produce

Piers Warren

Creating a Forest Garden
Working with Nature to Grow Edible Crops
Martin Crawford

Forest gardening is a novel way of growing edible crops – nature does most of the work for you! A forest garden is modelled on young natural woodland, with a wide range of crops grown in different vertical layers, with little need for digging, weeding, or pest control. Species are chosen for their beneficial effects on each other, forming a healthy system that maintains its own fertility, and also creating a beautiful space.

Food from your Forest Garden
Martin Crawford &
Caroline Aitken

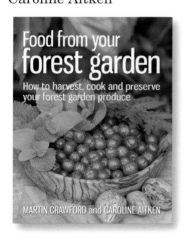

The Fruit Tree Handbook
Ben Pike

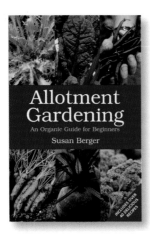

Allotment Gardening
An Organic Guide for Beginners
Susan Berger

Aimed at those who have not had an allotment before, *Allotment Gardening* is packed with advice: from choosing and planning your allotment through to harvesting and storing your produce.

It covers tools, growing techniques and solutions to common problems. Complete with a A–Z of vegetables, fruits, herbs and flwers, with growing instructions and recipes.

About Green Books

Environmental publishers for over 25 years.

For our full range of titles and to order direct from our website, see **www.greenbooks.co.uk**

Join our mailing list for new titles, special offers, reviews, author appearances and events: **www.greenbooks.co.uk/subscribe**

For bulk orders (50+ copies) we offer discount terms. Contact **sales@greenbooks. co.uk** for details.

Send us a book proposal on eco-building, science, gardening, etc.: see **www.greenbooks.co.uk/for-authors**

 @ Green_Books

green books

 /GreenBooks